Embodiment and
the New Shape of Black
Theological Thought

RELIGION, RACE, AND ETHNICITY SERIES

General Editor: Peter J. Paris

*Public Religion and Urban
Transformation: Faith in the City*
Edited by Lowell W. Livezey

*Down by the Riverside:
Readings in African American Religion*
Edited by Larry G. Murphy

New York Glory: Religions in the City
Edited by Tony Carnes and
Anna Karpathakis

*Religion and the Creation of Race and
Ethnicity: An Introduction*
Edited by Craig R. Prentiss

*God in Chinatown:
Religion and Survival in New York's
Evolving Immigrant Community*
Kenneth J. Guest

*Creole Religions of the Caribbean:
An Introduction from Vodou and Satería
to Obeah and Espiritismo*
Margarite Fernández Olmos and Liza-
beth Paravisini-Gebert

*The History of the Riverside Church in
the City of New York*
Peter J. Paris, John Wesley Cook,
James Hadnut-Beumler, Lawrence H.
Mamiya, Leonora Tubbs Tisdale,
and Judith Weisenfeld
Foreword by Martin E. Marty

*Righteous Content: Black Women's
Perspectives of Church and Faith*
Daphne C. Wiggins

*Beyond Christianity: African Americans
in a New Thought Church*
Darnise C. Martin

*Deeper Shades of Purple:
Womanism in Religion and Society*
Edited by Stacey M. Floyd-Thomas

*Daddy Grace: A Celebrity Preacher and
His House of Prayer*
Marie W. Dallam

*The Methodist Unification: Christianity
and the Politics of Race in the Jim Crow Era*
Morris L. Davis

*Watch This! The Ethics and
Aesthetics of Black Televangelism*
Jonathan L. Walton

*American Muslim Women: Negotiating
Race, Class, and Gender in the* Ummah
Jamillah Karim

*Embodiment and the New Shape of
Black Theological Thought*
Anthony B. Pinn

Embodiment and the New Shape of Black Theological Thought

Anthony B. Pinn

NEW YORK UNIVERSITY PRESS
New York and London

NEW YORK UNIVERSITY PRESS
New York and London
www.nyupress.org

Library of Congress Cataloging-in-Publication Data
Pinn, Anthony B.
Embodiment and the new shape of black theological thought / Anthony B.
Pinn.
p. cm. — (Religion, race, and ethnicity)
Includes bibliographical references and index.
ISBN-13: 978-0-8147-6774-0 (cl : alk. paper)
ISBN-10: 0-8147-6774-5 (cl : alk. paper)
ISBN-13: 978-0-8147-6775-7 (pbk. : alk. paper)
ISBN-10: 0-8147-6775-3 (pbk. : alk. paper)
1. Human body—Religious aspects—Christianity. 2. Theological
anthropology—Christianity. 3. Black theology. I. Title.
BT702.P56   2010
230.089'96073—dc22   2009050059

New York University Press books are printed on acid-free paper,
and their binding materials are chosen for strength and durability.
We strive to use environmentally responsible suppliers and materials
to the greatest extent possible in publishing our books.

Manufactured in the United States of America
c   10 9 8 7 6 5 4 3 2 1
p   10 9 8 7 6 5 4 3 2 1

For My Students

Contents

Acknowledgments

Delays occur and projects that are meant for completion linger, half developed in a folder on the desktop. This book was one such project. Jennifer Hammer and Peter Paris showed great patience, encouragement, and insightful suggestions for improving the project. Thank you for your encouragement and support. I must also thank the external readers for their careful review of this manuscript. What they suggested in terms of revision proved extremely helpful, and I am grateful for the time and energy they put into reviewing the initial manuscript. In addition, I would like to thank Despina Papazoglou Gimbel and Mary Sutherland for their hard work on preparing the manuscript for publication.

Some time has passed since those days, but I remain grateful for the brilliant insights of Richard R. Niebhur and Margaret Miles. As a student in their classes, I first developed an interest in embodied religion and the significance of the arts for study of embodied religion. It has taken time for me to express that interest in the terms presented here, but what they taught me shadowed all my work. Conversations with James Cone also helped me to think through the purpose behind my theologizing, and I am grateful for his assistance.

I would also like to thank Caroline Levander, Katie G. Cannon, Juan and Stacey Floyd-Thomas, Ramón Rentas, Benjamin Valentin, Eli Valentin, Ed Cox, and Alexander Byrd for their good humor and solid friendship.

Since my arrival at Rice University as the Agnes Cullen Arnold Professor of Humanities, I have had the good fortune to work with excellent graduate students. They challenge me, encourage me, and in so many ways force me to sharpen my thought. Their deep passion for the study of African American religion is inspiring and keeps me focused when the less compelling demands of academic life attempt to take center stage. To these students I dedicate this volume. In particular I must say a word of thanks to Margarita Simon Guillory, one of my graduate students, who provided a thoughtful and insightful read of this book. In making her suggested revisions, I believe the book has become more precise.

Preface

This book requires a bit of context, a framing of its intent in order to place it within the objectives that inform my larger intellectual concerns. How has a humanist come to write this book?

In important ways, this book has been more than fifteen years in the making, stemming as it does from my ongoing effort to do theology in nontraditional ways, and in light of overlooked but vital dimensions and schemes of African American life. Here I point to my concern with the presentation of an alternate black theology. While black and womanist theologies assume a limited range of religious orientations and creedal formulations, I continue to be concerned with religious pluralism marking African American communities as well as the manner in which theology serves as a way to query and articulate the religiosities of African Americans.

My 1995 book, *Why, Lord? Suffering and Evil in Black Theology,* attempted to begin this process through a theological and archeological discussion of African American humanism.[1] I continue to see that text as an extension of William Jones's *Is God a White Racist?*; it critiques Jones's theological assumptions regarding doctrine of God and pushes for the grounding of African American humanism in contemporary cultural production (such as hip-hop) through the use of a new hermeneutic—nitty-gritty hermeneutics.[2] And, it attempts to accomplish this in a way that acknowledges (while challenging) the centrality of Christ for those whom Jones critiqued in his brilliant study. The attention to the blues and hip-hop in that text was meant to problematize the inherent spiritualization of human existence through *imago Dei* rhetoric that dominated black and womanist theologies as I read them. *Why, Lord?* was my first attempt to re-envision the doing of black theology in ways that allowed for the centrality of the existential, human embodiment as the primary raw material for and concern of theology.

Although most have failed to recognize the central point of *Varieties of African American Religious Experience,* the authored volume following *Why, Lord?*, this book has served as an extension of my earlier theological arguments through the attempt to formulate a theological framework capable of holding in tension the various religious orientations present in African American communities. Critics often assumed this text (granted the title was less than ideal and failed to capture the larger, theological intent) was my effort to claim some expertise in various religious traditions without extending our understanding of those traditions.[3] This was far from the case. I attempted to provide a theological reading of those traditions—focusing on moral evil as a framework held in common. In the first four chapters; and, in the most important and final chapter, I suggest a way of "doing theology" that moves beyond the traditional limitations of black and womanist theologies. I made no claims then (and I make no claims now) to having a primary concern with the history of religious traditions in African American communities. Rather, I use attention to these traditions to push my points concerning religious pluralism and to problematize traditional ways in which African Americans have done theology. Attention to description of African American religiosity affords a useful mechanism by which to challenge black and womanist theology on their Christian bias. Furthermore, it provides opportunity to think through theological grammar and vocabulary better capable of speaking about African American religion(s) in substantive ways. (I should also note that I hoped a humanist scholar discussing in a serious manner theistic religious traditions would provide an alternate modeling of the role of religious commitment in African American religious studies scholarship.)

It became increasingly clear to me this theological work required some attention to theories of black religion that could inform my largely theological interests. In addressing this topic, my aim in *Terror and Triumph* was to think through Charles Long's classic assessment of black religion and extend it in ways sensitive to theological concerns and issues.[4] *Terror and Triumph* represented my effort to more forcefully articulate the theory of black religion (as quest for complex subjectivity) that shadowed *Why, Lord?* and *The Varieties of African American Religious Experience*. That book, based on the Edward Cadbury Lectures I gave at the University of Birmingham (UK), was not an effort to shift from theology to history of religions, as some critics falsely assume.[5] Instead, I sought to ground my work in a theory of religious experience that did not assume any particular religious tradition. Much of my subsequent work has attempted, never too far from my theological interests, to unpack various dimensions and locations of as well as the problematic associated with religious pluralism within African American communities.[6] In addition, *Terror and Triumph* meant to suggest my commitment to interdisciplinarity as the best way to approach the complex, shifting, and layered nature of African American religious experience and thought.

These various projects have over and over again brought into play black bodies. My effort to describe the religious diversity of African American communities, particularly its humanistic orientations, has centered on the presentation of the body as the center of humanistic practice and thought. Work toward construction of theology as a response to religious diversity has repeatedly turned on the black body as a common element within the various religious traditions marked by African American commitment; my theory of African American religious experience renders fundamental the manner in which bodies occupy time and space as the marker or sign of religion's nature and meaning. The theological and religious significance of embodiment is the sine qua non for my scholarship.

Terror and Triumph marks explicit attention to the visual arts and aesthetics below the surface in earlier work. Chapter 6 and the final section of that book deal with the nature of art and theories of artistic expression as a way of reframing notions of the religious, and that theoretical framework continues to inform my thinking. In *Terror and Triumph* I suggest that the arts provide a way of gauging the movement of bodies in time and space as marker of the religious. The decorative arts serve as a means by which African Americans have rethought and reformulated their contexts of existence through a re-presentation of themselves in new arenas of meaning through aesthetics. Materials such as quilts, during the period of slavery, served as a way to "speak" an alternate existence and to capture through the language of aesthetics their perception of self as vital and valuable. Essentialized existence is critiqued, and spaces of engagement and meaning are presented. More recent modalities of artistic expression, such as the work of Romare Bearden, speak of the black body in reshaped and reformulated ways. Thus the black body is given new meaning through artistic expression. Embodiment is highlighted. Artistic expression becomes a language of life and liberative hope through the arrangement of bodies in spaces of possibility. Art has a materiality that represents power relationships while also challenging those relationships. Within the realm of artistic expression, African Americans expose the structures of domination and portray alternate strategies for living life. As Houston Baker notes, art is "a product and producer in an uncasing struggle for black liberation. To be 'art' the product had to be expressivity or performance designed to free minds and bodies of a subjugated people."[7] This relationship between art and power, materiality and aesthetics is explored in several of the following chapters.

In this regard art and aesthetics become modalities of analysis useful in embodied theological thought in that they point to, through, and in bodies to express the wishes and fears of existence. To get at this dimension of meaning making through artistic expression, I rely heavily on the work of art critics such as Arthur Danto. For Danto much of what takes place in the art world of the twentieth century raises questions concerning the nature and meaning of art: What is art? How do the mundane materials placed in alternate time and space constitute art? Basic material, the mundane etches of human interaction and production, is transformed into the markers of deeper meaning. As Nicholas Davey remarks, "each aesthetic revelation not only extends the map of our seeing but also, in so doing, alters and extends our sense of self and how we understand our existential concerns and predicaments."[8] In like manner, the basic framing of humanity, of human relationships and construction—the body—within theology serves to mark the basic framing of life. Questions raised in light of Pop Art, for example, are relevant to the alterations of black theological thought in light of embodiment: What is the nature and meaning of theological thinking in light of the body as the starting point and purpose of theology?

In both instances, art/aesthetics and body/embodiment, there is a push to "'look' at it but, more importantly, to 'look' to it for what it reveals, and this became the pattern of exploration and criticism: content says something about form."[9] The body, like certain modalities of artistic expression, points to itself and beyond itself. In this way the body—as we see with art—becomes a proper source and framework for the exploration of our fundamental questions of existence and meaning. The body serves as both form and content of the *religious*. Through its preoccupation with embodiment, theology becomes a tool by which to surface and unpack the deep questions related to the *religious* and our experience of it.[10]

My colleagues have argued for a disconnection between my personal allegiance to African American humanism and my claims to do theology. How does a humanist, who does not believe in God, participate in "God-talk"? My efforts to rethink and reorganize the doing of theology in ways that render it a form of analysis without the need for Christian commitment has produced some space for my work. In both explicit and implicit ways, however, my response and effort to continue theologizing has revolved around promotion of embodiment as the central reality of theological work. Much of my work has suggested a turning away from the metaphysical assumptions and commitments marking a great deal of black and womanist theologies, and in place of these firmly held elements I have tried to situate embodiment and black bodies as the ground for theological inquiry.

This approach tied together even the most marginal elements of my descriptive work (i.e., attention to African American humanism) and my commitment to theological inquiry; this focus on the body allowed me to be both a scholar of African American humanism and a theologian—one who embraced nontheism and one who believes in the importance of theological inquiry. Attention to embodiment and black bodies offered a way to develop creative tension (and something resembling continuity) within my work.

While African American religious studies (particularly black and womanist theologies, history, and ethics) has given primary attention to the development of institutional forms and the doctrinal articulation or birth of religious sentiment within African America, I would raise questions—questions that motivate and guide much of what is in this present volume: Why would the embrace of borrowed creedal forms and institutional structures best mark the emergence and expression of a unique African American religious and theological ethos? Does not both the physical and "soul" movement typically highlighted when discussing African American religion/theology (e.g., Frederick Douglass's battle with the overseer; David Walker's *Appeal*; Sojourner Truth's work; the civil rights movement) exemplify the manner in which the quest for complex subjectivity (i.e., religion) is enacted as material demand and symbolic gestures, thus affecting a more complex arrangement and (re) presentation of the body?

Embodiment and the New Shape of Black Theological Thought is not the first text in African American religious studies to express concern with black bodies. The theological and ethical efforts over the past thirty years, for example, give at least implicit attention to the nature and meaning of embodiment.[11] One of the goals of this volume is to make embodiment not just explicit but also the central framework of theological inquiry: to do theology with embodiment and the body as the starting point and the end point.

One of the problems with black and womanist theologies is that they have not wrestled adequately with the dilemma of what can be known about the body. It is not clear what the body is, or how it can be realized or "known"— as biological or as metaphorical. As a consequence their liberation scheme is without a subject, the new spacing of life it seeks to champion is without a recognizable population. The "someone" or community associated with this new reality is missing.

This is not to argue that black theology and womanist theology are faulty in that they do not entail an extended theory of the body, although such might be helpful. Rather, what is said does not really take into consideration the nature and meaning, or the constitution or construction, of the black bodies that one would assume (as do these theologians) is the central concern. Appeal to the scriptures, as is often the case in black theology, fails to solve this problem in that this does not give attention to the "lived" African American bodies. The bodies of concern to black theology, or what one would posit as of concern, are missing. There are not even traces or shadows of these bodies, but instead there is an imposed discourse that yields little in terms of liberation as commonly understood in black theology in particular and black religious studies in general.

The inadequacies of the subject of theology and liberation as outlined by black theology was shown by the emergence of womanist thought and that, in turn, has been rendered inadequate on various fronts. What remains, then, is the unstable nature—if it exists at all—of a subject within black and womanist theologies. Is it the case that black and womanist theologies are not so concerned with saving bodies but rather are involved in a struggle over the power to name and create bodies? Or, perhaps it is an ill-defined combination of the two: black and womanist theologies are concerned with the welfare of the biological body and the control over the construction of the signifier or metaphorical body. For black theology a certain perspective on black bodies, often framed in terms of ontological blackness, serves as a totalizing force and one-directional pattern of relations, which does damage to the theological project black theologians hoped to develop.[12] Black theology and womanist theology believe the target for critique is clear and distinguishable from blackness and black bodies. But again, this is far from the case. The dilemmas identified by black and womanist theologies are in process, and define both blackness and whiteness and everything between these categories of epistemology. The target is uncertain and contained in fields of power and discourses of maintenance that reject the "stuff" black and womanist theologies prize and claim—stable identity—while also making possible to some degree the subject and object of theological discourse.[13]

What I present here is not a "fully" formed body theology along the lines of what has been offered by such scholars as James Nelson and Lisa Isherwood among others.[14] While *Embodiment and the New Shape of Black Theological Thought* shares Nelson's concern with sexuality and the importance of sexuality as a religiously charged and deeply vital dimension of human existence, it does not entail an incarnational approach to theologizing and, in this sense, does not offer an apologetic for sexuality (and embodiment) as a focus of Christian theology. I am more concerned with how the body and notions of embodiment might figure into theologizing (as a modality of analysis that does not entail of necessity a commitment to any particular religious organization) and less concerned with a more systematic presentation of a theological system as fitted into any particular tradition. One might say that this book is an example of theological experimentation (or thinking) as opposed to outlining a formal theological system.[15] *Embodiment* does not entail a body theology in a formal and systematic sense, but rather an interdisciplinary thought experiment regarding how the body and embodiment might inform the doing of black theology. It is my hope, however, that it might inspire more systematic efforts.

Furthermore, *Embodiment*, like much of Isherwood's work, is concerned with the manner in which the body figures into theologizing and religiosity, with some focused attention on issues of gender and sexuality; it seeks to reposition the body as religiously vital and significant. But, unlike both Nelson and Isherwood, I am less concerned with presenting this framing of the body within the context of the Christian faith. Hence, while I give some attention to the body/soul split as present in African American Christianity, I also make an effort to expand the discussion beyond Christian faith and other recognized institutionalized modalities of religious expression. This book also differs from M. Shawn Copeland's recent and important work, *Enfleshing Freedom: Body, Race, and Being*. While we are both concerned with the theological importance of bodies, unlike Copeland I am not concerned primarily with "the Christian question of what being human means on the body." My work is not grounded in the same theological anthropology, and it is not framed exclusively by the same "Christian belief."[16]

Within this book the body becomes an analytical tool and also the space out of which theologizing takes place. What results is the tying together of the various threads of my research. In the process, *Embodiment* points in the direction of a new black theology by offering an alternate orientation, a different posture toward the place of black bodies in the doing of theology that makes theological thinking contingent upon the nature and meaning of embodiment.

Introduction

Black theology is a mode of worldly theology, *worldly* in that it recognizes the manner in which the historical progress of humanity has taken place at the expense of particular groups not within the circle of dominance. Its existence is premised on a rejection of religious naïveté whereby human misery is covered by unrealizable hopefulness and theological slight of hand. While rejecting the extreme optimism generated by that position, black theological discourse also critiques unduly pessimistic depiction of human potential for initiating and sustaining socially transformative processes.[1] Human progress has indeed produced a bloody trail from Europe through Africa (and Asia), and into the Americas; furthermore, black theological discourse in the form of black theology seeks to acknowledge, confront, and address this situation—all under the belief that substantial social change is possible.

Theologizing consistent with this agenda exposes not only the messy nature of life but also the complex and layered ways in which religion serves as a response to the absurdity of our world. This posture and approach informed black theology's early rhetoric and stance toward the dominant American theological tradition, and it allowed for the rejection of that tradition's disregard for those in most need of freedom.

Few in black theology, or those familiar with it, would argue against these assertions as endemic to black theological discourse. And I have little interest in simply rehearsing this well-known and well-worn argument. Rather, I am more interested in the manner in which this fundamental framework shapes the reflexive process within black theological discourse and how that reflexive process might reinforce the importance of certain theological categories and highlight the implied importance of others.

Reflection and Assessment

Black theology is premised on the assumption that its effectiveness must be assessed in light of the manner in which its structure and content addresses the advancement of a liberative agenda. As a contextual note related to this section, some readers may raise questions concerning my frequent attention to some of the more established theologians and may find problematic the limited attention I give to more recent thinkers. I acknowledge that black and womanist theologies are undergoing transitions, and that new waves of theologians are challenging some of the assumptions regarding the doing of theology. Recent work by Monica Coleman, for instance, asserts the importance of *process thought* for the doing of liberative theological work, and for her this challenge includes attention to the religious pluralism that marks African American communities.[2] J. Cameron Carter's work on a theological assessment of race provides intriguing insights into the formation and theological impact of race within the modern world.[3] However, I would also argue that even more recent theological work all too often assumes the definition of the body and the framing of the body, which had been established decades ago. Hence, to break this practice and center black theological thought on embodiment/the body, it is necessary to first address the assumed understanding of the black body that informs the first two generations of black and womanist theologians.

Within black theological discourse all conceptual categories are tested in the arena of felt need and effectiveness—the ways in which meaning is made. From its early presentation some forty years ago to more recent efforts to expand and extend black theology's nature and meaning, there has been recognition of the need to test claims, demonstrate assertions, and adjust in light of one's findings. Or, as James Cone notes, truth is experienced and experience is truth.[4] What takes precedence, then, at all times is the "realness" of African American experience. Such a stance when held consistently must involve self-evaluation, an evaluation of black theology's form and content.

Self-critical exploration of black theology during the 1970s initiated by figures such as Gayraud Wilmore, Cecil Cone, and Cornel West produced greater attention to the importance of cultural production for the doing of black theology as well as the need for more explicit attention to social theory as a way to under gird a robust liberation agenda.[5] What is more, continued critical engagement by scholars such as Katie Cannon, Jacquelyn Grant, and Delores Williams produced a turn in black theology during the 1980s that resulted in the surfacing of black theology's sexism as well as a new theological model referred to as womanist theology.[6] These are just a few of the important and documented moments of introspection that have marked theological discourse in African American communities; they have resulted in the ongoing revision of its conceptual framework, content, and methodologies as well as expansion of its reach. In this book I suggest another important shift, one that will result in a new modality of black theological thought.

Context and Framework

Embodiment and the New Shape of Black Theological Thought is in part my effort at introspection, an attempt to present in a more sustained form theological concern with embodiment—with the body as the primary source and shape of theological inquiry—present in much of my thinking. My purpose is to point in the direction of a body-centered approach to theological thought whereby the body's meaning and lived experience are prioritized and used as a starting point for the doing of theology. Within this context, the body is interrogated for what it might offer in terms of the form and content of black theology.

One might assume black theology, over the course of four decades, has given significant attention to the nature and meaning of black bodies as an important theological issue. The sociopolitical context for its development and the liberative—pro-black and at times nationalistic and exceptionalist—focus of that discourse would suggest such a concern with bodies as a reasonable assumption. This is certainly a good way to understand the manner in which liberation has been presented in terms that speak to the materiality of black bodies. The demand for healthy life options, the challenge to environmental racism, the lament of inadequate employment all speak to an understanding of liberation theologically constructed as engaging the body.

Behind black theology's large claims regarding liberation is a troubled relationship to human flesh, to black bodies. Black theological thought related to issues of liberation and life meaning, when framed in terms of the body, tend toward the body only as abstraction, as symbol with little attention to the lived body. At best and with few exceptions, black theology and its claims made and agendas drawn do not typically emanate from the body.[7] Black theology is often a theology of *no-body*,[8] a system of theological expression without an organized (re)presentation of the body as body.

Black theology often lacks a clear subject of concern in that it gives so little attention to the body as material, meaning the physical dimensions of existence, the "stuff" of human beings. In black theology, the body is a vaguely presented and defined idea, a metaphor, a symbolic measuring stick used to debate the shape and purpose of social structures. (Regarding this understanding of the body Michel Foucault has been helpful to black theology, although black theology embraces a sense of liberation and a framing of ethics that would trouble Foucault.) In short, it is representational—a means of classification. Black theology, therefore, is materially empty. The problems with this approach are numerous. For example, from my perspective this perception makes difficult any clear assessment of liberation—its meaning and nature, its function and purpose. In addition, lack of attention to material bodies also warps the manner in which issues such as racism are measured, and progress against oppression marked. In other words, without attention to the physical, racism becomes a phantom reality; and like phantom limbs it is felt and serves as a source of pain or stimulation difficult to address. One is left with the sensation that racism is always present and impacting life in a reified manner, even when there are signs of its shifting importance. Tied to this perception of racism as fixed, a reality not dependent on observation, is the sense that blackness easily becomes "over present"—a concern that overshadows or shapes perception of all other concerns.[9]

Black theology, by highlighting the body as metaphor, as symbol of the meaning of blackness over against whiteness, is often an etiology of white supremacy, but one that fails to give sufficient attention to the *experiencing* (by material bodies) of white supremacy and, by extension, the materiality of liberation. The body becomes a symbolic measuring stick used to debate the shape and purpose of social structures. There are ways in which black theology concerns itself with the demand for agency; yet, "agency, of course, requires a body acting in time and space and is meaningless without it."[10]

The feel for life, the experience of living, is often addressed in black theology as an epistemological issue. Even M. Shawn Copeland's insightful analysis of the body in the article "Body, Representation, and Black Religious Discourse," seems to suggest primarily the body as mechanism of social regulation and control vis-à-vis racial stigma and racism/sexism. Even her discussion of sex/sexuality appears circumscribed to the body as metaphor through which the European sexual-self is worked out. The black body is shaped and defined by power dynamics. In a sense it is the cartography of power dynamics. The body, hence, is a story told to support the social system.[11]

What Is the Body?

What is meant by the term "body"? To what does this terminology refer? Efforts to explain and unpack this body have taken various forms—some privileging the body as epistemologically significant to a positioning of the body in terms of action. Yet others combine epistemological and action-based understandings of the body. Mindful of this perspective, and avoiding naturalistic arguments, I promote the body as developed and defined by social structures (e.g., discourse) and in this it is not a biological reality. I couple this with an understanding of the body as biochemical reality, as biological "stuff" that is not captured through abstract references to social mechanism and epistemological structures.[12] I work through this "combined" body or "meta" body by drawing from Foucault's work (and Foucault-influenced authors) for insights into the constructive nature of discourse and power relations, and by giving attention to sociology of the body's analysis of the materiality of bodies. The underlying conceptual commitment throughout the text is the suggestion that black bodies are material, are real, but what is meant by this and what is known/experienced about this body is not possible outside discourse (knowledge) generated in connection to power relationships. I do not want to dismiss the discursive body that is currently of concern to black theology but instead combine that understanding of the body with solid focus on the physical or material body.

To unpack the discursive black body, I make use of conceptual frameworks offered by Foucault within the three phases of his work devoted to (1) the production of knowledge; (2) the "conditions of knowledge," and (3) care of the self. These three stages might also be construed as being concerned with discourse, power relations, and the subject.[13] In the first phase of his scholarship, marked by *The Archeology of Knowledge*, Foucault concerned himself with an archaeologically identified manner of study, whereby he gave attention to the history and formation/transformation of knowledge.[14] At play here is not simply attention to "bodies" of knowledge but also to the discursive body as displayed through and by frameworks of thought. The "middle phase" of his work, involving *Discipline and Punish* and the first volume of the *History of Sexuality*, seeks to unpack the manner in which power shapes and controls bodies—rendering them docile—arranging them with political intent and through mechanisms of surveillance.[15] In short, the body is the location for the arrangement and display of power, producing a certain "art of the body." Through power, subjects are produced and these subjects come to represent various arrangements of power. The discursive body is "inscribed" by power relationships and modalities of discipline. As some scholars argue, though, this remains a matter of the discursive body in that "Foucault's argument that disciplinary power produced a certain 'art' of the human body challenges conceptions of modernity and only indirectly concerns empirical conceptions of the body."[16] The final phase of his work, framed by volumes 2 and 3 of *The History of Sexuality*, marks a turn toward care of the self, the manner in which the body is transformed by and through technologies that produce subjects. This is a less passive, less docile, and more active body, but nonetheless a discursive body. Through effort, individuals' work on themselves in ways meant to gain some relief, to achieve a certain level of contentment, if not happiness and advancement. For Foucault, in all phases of his thought, the body (particularly in the context of desire) is not hidden; rather, power and discourse shape and transform. Hence, the body is "real," but this realness involves its presence as a discursive construction, and it is monitored with regard to its development, (re)presentation, and control.

Embodiment and the New Shape of Black Theological Thought moves between these three phases because in each case Foucault remains concerned with the body: the construction of the body, the "placement" and "control" of the body, with (and finally) the management of the human being as a subject whereby individuals "act" on their bodies. The construction of black bodies through discursive means, in relationship to mechanism of power results in fixed "things"—black bodies that are rigid, truncated realities not to be viewed, understood, and appreciated in diverse ways. Rather, to draw from the quantum physicist David Bohm, they are the result of a unified and unique truth. This truth is built for the benefit of white supremacy, to limit the scope of black bodies. The dilemma for those possessing bodies so formed is that there is little "space" for a diverse range of opinions and perspectives on these discursive bodies. Their meaning is fixed—incoherent (again to borrow from Bohm), and dialogue concerning them is also fixed and limited to the "truth" of these bodies provided by those with the power to control the means of their production.[17] The discursive black body, formed as a matter of power dynamics and white supremacy, is a fragmented "something." This body is a mutation, a matter of warped reality representing a piece of black meaning that has lost its integrity and relationship to a more robust depiction of humanity. This discursive black body, then, is perceived as having no positive relationship to intelligence, civil liberties, privileged social spaces, and the like. And, the black material body, likewise, is believed, as a matter of social truth, to be understood as having no core relationship to beauty, privileged social spaces, and so on.[18] Theology based on these premises becomes a mode of interpretation whereby the forms of the body are exposed for their religious content.

Foucault's conceptual frameworks shake black theology's certainty, its somewhat arrogant claim to a special epistemology revolving around historical etiology upon which is harnessed its distinctive ontology. He points out that what they claim is not so unique and perhaps is not so liberative—but, sadly, may represent simply another working of power within power relations. But there were hints of this noticed early in the musical forms of the blues, and perhaps this is why black religion and later black theology needed to subdue the blues, render those bodies docile by spiritualizing them as secular spirituals.[19]

Perhaps the limited effect of black theology (and womanist theology) on the life circumstances of the most oppressed stems from misperceptions easily corrected by Foucault: fighting oppression as a form of power relations does not entail fighting particular individuals or groups. Power is a series of relationships found in everything and through everything. Hence, an attack on white supremacy as expressed in relationship to particular groups does not end the problem when one considers the fluidity of power relationships and the knowledge connected to them, as well as the manner in which these same power relationships flow from the oppressed. Struggle, then, takes on connotations and possibilities less robust and meaningful as that posited by liberation theologies. Nonetheless, struggle, as the effort to stem and alter the ways in which bodies are controlled and arranged, remains vital. It is only that the outcomes of such struggle must be less grand (a bit disappointing to old guard liberationists) and must revolve around greater spaces of liberty within the context of the system.[20]

Black theology and womanist theology seek to detangle black bodies from the power dynamics of oppression, but if Foucault is correct, such thinking is to misunderstand the nature of power and knowledge, and to assume the body has a pre-history reality and to assume that power does not flow through and by means of black bodies as well.[21] Furthermore, again turning to Bohm's provocative work on dialogue, one might also consider how the very form of theological discourse limits the outcome of its work. The type of freedom black theology claims to promote and seeks to make real is influenced by the limitations of our thinking, the limitations of our imaginative conceptualizations. This, however, is not the problem; it is simply the consequence of the limitations of thought. The problem is black theology's failure to recognize this limitation and to promote a rather troubled depiction of life and the issues confronting humanity.[22]

Black theology would be more helpful if it "goes into the process of thought behind the assumptions, not just the assumptions themselves."[23] Put another way, black theology has made its reputation on the ability to point out the bad faith of religion and certain forms of theological inquiry—the manner in which both reinforce oppressive political frameworks and restrictive social patterns. Black theology often fails, however, to recognize the ways in which it states its critique from within the very structures of knowledge it finds troubling. Black theologians' thinking is assumed free (for the most part) of the bad "stuff" and marked by liberative potential. Yet, their thinking is based on the same knowledge sources used to define and safeguard restrictive and subjecting arrangements. They believe they have the "right" religion, when in fact all religion participates in power relations and structures of knowledge. By implication, black theology must wrestle with multiple truths and avoid the tendency toward a resolution to oppression. The sexism and homophobia (as well as classism) that have plagued black theology's "liberative" praxis should be enough evidence to support this more moderate perspective on truth and resolutions.[24]

From my perspective, this "turn to the process of thought" within the context of black theology must include greater interrogation of embodiment (its meaning and practices) as thought experiment, as discursive construct. A greater range of resources and more intentional interconnectedness must match this. What I am suggesting is a pressing of black theology's assumptions concerning the body, assumptions that cloud black theology understanding, representation, and handling of the body as a "focus of life."[25]

There is more to the black body than this manifestation of discourse and thought. The body is also material, a "substance" without clear boundaries to the extent it is connected to the larger, natural environment.[26] The body is not simply discursive construction, as some critiques of Foucaultian analysis argue. For example, as philosophers like Susan Bordo have insisted, it is vital to recognize the materiality of the body. She remarks, "if the body is a metaphor for our locatedness in space and time and thus for the finitude of human perception and knowledge, then the postmodern body is no body at all."[27] While some argue even the materiality of the body is lodged in discourse, for scholars such as Bordo societal developments and the workings of power relationships have consequences that are felt, that impact the material integrity of people: bodies live, change, decay, die.[28] "Let's agree," writes Bordo, "we cannot 'get outside' the (historically sedimented) discourses and representations that shape our reality. Does this mean that all we are legitimately permitted to talk about is our reality as discourse and representation?"[29] In defining materiality, Bordo points to such markers as race, gender, biology, and the like, framing these markers in terms of "finitude" by which she references "our inescapable physical locatedness in time and space, in history and culture, both of which not only shape us but also limit us (which some postmoderns seem to deny)."[30] Material bodies engage culture and experience life through a range of activities and practices.[31] Our bodies are as defined and shaped by this materiality—the stuff of our practices—as by discourse and thought. Our bodies are both cultural product created through discourse, and material with "existential content" and "terrestrial weight."[32] In addition to this philosophical critique of strict attention to the discursive or thought body, sociology of the body informs implicitly *and* explicitly the concern for the material body marking this text. This is not to suggest a turn away from the body as cultural product, as discursive creation; but again I make an argument for understanding the body as both cultural production and material reality.

The benefit of turning to sociological concern for the material body is reasonable and productive because, according to Simon William and Gillian Bendelow, the body is "deeply embedded in the core problems of sociology."[33] As Bryan Turner remarks, sociology of the body is fundamentally "a materialist inquiry," but one premised on the importance of the body as regulated by discourse and as "vehicle of the self." The body is both "natural and cultural."[34] Like Bordo, certain figures in sociology have engaged but also critiqued Foucault and offered an alternate view of the body in that "Foucault's epistemological view of the body means that it effectively disappears as a material or biological entity. We can never know the biological or material body in the 'raw' so to speak, only through the filter of this or that discourse."[35] The body occupies a social space whose texture and tone cannot be fully assessed only through the workings of spoken language, but we also must be sensitive to the physical placement, condition, and actions of real and specific bodies. Meaning is embodied. Human experience, then, involves an array of factors only some of which are discursive in nature. Bodies serve as a nonmaterial text to be read, but they are also material realities that shape information within the context of the world. Whereas certain philosophical and phenomenological takes on this connection to and impact on the world is individual focused, Turner reminds us that sociology of the body places the individual within the collective. Sociology of the body recognizes the social nature of embodiment.[36] The benefits for black theological thought of this individual within the context of community are obvious.

As Bordo made clear and as further explicated in sociology of the body, physicality is necessary in order to understand and work through oppressive circumstances and address the pain and suffering promoted by those circumstances. Power relations are not simply thought but are performed through the placement of real, fleshly bodies in time and space. "The physical body," write Williams and Bendelow, "does not therefore simply reflect but actively contributes to social inequalities."[37] And Bordo's point is that these same bodies and their activities also ground efforts to resist those inequalities. As Gail Weiss writes, these bodies are "marked by assumptions made about their gender, their race, their ethnicity, their class, and their 'natural' abilities."[38]

Bodies that bend, scream, or act out when experiencing discomfort or pain cannot be ignored because oppression involves the visibility of all aspect of the body (or in fact the visibility of multiple bodies), thereby defying any effort to deny the materiality of physical bodies or the cultural/discursive creation of nonmaterial bodies.

As opposed to simply being the projection of thought, the "culture, too, becomes a projection of the body into the world."[39] The intellectual supremacy of the disembodied body has been challenged through recognition of physicality as shaping culture, rather than the body simply being shaped by culture. Therefore, the body, according to Mary Douglas, is a symbol of the social system and is also a material reality.[40] For Douglas and those influenced by her, the body affords an opportunity to challenge the dominance of the spoken and written word as the primary means of exchange: through the body, sociology depicts ways to analyze cultural arrangements and production. Concern with the physical body entails new insight into the lived dimensions of life—those elements of our existence not fully captured in what we think but more fully accounted for by what we do—our practices and existential interactions. "We," notes Bryan Turner, "labor on, in and with bodies."[41]

Theology and the Body

The reminder to engage the "fleshy" body is important for theology. Any effort to change the situation of embodied people must have litmus tests, benchmarks, and only attention to concrete conditions faced can give a sense of the "felt" consequences of struggle. We cannot step outside of power relations and the workings of discourse; it is only through engaging the markers of materiality that resistance can be assessed and strategies revised as necessary.[42] To the extent black theology avoids the existential and theoretical significance of the body, it fails to have an adequate object of exploration. One might argue that theistic forms of this theological discourse are grounded in a supreme subject—the divine—yet missing is the subject/object through which connection to and a mapping of the divine takes place. Hence, within the context of this book, the body is a tangled relationship of "thoughts" and "felts."[43]

What I am suggesting is recognition of multiple representations of the body, the manner in which the body is really bodies or "a multiplicity of bodies, inviting a great many disciplinary points of view and modes of interpretation."[44] The multiple meanings and references (metaphor and material) serve as the theory of the body framing this volume. In addition, this project is framed by an underlying argument: Theological and religious concerns, motivations, and formulations are present within this "give-and-take" between the metaphorical body and the material body. One might think of this tension between the discursive and the material body as the *me(an)ing* of embodiment. This tension highlights the connections between struggle for "place" or identity consistent with the workings and arrangement of the material body, and the manner in which discourse and power dynamics produce the meaning of the body both in thought and space. The black body—the changing sense of its biology and social construction/existence—provides a powerful example of the body as always under construction, never complete. The black body, so defined, "shadows" the evolving nature of religiosity and theology. The development of the New World, and the larger cartography of Africa and the African Diaspora, necessitated this black body.

Experimenting with Embodiment

In these pages, I make an effort to present examples of theological thinking that maintain the importance of theologizing the body as a symbol of the social system—as grand metaphor—but also theologizing the body as material, fleshy reality.[45] In this way, as noted in the preface, I am involved not in systematic theology (nor in the presentation of a formal constructive theology); but rather in experimentation whereby the body is central terrain, the place of contestation for all things sociopolitical, economic, cultural, religious *and* theological.[46]

The embodied approach does not maintain the assertive ethics of former black theology: it does not recognize as certain particular outcomes fully definable as liberation. Drawing from Foucault, it suggests instead that forms of identity cannot be addressed in isolation. They draw on and from each other in ways that keep them bound. Hence, positive movement regarding racism and other forms of discrimination might be a reinforcing of other oppressive patterns. Theology, done in light of and through embodiment, is content to point out the significance of bodies for the manner in which they provide an aesthetic of struggle that might inform our understanding and mapping of religion/religious experience. Such a perspective has implications for the outcomes of theological thinking through embodiment. The claims are not as grand, and the agenda less certain.

The rest of the book is divided into Body Construction and Bodies in Motion. Part 1 suggests a discussion of the body as metaphor or symbol, and part 2 concerns the body as material or as lived. This distinction marked by the two parts is organizational and not a firm epistemological and existential separation: together they serve to harness the importance of the complex body, as both metaphor and material. The chapters within these two parts are shaped by a question that undergirds in both explicit and implicit ways my main thesis: What is the look of theological thinking that takes as its starting point the religious significance and theological importance of the fleshy and metaphoric body? How does one think about theological categories such as "redemption," religious experience, evil, world, and so on, if the body is central?

Chapter 1 is followed by discussion of the troubled nature of identity as "blackness." Here I raise questions concerning how notions of identity, framed and embedded in black theological discourse as "blackness," have served to privilege the black male body by assuming the re-presentation and re-construction of that male body meet the liberation needs of all black bodies. Of concern is the manner in which this formulation of the (assumed male) black body hampers a full understanding of complex subjectivity as the shape of religious encounter because it fails to consider a sufficient range of the ways in which African Americans are dehumanized.

Chapter 3 focuses on the theological construction and deconstruction of the black male. I use Spike Lee's *Get on the Bus* to raise questions concerning the way in which even troubled notions of manhood are often interrogated within a limited context, based on a limited critique. Using womanist thinking as a lens, I offer an alternate perspective on the nature and meaning of gender. What results is an in/out orientation whereby the flaws of body construction are noted from within that very construction. I attempt to be mindful of this dilemma by pointing to cultural figures and developments as source material for theological inquiry rather than presenting them as normative models. The use of particular artists and other cultural examples does not suggest or imply a way of understanding embodiment. Rather, I want to suggest that attention to the blues and to rap or hip-hop does indeed break the monopoly held by what has proven a rather narrow range of source materials used in the doing of black theology (e.g., slave narratives, gospel music, a select range of literary sources). Black theology is often done in a way that privileges sources that do not trouble neat depiction of life (e.g., flat critiques of oppression that are no more than two-dimensional)—sources such as the spirituals and "race" narratives that affirm a liberation epistemology framed by a teleological view of history. However, attention to the blues (when not sanitized as "secular spirituals") and rap provides an alternate per-spective, one offering a look into the "messy" nature of life. But this depic-tion of source material, and the suggested framing of the black body when referenced using music, is best read in conjunction with the insightful work being done in relationship to the presence of black female bodies. [47]

Chapter 4 wrestles with the theological import of bodily pleasure by rethinking the nature of sex(uality) as theological category. Following Kelly Brown Douglas's lead, current discussions of sex(uality) within black theology all too often maintain unchallenged moral codes and frameworks that buttress a mind/body dualism.[48] In something of a departure from Douglas, however, I do not understand black churches as victims of a generic Western framework of proper relationship, but rather that this problematic stance stems from black theology's uncritical epistemological link to and enabling of black churches.

Chapter 5 discusses the body as the site of religious struggle. This chapter focuses on the nature of encounter with good and evil—the body's troubled occupation of time and space through attention to a question: How does one articulate and live the struggle for life meaning, or complex subjectiv-ity? My response is shaped by attention to musical production—the blues and rap music—as source material. Use of musical production as theological resource continues in chapter 6, where the rap artist Tupac Shakur frames perspective on redemption as outcome of religious struggle. Chapters 5 and 6 seek to wrestle with traditional questions of religious struggle and redemp-tion (what some might call conversion and salvation), but in a way that never loses focus on the body.[49]

Chapter 7 highlights the body's relationship to the world by exploring the theological nature and meaning of the effects of Hurricane Katrina. The chapter seeks to think about pain and suffering in ways that center the mate-riality of the body and its connection/relationship to the materiality of the world. That is to say, evil is discussed here, based on the assumption that the body and world influence and inform each other, without clear boundaries between the two.

Chapters 2 through 7 end with a short statement ("Prospects for Future Study") offering suggestions concerning what embodiment might entail, the look of embodiment within black theological thought. This material is not meant to imply the formal look of an embodied theology, and because of this I do not offer full explication of these possible turns in the doing of black theology. Again, I do not provide an embodied theology in this book. Rather, in a somewhat heuristic manner these thoughts at the end of chapters are meant to simply offer possible directions and topics for further work.

The Goal

My claim is simple: The body (metaphor and material) has profound theological importance. And here I make an effort to give some shape to this claim, to explore the ways in which this claim effects and influences the form, content, and tone of black theological thought.

Embodiment and the New Shape of Black Theological Thought is really a work in progress because it does not provide a full articulation of the complex body in/as theology, and in some cases readers will likely point to the manner in which the chapters talk about the body rather than represent theologizing from the body.[50] My goal here is to simply point to the importance of such as a move toward embodiment and to provide examples of how this might occur: To the extent the ordinary definition of theology as "God-talk" is still used by black theologians, I would note even this framing of theological discourse as "story-*ing* the divine" stems first from relationship to the human body. It is the discomfort, *dis*-ease, and joy of embodiment that promotes reflection on transcendent concerns in connection to the world. Attention to the body, then, points *in* as well as *out*.

I must also acknowledge the manner in which this book frames much of this discussion in ways meant to decenter the male body through an alternate attention. This is not to dismiss black female bodies as important. Rather, I make an effort to include sources and to note the importance of gender discussions extending beyond the frameworks of masculinity. The assumptions concerning the nature and look of black bodies must be challenged and broken, and in part this must involve the exposure of the problematic of the male body related to both the historiography of black theological thought and also as a matter of challenge to my theological autobiography. Hence, my discussion of the black male body does not solidify its centrality but rather serves to challenge this centrality.

Understanding and addressing the concerns of black theological thought as they involve altered states of existence—marked by greater freedom and liberty—requires attention to the material body as the source and recipient of social regulations and controls. The lived body must be tracked.[51] After all, it is reasonable to assert the corporeal body was the first and primary instrument of construction (their bodies for the benefit of others within an oppressive system) *and* resistance—of "being"—available to people of African descent within the ontological and existential disorder of diaspora environments.

Part 1

Body Construction

Theological Posturing

The modern world focused a new type of attention on the difference of bodies, and created a hierarchy of bodies that gave felt or lived meaning to aesthetics.[1] Enslaved Africans and their descents as victims of this discursive arrangement sought and continue to seek (in that the process is ongoing and always unfinished) to transform this discourse by turning it on its head and by gaining new visibility and new spaces of life for their natural bodies. The materiality of the body, both the individual body and the collective body, became a venue for struggle against the damning effects of language and modalities of knowledge.

While institutions and discourse place certain restrictions on particular groupings of bodies, forcing them to be perceived in relationship to the restrictive arrangements (e.g., stigmas) of the recognized social order,[2] resistance or struggle involves the very effort to expose and undo this coercion within the social context of everyday patterns and practices. Thus, according to Sarah Nettleton and Jonathan Watson, "everyday life is therefore fundamentally about the production and reproduction of bodies."[3]

Effort to reconstitute the body does not produce a unified self and no single "truth" upon which to rely. As the body is really bodies plural, the relationship between the body and the self must also mean multiple selves; therefore multiple ways of viewing the world and the demands for justice placed on the world. Agency is not lost, nor is the desire for transformation diluted. Rather, this recognized need to challenge everything changes black theology—stripping away its certainties and its rather flat depiction of the history of struggle—but it does not destroy the ability to do theology. It is simply the case that embodiment must mean a new kind of theological posture.[4]

I found useful insights for such a theological posture in a newspaper article read some years ago. The February 28, 2003, issue of the Minneapolis *Star Tribune* contained a story titled "Modern and Muslim" describing the "Scheherazade: Risking the Passage" show in which Muslim women used their artistic creativity to explore the intersections between personal faith, culture, and world developments. Of particular interest, because of its controversial nature, was the photo exhibit by Lalla Essaydi.

The context for one of Essaydi's photographs is a "'House of Obedience' belonging to Essaydi's family in Morocco." This refers to the place where women are imprisoned for "extended periods, apparently to compel repentance after they've broken an Islamic custom." This "space," as Foucault might note, is meant to individualize (as problematic), manipulate, reconceive, and reconstitute the body as docile. Within the context of this confinement or discipline, the practices and movements of the body are defined and surveyed. Bodies enter that space through a discourse of knowledge depicting them as "sinner" or "disobedient," and they are to exist supple and easily controlled. These houses are local points of power, offering specific examples of force—a type of "spectacle." Within this space of confinement, the body "is caught up in a system of constraints and privations, obligations and prohibitions."[5]

While physical pain may not be the primary mode of punishment with respect to the discursive body that concerns Foucault, the physical body is also present within that confinement. The bodies entering or displayed in these "houses of obedience" are also material; they are physical beings that experience pain, suffering, and demoralization in order to control the manner in which they respond to traditional authority. In short, within these spaces of confinement, bodies—discursive and material—are trained to accept the "truth" of the structures and institutions defining and guiding their discipline and punishment. Hence, punishment within the houses of confinement might entail privation of movement as a form of discomfort or suffering. Pain is an unavoidable dimension of confinement.[6] The point in either case, in this context of punishment as religious process, is not to destroy but rather subdue the body, to determine how the body occupies time and space and what the body does within time and space. Both the symbolic and the expressed dimensions of the body are captured through punishment. As Foucault notes, "it is always the body that is at issue—the body and its forces, their utility and their docility, their distribution and their submission."[7] Confinement in this case is meant to produce discursive bodies marked by the "truth" of the socioreligious arrangement of society, and material bodies equipped and willing to work for the safeguarding of these power relationships.

Punishment must be perceived, through the mechanisms of implementation, as natural, as "right," and beneficial.[8] In a certain way, this punishment is meant to produce a "soul"—a modality or residue of power over the body represented through habits/behaviors that is present "around, on, within the body by the functioning of power that is exercised on those punished . . . born . . . rather out of methods of punishment, supervision and constraint." The "house of obedience" forges within and on those women punished a mechanism facilitating surveillance and ongoing confinement. Through the soul (being fine tuned as necessary), punishment reaches beyond the particular moment and gains a more lasting and more embedded control over the body.[9] These disciplined bodies were to teach lessons to those within the social body, and these lessons revolved around issues of placement and practice with respect to religion, gender, and politics.

Essaydi "persuaded Moroccan women friends to pose for her in that beautiful prison. Naked, their bodies are painted."[10] This presentation would be interesting but less confrontational if it involved an arrangement of colors and designs, but instead the artist clothed the bodies in "lacy calligraphy that includes floral designs and quotations from the Qur'an."[11] This was considered an outrage in that calligraphy "is a sacred Islamic art forbidden to women," and "by literally robbing themselves in the words of the Qur'an, the women are both submitting to and violating Muslim strictures."[12] There is a certain type of defiance at work in this picture, a signifying of power relationships, a layering of "texts," through a presentation of the body as resilient against efforts to inscribe it. The body as symbol of the religious system is exposed as such, but the visibility of the marked body also points out the fragile nature of religious discipline in that it raises the question of necessity: Must this situation be? Against the purposes of the "House of Obedience," women turn themselves into subjects in that they work on their bodies and shape their conduct as individuals but within the context of others, and in this way they secure a measure of contentment not intended for them.[13] One might suggest that their presentation as text-within-text, within materiality, exposes the "made" nature of power regulations and suggest an increased range of life opportunities. Or, to borrow Foucault's wording in *Technologies of the Self*, people "are much freer than they feel, that people accept as truth, as evidence, some themes which have been built up at a certain moment during history, and that this so-called evidence can be criticized and destroyed."[14]

Without the intent of a theodical argument, there are ways in which the (re)presentation of these women as embodied and defiant exposes "houses of obedience" as somewhat arbitrary and open to historical manipulation. Molding of the body through discipline is replaced by an aesthetic construction of the body. Fractures in social arrangements and religious knowledge occur as a result. The former, molding through discipline, involves techniques/principles (for Foucault an "art") of obedience and the latter tech-niques/principles of disruption. Both are intentional modalities of think-ing and behaving. Punishment is meant to mark the body in ways enabling control over it; however, these particular bodies displayed in the image are marked in ways that challenge socioreligious and political obligation and control. They signify subjection by bringing into view and question efforts to normalize certain mechanism of individualization and social existence. Claiming their bodies, they fight tendencies to have their bodies conspire against them. In this respect the body is political.

Both the discursive body and the physical body can participate in this challenge to the framing of power in that they are each the target of disci-pline. Yet, these bodies do not resist in ways that remove them from power relations and outside the reach of knowledge, beyond the view of society; but their working against or refusal to comply with power through changes to their bodies (e.g., nude and covered with sacred text) does involve rec-ognition of the "self."[15] By their creative disregard of power, they "become." Nonetheless, even this subjectivity, this self, must be interrogated in that it resided within and not outside power relations. What is more, this subjec-tivity is not unknown but stems from choices present within the discourse of knowledge framing the social body. Self-government through this act of resistance is limited. If this reach toward self is meant as a lasting strike against gender-based discrimination or against religious oppression, it fails to root out fully these discourses. This turn toward the self cannot be under-stood as the attainment of an alternate but unified truth about the self that is lodged in the body.[16] One must neither make too much, nor too little of creative disregard in that bodies are double-faced, they are "both sacred and profane, purity and danger, order and chaos."[17]

The challenge to socioreligious regulation and knowledge found in these embodied women fractures the assumption of necessity behind spaces of docility; it urges the construction of "spaces of freedom" despite efforts to write and subdue these same bodies. It is possible to further suggest that the "secrecy" or obedience intended is exposed and challenged.[18] The "tech-nologies of power" represented by these houses of obedience are signified through manipulation of other technologies—of production, sign systems, and the self—for work against prevailing knowledge-power discourses.[19] Stigmatized (by gender) bodies, to borrow Erving Goffman's language, are transformed through an altered meaning for their embodiment; they are not presented as failed or sinful. They do not view themselves as "discredited" in that the marks on their "natural," naked bodies are not signs of abomination but instead are the language of beauty. An altered aesthetic transforms their bodies into something visible for their beauty, their happiness. Social identity is challenged and interrogated to the extent it does not fit this new self-identity.[20] If "obedience is a sacrifice of the self," this image suggests a break with the demands of certain power relations through recognition of these very relations as open to shifts and changes.[21]

The body may be culturally framed and formed, but the body is also material realities and never fully controlled. It is the reality of this physical body that gives this challenge to authority its political weight and importance. Power and knowledge (working together) allow the body to be present physically and known, but it is known in a certain way: Gender is a real issue to address because the bodies within Essaydi's photograph are material bodies experiencing the dynamics of gender discourse, feeling the discomfort and limitations involved. The problematic of agency and control is in play here to the extent this effort at discipline and presentation of the body is focused on the material body.

Of Disobedient Bodies

I find the content of Essaydi's artistic statement intriguing, in part because of the theological paradigm implied by the form of expression used.[22] I suggest Essaydi affirms creative disregard—what might be described as a photographic challenge to staid notions of the body and its proper construction and meaning—as an important source of transformation: it serves to reconfigure societal margins or boundaries using the despised to reshape the language and grammar of beauty in terms of both body and "soul." Creative disregard means, in this context, those attitudes and sensibilities that run contrary to the normative workings of societal arrangements/regulations and are therefore considered problematic because they question what discourses of power and restrictions on life practices are meant to enforce. By "unacceptable" presentation, creative disregard as process and posture challenges the construction of the body as metaphor for the social system and the denied importance and place of the body as material.[23] This sense of disregard involves a re-presentation of the complex body in ways that allow for alternate life meaning(s).

Attention to body aesthetics and the look of the body has implications that are far ranging. Because the display of the body either affirms or challenges cultural arrangements and assumptions affecting both the individual and the group, decoration or alteration is never a merely superficial and personal development. If the philosopher Terence Turner is correct, the decorating of these bodies with sacred texts exposes and brings into play both the individual physical body and the social body—both open to interrogation in that "the surface of the body seems everywhere to be treated no only as the boundary of the individual as a biological and psychological entity but as the frontier of the social self as well." What is more, Turner continues, "the surface of the body, as the common frontier of society, the social self, and the psycho-biological individual becomes the symbolic stage upon which the drama of socialization is enacted, and bodily adornment . . . becomes the language through which it is expressed."[24] The body becomes artistic, an aesthetic framing of meaning in the form of a work of art. Hence, adornment, in this case through the body inscribed with verse, is no small matter. This is a double "reading" in that the photographic image is to be read and the body containing verse must also be read.

Altered body images challenge normalized images of these women's bodies that seek to reify stigmatized and oppressive life schemes meant to house controlled and docile bodies. The body "redrawn" alters perceived and felt identity, and challenges (although also representing) societal interests.[25] Something of fundamental importance is involved in this adornment of the body with the written words of a holy text: the body is given a new ordering that in this instance (perhaps more than in others) connects it to perception of and a discourse on a more stable beauty and wholeness.[26] Adornment, hence, gives the body visibility and importance not intended by the mechanisms of punishment.

Furthermore, there are ways in which one might consider the action of this artistic presentation a strike against the assumed authority of a particular discourse of beauty and merit through which women "act" on themselves, (re)present themselves as something other than "sinners" in opposition to traditional power relationships (authority) vis-à-vis religion, and in the process become subjects. Power is stretched thin: The "house of obedience" does not produce docile bodies as intended; obedience does not become solidified as the shape of socioreligious relationships. Defiance in the context of this presentation of women as embodied and as texts over against certain modalities/forms of authority involves an alternate morality and ethic premised upon intentional "practices of freedom," which recognize the plastic nature of the self and the dynamics of power relationships from within which one labors for life.[27] Essaydi's work entails an act of defiance, a creative disregard, not the final dissolution of all power relationships, but hopefully the development of new, local power relationships that offer alternate "truths" in response to a socioreligious and political issue. There is, then, an always and ongoing process of construction and deconstruction.[28]

While the implications of gender in this practice of resistance is not explained through a Foucaultian challenge to the assumed necessity of the power relations currently in place, there are ways in which the positioning of the women in the image and the writing on their bodies makes visible their bodies as cultural constructions upon which are written the "laws" of life, but also these bodies challenge those laws through their materiality—the manner in which their resistance of traditional religious aesthetics disrupts efforts to keep them docile.[29] These bodies, gendered bodies, are not merely slates upon which power relations are drawn; they are "natural" bodies that shape knowledge through their demand for "space" once denied them. They are never completely controlled, never fully subjected to the structures of domination in that their visibility disrupts the taboos under girding religiously arranged power relationships. These houses of obedience were meant to render bodies subdued; yet their aesthetic presentation troubles this modality of punishment.[30] Something useful comes from this, as Susan Bordo remarks that "the fact that resistance is produced out of a hegemonic order does not preclude it from transforming that order."[31] The possibility of reconstituted and varied approaches to life remains.

What is so brilliant about this photograph and its underlying paradigm of creative disregard is the manner in which holy pronouncements of a disembodied deity are placed on the supple curves and sensuous places of the human body provoke in the viewer a reaction: Is this permissible? If it is not, what does it say about the creation of this god, the female body, through its inability to house or display the sacred? Ultimately, I imagine, what lurks behind such questions is an unspoken discomfort with embodiment and an effort to "apologize" for it in the presence of the transcendent. But this is an odd dilemma in that the words of both the Qur'an and the human body can be said to speak, albeit in different ways, to the presence of the divine in history. Both the body and words have a materiality, a firm presence, realness that in turn speaks to the realness and ultimate intentions of the divine, according to theists. Even so, there is a tension here: the words of the divine illicit a striving for more, a push through history, and a type of embrace and conquering of ourselves and our socioeconomic, cultural, psychological, and historical environment. The body, the flesh, elicits discomfort through a sense of being that runs contrary to the objectives of the sacred text. The sacred text, in this case the Qur'an, pushed beyond history, and the human form embodies history.

Reading the Marked Body as Art

The implications of Essaydi's work for black theological thought are here explored through an examination of the manner in which black theology might gain a posture of creative disregard through attention to the visual arts.[32] My goal here does not involve the presentation of art criticism, an articulation of the "good" and "bad" of various styles of artistic production or particular artists or pieces. However, I suggest that attention to the visual arts may help theologians recognize the manner in which theology (perhaps as an artistic process itself) might force new understandings of reality, in particular the relationships and interactions that mark the formation of life's meaning.[33] A proper posture for embodied black theological thought must involve a form of creative disregard.

Such a posture must involve a bold questioning of what is "real" about social order and existing social structures; thereby, to borrow from Foucault, exposing as contingent structures we have traditionally assumed as necessary and unshakable. Creative disregard within the context of theological work entails an uncovering and bringing into question modalities of interaction and relationship that give "meanings that we have come to attach to our bodily life."[34] It involves a rejection of metanarratives, i.e., the framing or scripting of life in rigid ways that encourage us to exist happily in "houses of obedience." Put another way, it involves the interrogation of narrow assumptions of truth and recognition of the manner in which theologizing might serve to trouble the power relations that define, shape, and confine black bodies.

Why this turn to art? I am in agreement with those who argue that artistic expression speaks to and about, from and within, the fields of power and structures of knowledge that inform and shape social interactions. Therefore, it provides an important way of viewing and exploring intersections between experience and representation, including exchanges between the body (material and discursive) and the social body. There is interplay between art and the world—as culturally constructed and as encountered in nature. Art says something about our makeup and the operation of our bodies.[35] What is more, art also becomes a way of disrupting social authority and troubling dominant modalities of knowledge—working at the boundaries and margins of thought and action. In this regard, art explores "the presentation of creative disregard"; hence, art becomes a vital means by which to set the theological posture informing this project.[36]

There are ways in which art might become the form of meaning as the body emerges and re-presents itself to itself and others. Art has served to hold together and pull apart the body as metaphor and the body as material, investing and challenging the positioning of each/both in time and space. Art can confirm problematic understandings and representations of black bodies as one finds in depictions of African Americans as aesthetically question-able and in depictions of African Americans as socially troubling. Or, art can challenge these framings of the body.[37] In a word, art "heightens awareness" of life.[38] Mindful of the work done by the art historian David Morgan among others, art bumps up against the religious and theological within the body social.[39] Perhaps it is for this reason that the philosopher of art Arthur Danto could label the museum "a kind of secular church, where the congregation affirmed and reaffirmed its identity."[40]

Post–World War II Art

Prior to the advent of the twentieth century much of what was done within the visual arts entailed a mimicking of historical reality, the presentation of what *is* exactly as it meets the eye, in accordance with the established rules of aesthetics and practice. With the creation of cinematography, the ability to capture reality was perfected, and the artist was free to impose his or her own sensibilities on art, giving the world captured a new quality of presenta-tion and meaning. Within this new artistic freedom, imagination, a creative "what if" was applied to the artistic representation of the world. In other words, the visual arts after cinematography, such as painting, did not simply copy moments and structures of life. Rather the visual arts could be used to raise questions concerning sociopolitical, religious, cultural, or economic matters; but this was done within the context of accepted rules governing the world of art and the social sensibilities that informed the art world's regula-tions. Artists, then, were "free" only to a degree.

Even Picasso's cubism paintings maintain something of the familiar in that the existing language and grammar of the social system and the art world still apply without great effort, although filtered at times through his attention to the sensibilities of the outsider—the African. Picasso was clearly influenced by and borrowed from the work of African artists. Or, think in terms of the settings presented by Henry Ossawa Tanner, the African American artist who captured perfectly the tender moments of life within the context of a larger society seething with ill will. There is something comforting in Tanner's pre-sentation of reality in that it is, although nuanced, familiar and recognizable because it uses the accepted tools of social interaction. More recently, the sensibilities and positioning of what is referred to as "Outsider Art" called into question aspects of arts production, presentation, and "refinement," but this style still works within the confines of the established system. It, like Picasso's cubism or Henry Ossawa Tanner's life settings, can involve an imaginative presentation of social realities in such a way as to signify or veil them without a fundamental frustration of said realities. The work of "Outsider Art" seeks to create additional space, to re-conceive the geography of life, but without fundamental challenge to the basic structures used to describe life. In a sense, it is an acceptable rebellion.

With the emergence of abstract expressionism in the 1940s, the relationship between the artist and the expression of reality changed. Imagination as the aesthetic practice of re-creating the historically real was questioned and problematized, but never fully conquered. Transcendent reality and surrealism were combined in this new art form in ways that brought into question basic structures of reality and the ways in which they might be depicted or captured. Artistic representation took on a new meaning, new possibilities. As shepherded by Jackson Pollock, abstract expressionism did not simply present historical reality in creative ways. Instead, it marked a vision inscribed by freedom because, "for Pollock the acceptance of freedom, the striving for fluidity, is and has been the supreme discipline."[41]

This form of painting sought to demonstrate that reality was found within the "hidden consciousness," and this was projected onto the canvas. In Pollock's words: "The source of my painting is the unconscious. I approach painting the same way I approach drawing. That is direct—with no preliminary studies. The drawings I do are relative to my painting but not for it."[42] This practice brought into question the established framework of artistic production, its language and grammar. Pollock remarks concerning his style that

> My painting does not come from the easel. I hardly ever stretch my canvas before painting. I prefer to tack the unstretched canvas to the hard wall or the floor. I need the resistance of a hard surface. On the floor I am more at ease. I feel nearer, more a part of the painting, since this way I can walk around it, work from the four sides and literally be *in* the painting. I continue to get further away form the usual painter's tools such as easel, palette, brushes, etc. I prefer sticks, trowels, knives and dripping fluid paint or a heavy impasto with sand, broken glass and other foreign matter added.[43]

This sentiment was echoed by Bruno Alfieri who wrote: "It is easy to detect the following things in all of his paintings: chaos, absolute lack of harmony, complete lack of structural organization, total absence of technique, however rudimentary, once again, chaos. . . . Pollock has broken all barriers between his picture and himself."[44]

Pollock was in a sense absorbed by the process of painting, while he also absorbed it. Because it required attention not to particularly recognizable entities, it became necessary to work with this art in terms of "objectless feelings: joy, depression, generalized excitement, etc." This required "a totally different structure" for understanding the history of art as something other than "a progressive history," as Arthur Danto remarks.[45] I am not suggesting that abstract expressionism entails an escape from the influence of others, from attention to existing structures of production. To the contrary, the artist does not work in a vacuum, completely independent of others, "generat[ing] art from nothing."[46] But abstract expressionism involves recognition of regulations on production as interference as opposed to necessary influence. Perhaps this is the meaning behind Pollock's eventual rejection of two traditional tools of painting: brushes and easel. It is through his effort to dismiss standards by "negating the practice of his precursor [Picasso], Pollock seeks to negate all precursors, as if endeavoring to be the first artist to paint a picture entirely from within himself."[47] The nature of relationship (in this case between artists and product) is changed, radically reinvented. While it speaks more to the discursive body than the material body, Pollock's work might be said to teach creative disregard. And *this* is the important point for this chapter.

How well this reinventing took place is uncertain when one considers the emergence of pop art during the 1960s, which demonstrates the degree to which even abstract expressionism involves a masking of realities.[48] There are ways in which dimensions of abstract expressionism are viewable as a mistake, as being a misunderstanding or an abuse of artistic language and symbols rather than a rejection of this language and these symbols.[49] Hence, even abstract expressionism's critique of the art form implies recognition of the traditional structures, but distorted, deformed. It leaves damaged but intact the metanarrative of art's meaning and modalities. Its advocates who subtly affirm social tradition by proclaiming pop art a "blemish" express the degree to which abstract expressions is, indeed, status quo.

Training its attention on commercial developments and symbols of commercial acquisition, pop art challenged the substance of human life and the ways in which the meaning of life is constructed. In so doing it fostered sensitivity to previously ignored or even despised relational qualities of life. This, for example, entailed an appreciation for the erotic qualities of life to the extent such realities focus on the expression of beauty through relationship, particularly those often ignored. This was troubling for some and indeed Warhol is said to have been a killer of art, "a killer of beauty."[50] But perhaps pop art as produced by Warhol really entailed recognition of beauty within the traditionally ignored items and relationships that mark typical moments of life. Perhaps this is one of the challenges posed by his instillation of the Brillo boxes.

In either case, abstract expressionism or pop art, the relationship between "things" is broken and exposed to new possibilities, and it is this development that interests me. Both suggest new possibilities of meaning. For abstract expressionism, this involves diving deep into the inner self; for pop art the external world of images and objects says a great deal. Pop art, as did abstract expressionism to a certain extent, critiqued stilted depictions of humans in relationship with other humans and materials. Each form of artistic presentation dislodged the beautiful from traditional structures and thereby allowed for the formation of new modalities of connection with ideas, objects, and other persons. In this sense, both raise questions concerning the manner in which social structures create icons of life that prohibit other ways of being and doing. While different in numerous ways, both abstract expressionism and pop art share an attitude of disruption with respect to the typical manner in which content and form relate. Thereby both, to varying degrees, teach creative disregard.

Art as Challenge to the Perception of Meaning

Both abstract expressionism and pop art require of viewers a surrender of the safety of visual comprehension. One cannot fully understand such art using the eye, because the eye allows distance and disconnection. Both of these art forms challenge basic assumptions, established sensibilities, in ways requiring different relationships to the work of art. For some, this process begins with an altered relationship to the artist through rather crude but common questions: Couldn't I make this? (This is in part a question of quality—the true artist produces what I cannot—vs. quantity—anyone can make this.) What was so offensive about pop art was the manner in which it boldly presented such established commercialized realities as cartoons, Brillo boxes, and soup cans, and through them raised questions concerning the meaning and context for art. For those who disliked pop art, such a display lacked necessary sophistication—the veiling or presenting as interference of established schemes and structures. By raising the question of what is beautiful, phrased in terms of the question what is the nature of art, whether intended or not, pop art allowed for a disregard of established norms considering what can be approached as interesting and worthy of attention. In other words, what is the proper subject of relationship or connection? According to Andy Warhol, "Pop art is a way of liking things."[51]

One of the great appeals of pop art is the manner in which it calls into question the nature and meaning of relationships: the artist to the art; the art to the public; the meaning and nature of art over against traditional perceptions of the "real." "What is art? Does it really come out of you or is it a product?"[52] Does integrity—the self as a self in relationship to other selves—exist only within the geography of the established order and its standard of acceptable behavior, or does it exist only through the destruction of this established order? Is the latter the actual nature of embodiment?

There are ways in which some of this art and these questions bring the sexual into play in both overt and subtle ways, and by so doing make visible various dimensions of bodily (body as material) pleasuring. I mention this because the sensual nature of human interaction as lived or "flesh" experience expressed in Warhol's work, for example, holds great promise that can be used to push for a more inclusive presentation of black theological embodiment through an embrace of the erotic as an important modality of meaning and relationship.[53] Take for example Warhol's post-1960s work such as his "piss paintings," so named because of the technique involved. The following statement outlines this process of blending the sex(ual) body and the visual arts within Warhol's depiction of young artist Jean-Michel Basquiat:

> In this extraordinary picture, a screen print based on a Polaroid photo of Basquiat's face has been layered onto the field of one of Warhol's *Oxidation Paintings*. The result combines Warhol's standard portrait format of celebrities and socialites with the oxidation technique in which a male urinates on a copper field, producing a so-called "piss painting." The urine stains now take the place of the typical multicolored brush strokes that were applied to the ground of Warhol's society portraits by his assistants. Warhol's usual oxidation process provides only the trace of a performance in which young men put their genitals to work for Warhol. The *Oxidation Paintings* are like the stained sheets of an erotic encounter.[54]

Warhol is not the only one to make use of the body in ways that emphasize its functions, its often despised or segregated functions.[55] But by so doing, in Warhol's work, the body gains importance as a multidimensional reality, the basis of art and the tool for its construction. One might say this is another example of the irreverent as the ability not to find "beauty in the banal" as much "as to find the banal as beautiful," and in the process to find "the ordinary extraordinary."[56]

Pop art raised questions concerning the content and location of reality as well as the source of pleasure associated with visual images. This, I believe, is the basic assertion made by Nicholas Davey that "art works do not merely reinterpret and represent subject matters but extend and alter their being. . . . It is in the notion of subject-matter . . . [that we gain] insight into how an art work can transcend the temporal restrictions of its historical origin and affect the contemporary world . . . and it can only do so if it successfully enables us to understand that there is something more to be seen in it than what is immediately before the eyes."[57] Pop art moves close to capturing in the world of art what body theology seeks to accomplish within the religious realm, and that is to uncover deep meanings through the obvious. For pop art the obvious means common items, and for body theology the obvious is the body. But there is even a relationship here if one pushes Arthur Danto's labeling of artwork as being "embodied meanings."[58]

Changing of reality's substance points to tension between imagination as defined above and a type of creative disregard. One also gets a sense of this tension between established and possible realities, and more challenging possibilities in the collage style of Romare Bearden. According to Bearden, his work presents and surfaces the hidden possibilities of life in that it acknowledges the various "roads out of the secret places within us along which we all must move as we go to touch others."[59] Through his art, revelation becomes a type of existential encounter, one that raises questions concerning acceptable presentations of life by taking objects and making them serve new purposes—an irreverent act to be sure.

Bearden constructs the conjure woman collages, for example, out of bits and pieces of other "bodies" or realities, pieces of paper and the like. There is something sensual, very material, about this process and its outcome. There is an interchange-ability at work that calls into question the nature and shape of realness. Bearden accomplishes through the collage what black theology attempts through various mediums: taking bits and pieces of fragile cultural and historical memory and expressing a reality that counters the dominant perception of the world and its content. Such a move raises important questions: What is a subject, its form, and its content? Are there set ways in which a subject must occupy space, or define space, even be distinguishable from space? On one level, the "conjure woman" is the realness of social sensibility as it relates to long-standing folk community and culture; but she is also unreal in that she is an odd configuration of pieces that, taken alone, hold little meaning. Perhaps in this way, the "conjure woman" is metaphor—constructed representation of the human body—and real material arranged in a particular manner.

Ultimately, abstract expressionism and pop art damage narratives of art and artistic production in the same way theology should question narratives of certain life interactions and relationships. The work of art demands a different perception of the history of an object or subject, an intense inspection of its contours. That is to say, "by bringing to fruition potentialities for meaning hidden within ourselves and actuality, art, far from distorting reality, brings it to an even greater fullness of being."[60] It is a provocative type of embodiment. Regarding the primary concern of this chapter with black theology, embodiment as a theological posture and concept must involve fully approaching the body in all its possible relationships. Black theology should, like these art forms, involve re-presenting of the real in time and space, and the manner in which the real is "real." Of necessity, this would involve reformulation of the form/content of the body to itself and to others.

Theological Posturing

Liberation theologies, such as black theology, raise questions concerning the likeability of despised bodies (e.g., "Black is beautiful!"), but without going so far as to question the fundamental nature and meaning of beauty. This being the case, theological discourse has much to learn from artistic developments of the twentieth century. The uncomfortable questioning of art's nature, source, and meaning holds useful implications for theological discourse's struggle over narratives of life's meaning and purpose. Black theological thought, like the art discussed above, should push beyond imagination through acts of creative disregard, acts that push against existing social structures and symbols not by an effort to jettison them but by using them.

Whereas the social system projects the world as complete—things are forever as they are–the visual arts remind us that the world is in process, meaning remains to be made. Art can involve imagination to the extent the artist seeks to give new dimension to reality as encounter by the observer, but it is not content with this process because it also pushes the boundaries of what is real about reality, and what is the nature and meaning of relationship between humans and the world. So conceived, this turn to art as a way of understanding the makeup and framing of black bodies offers strategies of creative disregard that recognize the complex nature of embodied life. While maintaining awareness of modalities of harm, attention to creative disregard vis-à-vis the arts (e.g., visual arts and musical production) also pushes for approaches to the production of healthy life options and opportunities that are not restricted to limited and limiting framing of life experiences. Rather, creative disregard as theological posture viewed through the arts recognizes the tangled nature of human relationships and the ways in which attention to these relationships should involve more than advocacy of simplistic "right" and "wrong" sociopolitical and religious perspectives and opinions. For instance, a theological posture of creative disregard within the context of hip-hop/popular culture in chapters 5 and 6 involves recognition of sexism and misogyny found in rap music, but it places these modalities of harm within a larger framework of expression and meaning. The attention to sexuality in chapter 4 turns on more than a reaction against homophobia: it critiques homophobia but places this issue within a larger framework of desire and pleasure. In short, this theological posture of creative disregard troubles a limiting and linear sense of liberation as the litmus test for proper body construction and embodied relationships.

Even when the art is figurative, there is a quality to the work that seeks to create new spaces of interaction, of connectedness to the world, done through erotic realities as pleasurable. I find value in re-conceiving black theological discourse so as to better address what Arthur Danto has termed an "aesthetic of meaning."[61] Attention to the manner in which these two forms of artistic production, abstract expressionism and pop art, raise questions concerning the nature of art and the nature and meaning of relationship to art may help black theological thought push beyond the boundaries that prevent proper recognition of a much fuller range of relationships and perceptions of the body as/in time and space. Pop art, for example, suggests that in the realm of art anything is possible because the traditional indicators of a work of art have been disregarded.[62] In the same way, application of this sensibility in the work of black theological thought could stimulate openness to acknowledgement of interactions and modes of be-*ing* that extend beyond those traditionally described and embraced. There is a sense in which the forms of artistic expression briefly depicted here, from the perspective of a theologian, push toward a new process: depiction of life in tune with the truth of our complex relational possibilities.

Guided by this sensibility, the task for black theological discourse is simple. Look deep. See the alternate possibilities; see the placement of bodies in time and space in new ways, ways that push our thinking forward. Challenge the norms of interaction and celebrate the emerging possibilities as we, to borrow from Frantz Fanon, restructure the world and the bodies it creates and sustains. So conceived, black theology becomes equipped to challenge both historical conditions and the assumed proper "attitudes toward these conditions."[63]

Stepping away from more traditionally cosmological sensibilities, I promote a theological posture that is embedded in the body and that seeks to uncover the significance of human experience as it relates to the world we structure through thought and the world experienced. The conceptual framework described here serves as a general theological rubric informing the remaining chapters and allowing for a multidimensional interrogation of the body as the main focus of black theological thought, thus promoting recognition of the manner in which bodies are constructed and experienced in time and space as of profound and foundational religious importance.[64] Religion inscribes the discursive body, and the material body plays religion out in lived experience. Theology represents and interrogates this process of interaction. And theological thinking comes to involve demanded visibility of the body, interrogations of the body many African American religions often seek to hide.[65]

It is because religion involves both the discursive body and the material body that theology can lodge itself in concern for "stigmatized" bodies, and from that position advance efforts to transgress situations that do not promote moments of freedom.[66] In this way, religion is mundane, embroiled in the structures and frameworks of how we conceptualize and live life. Destructive tension between religion and the body is lost. Furthermore, the new mode of theological thinking proposed here does little to safeguard religion from such "soiling." It cannot offer a rationalization for religion conceived in another way.[67] Hence, religion and the theological interrogation of the religious take place in a variety of venues and hold to an array of materials. This theological thinking (and acting) marked by creative disregard is, in short, embodied thinking (and acting) that concerns itself with bodies and the problems and possibilities associated with and experienced by bodies.

$$2$$

Blackness and the
Identifying of Bodies

For over a century W. E. B. Du Bois' haunting proclamation has shaped epistemological and existential discussions about African Americans.[1] In his words:

> Herein lie buried many things which if read with patience may show the strange meaning of being black here in the dawning of the Twentieth Century. This meaning is not without interest to you, Gentle Reader; *for the Problem of the Twenty-first century is the color line.* . . . Leaving, then, the world of the white man, I have stepped within the Veil, raising it that you may view faintly its deeper recesses,—the meaning of its religion, the passion of its human sorrow, and *the struggle of its greater souls.*[2]

Suggested here is a felt/lived importance given to race that runs contrary to the more discursive take on gender and race offered by Michel Foucault, or the manner in which Foucault influenced such scholars as the philosopher Judith Butler, who understand these as something of a fantasy. For those prioritizing the discursive body, a turn to a "natural" body would constitute a metaphysical foundationalism deeply troubling and misguided when such a turn assumes a pre-discourse existence of the body (without recognizing the manner in which the culturally constructed and bound perspective on the body can also entail a metaphysical foundationalism).[3] Yet, it is the material body as it occupies raced and gendered time and space that concerns Du Bois and that, from his perspective, dominants the development of localized geographies of life meaning and practice.

This is not to say discourse and thought (power and knowledge) play no role in Du Bois' work. Both are present and have impact, but they have impact on real, physical bodies. There is at least a hint of this within Du Bois' oft-quoted words: "One ever feels his two-ness,—an American, a Negro; two souls, two thoughts, two unreconciled strivings; two warring ideals in one dark body, whose dogged strength alone keeps it from being torn asunder."[4] This statement sets up much of the work untaken in the remainder of Du Bois' famous book; and what Du Bois recounts in those pages is the pain, struggle, happiness, joy, and uncertainty experienced as the life of material bodies making their way through a world both constructed and natural.

Gendered and raced flesh gives a certain type of purpose to the construction and workings of history. There are some aspects of Du Bois' insights that suggest effort to render the body more happy and free as it responds to structures of knowledge impinging upon and informing it.[5] Yet, it is clear from Du Bois' perspective that one does not simply think or offer language to explore such bodies; rather, these bodies are invested with an experiential quality: real bodies move between these two somewhat distinctive worlds.

For Foucault care of the self is directed at the soul, not at a substantive body and issues or items used by the body.[6] Du Bois also speaks of the soul with a few differences. For Du Bois the soul references elemental and somewhat unifying impulses toward life.[7] The soul(s) accounts for the more opaque impulses guiding the ways in which bodies occupy time and space, and that push toward a more developed self in relationship to other selves. In this regard, unlike Foucault, Du Bois would most likely not recount the soul as the prison of the body, but rather as the force guiding the body into greater spaces of freedom or be-*ing*. Such differences stem largely from Foucault's lack of attention to the material body and preference for the body thought and written, and Du Bois' concern extending to the body lived and experienced. "How does it *feel*," asks Du Bois, "to be a problem?"[8] This question draws from a history of both the ownership of physical bodies and the discursive construction of bodies. Real bodies experience and feel the discomfort, suffering, sorrow and moments of joy involved: they are disciplined and punished for the disruptions they cause to the social body and its logics.

Bodies experience the tensions and dilemmas of the "veil," and relationship to this veil signals certain types of bodies having different connections to the social body. The veil had multiple meanings, arrangements, and purposes one of which is clearly that of prison, a more far ranging mechanism of control than the "house of obedience" described in chapter 1.

It is prisonlike in function in that it serves to arrange black bodies, to position them properly and to fix them as docile. There are cultural arrangements and physical bodies on both sides of the veil, but in itself the veil establishes and outlines the proper relationships between those bodies through depiction and practice. "Leaving, then, the world of the white man," writes Du Bois, "I have stepped within the Veil, raising it that you may view faintly its deeper recesses,—the meaning of its religion, the passion of its human, sorrow, and the struggle of its greater souls."[9] As the view Du Bois provides would suggest, the work of confinement pretended by the veil is not fully successful as a process of negation. And as Foucault reminds, the tandem of power and knowledge are not one-directional, understandable simply in negative terms, but there are always ways in which power can be turned to one's benefit.

The tangled mess of life in light of the veil further points out the tangled nature of the material and discursive bodies. This is because the veil entails a boundary of sorts, a porous means of distinction, surveillance, and valuation. Behind the veil black bodies have double vision—seeing themselves within a localized geography of meaning and place, and also seeing themselves within an elusive larger ethos of identity. Framed in psychological terms, the racialization at work here "is the process whereby the psychological suturing effects that meld self-perception with an idealized image of wholeness dissolve."[10] It is in large part here that race (and gender) has discursive and existential force. Bodies, white bodies, more closely resembling the ideals embedded in the social body, have the luxury of subject status with a smaller range of stigmas with which to contend. Whereas black(ened) bodies encounter race and experience race as "the dividing force that splits the self beyond (unconscious) suture. For the racialized subject, both the splitting and the suturing of the ego are made apparent, visible, conscious."[11] White bodies were protected for the most part from this particular form of disturbance and needed only to abide by their rather privileged role in the social system, a role that by its very nature served as a means of surveillance and discipline for dangerous "non-white" bodies.[12]

The context of the colonial period, and with respect to sociocultural distinctions between bodies, provides a related and useful way to think about this differentiation of bodies through discourse and practice. White bodies were to be defined by the perception and practice of "civility, self-control, self-discipline, and self-determination" over against black bodies defined in terms of the opposite of those traits.[13] They were marked by an aesthetic involving dress, work, and the like with wide-ranging implications. And mechanisms were in play to prevent the blending of black and white bodies, thereby seeking to safeguard the categories of membership within the social body in general and family structures in particular. This involved narrowing (by violence when deemed beneficial) of the opportunities available to black bodies and an expansion (by violence when necessary) of the practice of white bodies.[14] Du Bois' perception of a two-ness, of double-consciousness, speaks to the workings of this stratagem of identity formation and the structuring of relationships. In response, through aesthetics, language, and practices Du Bois "aimed to reanimate the African American body, transporting it from the realm of (racist) science to that of class and culture."[15] Nonetheless, this effort to "reanimate" black bodies predates Du Bois: during the antebellum period the significance of the material body for demands made regarding sociopolitical space was well known and served as the focus of efforts to experience greater subjectivity. Looking both backward and forward, Robert Reid-Pharr argues the "spectacular display" of the corporeality of black bodies expressed the delicate status of "that body's being" but also marked recognition that an "ontology of blackness" must rest on reference to a black body.[16] Hints of a similar awareness continued into the late twentieth century in rebellious grammar (e.g., "bad" as good; black is beautiful), aesthetics, expressive culture, religion, and theology.

To the question posed by Du Bois "How does it *feel* to be a problem?" black theology (and black religion) forged answers. The impact of power on real, material, and black bodies has concerned black theology from its earliest phases to the present, providing in turn its possibilities and its shortcomings. "Certainly, we are embedded in language," Susan Bordo argues, but "we are also creatures with a physiology that limits us, even in the kinds of languages we have developed."[17] Language becomes a useful tool *and* a method of suspicion. In both cases language was manipulated and conceptual frameworks altered for new purposes. One should place early theological thinking on blackness as marker of identity within this embodied context of struggle over lived experience and how to speak that experience.

Theologizing "Black"

Even a quick survey of twentieth-century writings related to African America surfaces countless arguments, all framed by racial dichotomy and by subsequent efforts to address this dichotomy in ways that foster the emergence of selves enjoying a greater range of freedoms.[18] Discussions concerning black religion and its relationship to African American communities, a major component of conversation in African American scholarship, embrace this dichotomy and define liberative praxis based upon its assumed legitimacy. Pointing to this very thing, the National Committee of Black Churchmen, the first organizational locus of African American liberation theology, says the following in its 1969 statement: "Black Theology is a theology of 'blackness.' It is the affirmation of black humanity that emancipates black people from white racism, thus providing authentic freedom for both white and black people. It affirms the humanity of white people in that it says No to the encroachment of white oppression."[19] By means of this early articulation of a theologized black aesthetic, it was clear this affirmation of blackness as an alternate discourse of power was lodged in both abstract structures of authority and referenced in/by the materiality of black bodies. This positive blackness shaped and was shaped by bodies. It was a pronouncement to be heard and to trouble the prevailing story of stigmatized bodies. In this regard, black identity as blackness was not simply a discursive device but was also embodied and practiced.

The nature and intended audience make this process in religious studies, especially theology, of particular importance. With respect to this, the theologian Cecil Cone raised important concerns in 1975. He brought into question the "blackness" of Black theology based upon its intellectual framework's reliance on European resources. Making direct reference to his brother, James Cone, a professor of systematic theology at Union Seminary in New York, Cecil Cone says the following:

> For Cone . . . and others who are infatuated with the themes of liberation, freedom, and equality in social structures, this means that they must begin to realize that they are being influenced more by Euro-American conceptions of freedom than by the religious freedom of the black religious experience. Black Power, despite its positive affirmations of blackness and freedom, owes more in its origin to Europe than to Africa.[20]

Cecil Cone's cautionary comments are echoed in the work of many others who argue for maintenance of the racial dichotomy as the epistemological map for liberation movement. It has, hence, remained the prevailing assumption that black theologians must, when dealing with the needs of African Americans, think in terms of racism: Black v. White. The resolution of American absurdity entails a response to the race question. Even when this question was complicated by recognition of classism and sexism, these forms of oppression were understood in light of racism. The charge to "get black together first" had been softened but not forgotten.

For many, blackness was the central aesthetic concern in that it was the most telling and significant marker of black bodies. "Black is beautiful" became an extremely powerful discursive device, one that also had felt consequences for material bodies. Power played on knowledge through this slogan resulting in an alternate type of visibility whereby the conditions of blacks could be forcefully critiqued in light of a variety of scripts, including theo-religiosity. Even the most significant symbol of Christianity was reformulated in light of this new discourse as images of Jesus went from blonde and blue-eyed to darker skin with an Afro and brown eyes.[21] Jesus, both bodily and epistemologically, *is* black. "The black community," writes James Cone, "is an oppressed community primarily because of its blackness; hence the Christological importance of Jesus must be found in his blackness. If he is not black as we are," he continues, "then the resurrection has little significance for our times. Indeed, if he cannot be what we are, we cannot be who he is."[22] This controversial Christology had to be matched by a comparable anthropology—one connecting the epistemological power of blackness with a similar aesthetical value. Blackness defines God, defines Christ, and gives meaning to the struggle for existence in the contemporary moment. Such a pronouncement was not intended to have only shock value; rather, it was meant to highlight the manner in which blackness was to serve as the primary logic of contemporary (Christian) religiosity as well as the defining feature of a particular community. The discursive significance of this take on Christ had to be worn on the black body and as the renewed black body (unfortunately often limited to discursive bodies). In positioning this claim theologically, black theology was not creating a particular aesthetic and framework of authority. To the contrary, black theology was drawing from a popular discourse already underway.

Physically framed and highlighted during the 1960s and 1970s by distinctive clothing meant to critique Eurocentrism and its preferred styles of grooming, the markers of "black as beautiful" would alter with time.[23] And, as this alternate discourse can only disrupt and not destroy power relationships embedded in the social body, black is beautiful also at times reinforced the very mechanisms is sought to challenge. This was first accomplished through the unavoidable highlighting of European standards of beauty and be-*ing* through a reframing of black bodies over against these standards. This new discourse and the physical bodies engaged resulted in the heightening of individuality, but these individuals/selves were coerced into surrender to a collective. "We black people," became a linguistic referencing of the submission of the individual to a communal will. In addition, while this shift had clear ramifications for both black males and females, the dominance of black males in crafting this discourse resulted in a perpetuation of patriarchal strategies in the midst of calls for transformation (see chap. 3). Black was beautiful, but within the gender roles and patterns of relationship inherited from a time when blackness wasn't so widely accepted. Rather than consistently challenging these flaws in discursive strategies and lived practices, black theology of the late twentieth century often reinforced them.

As a result, a complex situation of conflicting strategies arose that promote some concern in late twentieth and early twenty-first century theological thought. Many members of a new generation of religious studies scholars are currently involved in constructive tasks, yet few have challenged, in a sustained way, this sense of blackness as the defining physical character and dominant discourse of African American identity and community. It is for this reason, among others, that the works of the theologian Victor Anderson (*Beyond Ontological Blackness: An Essay on African American Religious and Cultural Criticism* and *Creative Exchange: A Constructive Theology of African American Religious Experience*) are important challenges to black religious thought, which should inform the theoretical underpinning and sensibilities of the study of black religion.[24]

Anderson is not the first to question the reduction of black life to blackness; to think so is to dismiss womanist scholarship, among other subversive discourses.[25] Nonetheless, Anderson's texts are engaging because they recognize the weblike structure of African American life while holding in creative tension its demonic and productive aspects, dethroning the framework of race as identity and blackness as the *only* way to mark the bodies of African Americans. Informed by his commitment to pragmatism, Anderson's two texts offer a more firmly historicist interpretation of black life, thereby avoiding some of the more questionable assumptions (such as the certainty of black identity and the firm nature of history) marking many black and womanist theologies. Difference and change represent the logic guiding Anderson's thinking, and they connect in a framework defined by ambiguity and unresolved tensions. In this way he seeks to rethink the terms of identity formation and community participation in order to allow embodiment the broadest possible assorted points of contact with ideas and experiences. Whereas black and womanist theologies have wanted to clean house, as it were, removing the clutter and reducing frameworks of knowledge and activity options to an approved few, Anderson seeks to maintain the messy nature of the quest(s) for fullness.

What is blackness? How is blackness presented and measured? Does blackness offer an adequate summary of what it means to be included in the African American community, to have a body recognizable and celebrated? If not, what are possible alternatives to this notion of blackness? Response to these questions is important in that it provides a way to trouble long-standing but flawed structures of embodiment—blackness is the black body—and opens new possibilities of theological engagement.

Challenging Essentialism

Victor Anderson argues, in *Beyond Ontological Blackness*, that notions of white superiority and categorical racism have profoundly influenced America, and this preoccupation with race has resulted in African Americans using tremendous intellectual energy to debunk the legacy of modern racism, that of racial apologetics. Anderson rethinks this internally inconsistent form of criticism and its reified sense of blackness. Pushing beyond racial apologist's limited vision, he seeks to foster an appreciation for life as a full range of individually selected and community nurturing actions, attitudes, stances, objectives, and goals (i.e., cultural fulfillment). For Anderson there is a dynamic and meaningful connection between religious criticism and cultural criticism. This point has, however, been debated. Prior to diving into a discussion of race in Western culture and the outgrowth of religious criticism (informed by cultural criticism) in a racialized society, he discusses the nature of modern critical theory within Western culture. Moving through thinkers such as Clifford Geertz, Richard Rorty, Hans Blumenberg, Jürgen Habermas, and Edward Said, Anderson points out the struggle between an appreciation for religious criticism and the development of a postmodern and oppositional secular criticism. Anderson seeks to point out possible problems in developing a critical stance that does not collapse into self-referential inconsistency, which does not require violence to one's argument in making one's argument. He asserts that black cultural/religious criticism and black theology specifically (because of a narrow framework and oppositional to their European theological roots) are victims of this self-referential inconsistency.[26] To avoid this, black religious criticism must attack all attempts to essentialize through iconoclasm while being sensitive to its internal workings. Anderson establishes the legitimacy of seeing religious and secular criticism as compatible, not oppositional. Black religious criticism contains an iconoclastic sensibility but also contains a religious zeal for utopian vision of what exist beyond the immediate. Religious criticism can allow for cultural fulfillment because it is informed by critical theory and the "sociological tradition"; it holds a healthy distrust of "cultural heroes and idolatry," while appreciating the human impulse toward creative transformation.

Yet, African American critiques cannot ignore black life as conducted in context of a country indebted to African Americans but skeptical of their humanity. He places criticism within the "racialized culture" of the United States by developing a racial genealogy (in keeping with Cornel West's *Prophesy Deliverance*). He contends that categorical racism and white racial ideology are part of a long list of exclusionary tactics justifying differentiation of humanity for overt economic, political, social, and spiritual goals. Categorical racism entails membership within a species based upon the possession of certain characteristics and qualities that are not subject to circumstance. The process of ontological and physiological differentiation was undertaken during the Enlightenment with respect to the argued specialness of "European consciousness," and this was, in turn, based upon rationality, aesthetics, morality and race. What naturally develops, via the humanistic sciences and grounded in a theory of natural inequality, is a European genius (i.e., spirit of the age) anchoring the bloody movement of European modernity. Anderson traces the development of this reasoning in Europe to such figures as Immanuel Kant. In his writings Kant gives full expression to the aesthetic distinctions between "Negroes of Africa" and those of European descent:

> The Negroes of Africa have by nature no feeling that rises above
> the trifling. . . . So fundamental is the difference between these two races
> of man, and it appears to be as great in regard to mental capacities as in
> color.[27]

This formulation was actualized outside of Europe because it served as the bases for relations in what became the United States. Through the rhetoric of figures such as Thomas Jefferson, for example, aesthetic and intellectual distinctions between Africans and Europeans are accepted and used to rationalize slavery as the basis for economic growth and social codes of conduct (Jefferson, *Notes on the State of Virginia*, 1787). African American philosophy has spent much energy engaged in racial apologetics because of the successful transposition of the European genius to the New World. In response to this European spirit of the age, Black criticism developed a counterdiscourse that Anderson labels *ontological blackness*. Generally, black apologists have refuted claims of white supremacy by presenting black cultural genius—the uniqueness of African American contributions to culture—as grounds for black participation in social progress and democratic humanism, and the race's eventual uplift. Although one might initially recognize the appealing quality of this argument with respect to black survival, it is fundamentally flawed because it is predicated upon acceptance of the whiteness—white superiority—black apologists reject.

Albeit passionate and reasoned, Anderson argues that versions of this argument from the likes of David Walker, Maria Stewart, and Reverdy Ransom inadvertently reinforced racial ideologies, thereby damaging life options available to African Americans. Only those activities mirroring and advancing this particular sense of black genius are acceptable; other activities exist outside of "black life." In a very real way African American collective identity so defined creates internal conflict because individual desires and styles are always subject to the black "party line." The "conscious lives of blacks are experienced as bound by unresolved binary dialectics of slavery and freedom, negro and citizen, insider and outsider, black and white, struggle and survival."[28]

Viewing these issues from the context of overtly religious thought, it is reasonable to say that black religious studies participates in this ideological game by demonstrating the uniqueness of black religion in opposition to white religious expression. Ontological blackness denotes a provincial or "clan-ness" understanding of black collective life, one that is synonymous with black genius and its orthodox activities and attitudes. Blackness is reified, that is, treated as an "objectively existing category independent of historically contingent factors and subjective intentions in the writings of historical and contemporary African American cultural and religious thinkers."[29] In Anderson's *Creative Exchange*, ontological blackness truncates black (religious) experience by smoothing over its roughness and inconsistencies, its competing elements, its delights, and its dilemmas. Ontological blackness limits the range of this experience and thereby misrepresents its glory by highlighting only its flaws. While recognizing the changing nature of theological discourse over the years since the publication of *Beyond Ontological Blackness*, Anderson remains concerned. "I have witnessed," he writes, "great attention among black liberation theologians and womanist theologians to move beyond any ontologizing strategies that essentialize black experience." However, this is met with a bit of caution. He goes on to state that "yet I am still suspicious of their persistent defining of black experience as the experience of suffering, humiliation, struggle, survival, and resistance."[30] In short, the discourses of black and womanist theologies fail to adequately appreciate the ambiguity (or continuing tensions) marking the religious experience of African Americans.[31] Rather, these theological discourses circumscribe black bodies (both metaphorical and material) through a language of belonging, a language centered on a grammar of blackness. In this way, many scholars miss opportunities for profound creativity available when difference is not collapsed but allowed to persist as the mark "of experience before it is captured, frozen, and domesticated by our clear, distinct, exceptional racial descriptions."[32]

Anderson grounds his corrective to this failed approach in Howard Thurman's theory of radical consciousness and human action, Cornel West's prophetic pragmatism and politics of difference, and the literary criticism of Toni Morrison and bell hooks (Gloria Watkins). Anderson highlights the manner in which these thinkers promote the existential condition of black people as informed by race, but not limited to race. For them, life is not binary nor communal at the expense of individual choices and rights. Again, "blackness" is understood as an element of African American identity. "Both Thurman and West," Anderson remarks, "hold open the possibility that the apparently binary oppositions that characterize racial discourse can be transcended. But transcendence requires a cause or loyalty that is sufficiently categorical to include within itself both the cultural aspects of group life and personality. . . . For Thurman the dialectics of race is transcended in the idea of the beloved community. For West, radical democracy serves the function of transcendence. I call the elements of transcendence that these thinkers commend *cultural fulfillment*."[33] Anderson recognizes that their claims do not parallel fully his sense of cultural fulfillment (as transcendence), complete with both its religious and cultural criticism components. Nonetheless, they do provide a pragmatic sensibility and a new cultural politics of difference, which are more than useful. At its best, African American criticism draws from critical theory and has an appreciation for the human impulse toward creative transformation. Cultural fulfillment, not illusive blackness, is normative. The end product is a utopian yet pragmatic vision of life—fulfillment—forged in the arena of public (politicized) scrutiny, allowing for solid responses to the facts of contemporary black life. A question remains: "What should African American cultural and religious criticism look like when they are no longer romantic in inspiration and the cult of heroic genius is displaced?" (ibid., 132).

Connection between ontological blackness and religion is natural because "ontological blackness signifies the totality of black existence, a binding together of black life and experience. In its root, *religio*, religion denotes tying together, fastening behind, and binding together. Ontological blackness renders black life and experience a totality" (ibid., 14). Black theological discussions are entangled in ontological blackness, Anderson states. And accordingly, discussions of black life revolve around a theological understanding of black experience limited to suffering and survival in a racist system. The goal of this theology is to find the "meaning of black faith" in the merger of black cultural consciousness, icons of genius, and post–World War II black defiance. An admirable goal to be sure, but here is the rub: Black theologians speak, according to Anderson, in opposition to ontological whiteness when they are actually dependent upon whiteness for the legitimacy of their agenda. Furthermore, ontological blackness's strong ties to suffering and survival result in blackness being dependent on suffering, and as a result social transformation brings into question what it means to be black and religious. Liberative outcomes ultimately force an identity crisis, a crisis of legitimacy and utility. In Anderson's words:

> Talk about liberation becomes hard to justify where freedom appears as nothing more than defiant self-assertion of a revolutionary racial consciousness that requires for its legitimacy the opposition of white racism. Where there exists no possibility of transcending the black-ness that whiteness created, African American theologies of liberation must be seen not only as crisis theologies; they remain theologies in a crisis of legitimation. (ibid., 117)

This conversation becomes more "refined" as new cultural resources are unpacked and various religious alternatives acknowledged. Yet the bottom line remains "blackening" of issues and agendas, life and love. Falsehood is perpetuated through the hermeneutic of return, by which ontological blackness is the paradigm of black existence and thereby sets the agenda of black liberation within the postrevolutionary context of present-day America. One ever finds the traces of the black aesthetic that pushes for a dwarfed understanding of black life and a sacrifice of individuality for the sake of a unified black faith. Yet differing experiences of racial oppression (the stuff of ontological blackness) combined with varying experiences of class, gender, and sexual oppression call into question the value of their racialized formulations. Implicit in all of this is a crisis of faith, an unwillingness to address both the glory and guts of black existence, those nihilistic tendencies that unless held in tension with claims of transcendence have the potential to overwhelm and to suffocate.

At the heart of this dilemma is friction between ontological blackness and contemporary postmodern black life—issues, for example related to "selecting marriage partners, exercising freedom of movement, acting on gay and lesbian preferences, or choosing political parties" (ibid., 17). How does one foster balance while embracing difference as positive? Anderson looks to Friedrich Nietzsche. European genius, complete with its heroic epic, met its match in the aesthetic categories of tragedy and the grotesque genius revived and espoused by Nietzsche. The grotesque genius served as an effective counterdiscourse by embracing both the light and dark aspects of life, and holding in tension oppositional sensations: pleasure and pain, freedom and oppression (ibid., 127). Utilizing Nietzsche's work, Anderson asks "[W]hat should African American cultural and religious criticism look like when they are no longer romantic in inspiration and the cult of heroic genius is displaced by the grotesquery—full range of expression, actions, attitudes, behaviors everything found in African American life—of contemporary black expressive culture and public life?" (ibid., 132).

Applied to African Americans, the grotesque embodies the full range of African American life, all expressions, actions, attitudes, and behavior. With a hermeneutic of the grotesque as the foci, religio-cultural criticism is free from the totalizing nature of racial apologetics and the classical black aesthetic. By extension, black theology is able to address both issues of survival (Anderson sees their importance) and the larger goal of cultural fulfillment, Anderson's version of liberation. Placing "blackness" along side other indicators of identity (beyond what is visible on the flesh) allows African Americans to define themselves in a plethora of ways while maintaining their community status. This encourages African Americans to see themselves as they are, complex and diversified, no longer needing to surrender personal interest for the sake of monolithic collective status.

Anderson's aim, with a bit of the autobiographical grounding it, is to provide a way by which to think about and live African American religious experience without truncating its tone and texture, without overdetermining the bodies that move within these spaces of exchange. Blackness, set alone, tells us very little about the bodies inhabiting African American religious experience. Rather than suggesting what is the actual array, turning to blackness as the central category of identity promotes the construction of discursive bodies that are defined by maleness and a certain relationship to a limited range of cultural markers. In addition, this turn to blackness connects to material bodies that experience happiness, sorrow, joy, fear, and the like in a limited range of ways and in light of a rather questionable and much too clean read of history as involving a limited grouping of players (heterosexual males for the most part) and without full attention to the messy and uncertain nature of outcomes. So arranged, blackness rather than opening us to a complex world of relationships is a prophylactic preventing contact with *dis-ease* that might weaken or pollute identity. Critiquing blackness as a category of identity does not rule out attention to race. Whereas ontological blackness restricts and prevents fulfillment in complex ways, race according to Anderson signifies opportunity for fruitful encounter, encompassing both difference and similarity within the context of dialogical exchange and embodied practices. As Anderson cautions, race has the potential to expand and enliven our human interactions; however, this potential must be monitored in that race can also truncate relationships and limit the structuring of identities.[34]

Anderson privileges those symbols and signs that promote complex identities and rich conversation. And he sees African American religious and cultural criticism as a useful mechanism for pointing out and putting in play such symbols and signs. African American criticism, as Anderson's preferred approach, must be pragmatic enough to subvert all racial discourse and "cultural idolatry," and sensitive enough to appreciate diverse and utopian or transcendent visions of life (*Beyond Ontological Blackness*, 37–38, 80–86). When this is done, both the friction between cultural and religious criticism highlighted by Said and the preoccupation with blackness—physically and culturally—are resolved. Room is made for a religiously informed cultural criticism that is not limited to the space available though blackness, but grows to include his more recent commitment to the symbol race. This is because race has the potential to enliven and enlarge, hence it can figure significantly into the mechanisms and structures we utilize when discussing and appreciating our bodies within the context of "circles of relations" (*Creative Exchange*, 50). In this way, unlike the discourse of blackness, the discourse of race does not require reduction of explanatory frameworks, limiting of commitments, and the stultifying of social relationships. As Anderson proposes it, race becomes a way of thinking about and experiencing engagement of life on multiple levels and taking our bodies with us.

One will notice Anderson does not actually redefine blackness. He does, however, shift emphasis by understanding racial indicators such as blackness as only one of many spokes in the wheel of African American identity. Hence this identity becomes flexible and fluid, neither binary nor communal at the expense of the individual nor radically individualistic. Identity continually evolves and indicators are continuously uncovered. Fruitful self-identity is based upon a flexible humanization process extending beyond discussions of one's blackness, one's sexuality, one's class, and so on. This, it appears, allows cross-cultural contact and discussion in keeping with the best manifestations of multiculturalism because "African American-ness" develops from combinations of an endless number of social, cultural, economic, political, and psychological possibilities.

Prospects for Future Study

In what remains of this chapter, I briefly address theological ideas of subjectivity and community, alluded to in the above discussion, in keeping with a concern for the body as metaphor and material.[35] I do so in order to push the theological consequences of embodiment connected to Anderson's critique of black theology and black theology's essentialism (e.g., reification of the body-metaphor as counter whiteness). The assumption of the male body as normative black body found in black theology (and to some extent in Anderson's work) is exposed as a religious-theological problem. This, in turn, makes possible the work undertaken in chapter 3 and provides possible direction for the content of new black theological thinking.

Within the context of black communities, religious experience serves to define recognition of and struggle not for simple subjectivity but for a complex subjectivity marking robust life meaning and movement; it is the struggle against essentialism, a fixing/reification of bodies in time and space.[36] Religious experience is an assertion of being/meaning in face of oppressive essentializing and dehumanizing forces, shifts, and changes. It is, in effect, a new construction and placement of bodies in time and space that is plastic in nature, entailing flexibility.[37] When complex subjectivity, or existence as an actor in human history, is considered in light of community, tendencies toward extreme individualism (or reactionary cultural nationalism) are checked; they fall outside the scope of the accepted norm. Self-consciousness is moderated by responsibilities to community (external commitments). This is a measured sense of autonomy, an autonomous existence associated with freedom from essentialism (as expressed through sexism, racism, classism, homophobia, and environmental destruction), yet is does not entail a freedom from relationship and the obligations entailed by relationship.[38] The key is individual subjectivity in creative tension with the demand for quality of relationship (community), an alternate framing of the body and the body with other bodies. What I suggest here is the manner in which we move within various spheres of influence and commitment, marked by a wide range of circulating power relations and frameworks of knowledge. In all cases we move with the hope of fostering greater and localized spaces of engagement, and care for self and others. Recognition of various points of contact becomes vital as rich interaction is marked by engagement that recognizes the dynamics of language and the presence of the body.[39]

In contrast, essentialism is the reduction of a group or class of people to a single category or cluster of categories that promotes through law, social arrangements, and so forth their subordination and the subordination of their power to define themselves in more holistic terms. Their bodies are fixed, and limited in scope and reach.[40] What guides this process are modalities of discipline, to borrow from Foucault, whereby the restrictions are rendered natural and necessary—for the good of all involved.[41] This is most often caste in anti-black terms, yet essentialism can manifest as a pro-black stance, as in the case of the Nation of Islam, based on a racial or cultural essence. The latter is also harmful because, as the philosopher Robert Birt notes, "it tends to preserve (however clandestinely or in black face) all the conservative values of the white cultural hierarchy, and sometimes harbor[s] a secret contempt for black people concealed behind a rhetoric of glorification."[42] In either case, the significance of the body as complex conveyer of meaning is lost, and the material body as means through which we experience the world is circumscribed and confined.

I am not suggesting a crude anti-essentialism that denies the impact of blackness on African Americans. This impact is, to the contrary, recognition of blackness but as only *one* of the many factors affecting subjectivity in the context of the United States. Essentialism is oppressive because it seeks to falsely restrict being/identity to a narrow range of options—to objectify the body or body collective in such a way as to render its signification relegated to its one dimensionality as an instrument of others enjoyment or abuse. Remember that essentialist notions of black identity entail not only the "thing-ness" imposed by external oppressors but also the reification of a certain sense of blackness promoted from within. This would include the various forms of oppression discussed in black theology, but it would also protect the individual's quest for "cultural fulfillment" that concerns Victor Anderson. As Anderson notes, black and womanist theologies have unwittingly enforced forms of essentialism in ways that actually counter the struggle for a liberated existence. Think, for example, of black theology's early focus on the black male body and its need for liberation against racism. This preoccupation, of necessity, meant little attention to the black female body and the sexism implicitly accepted by black male theologians and the churches they claimed to represent.

The insight and warning offered by Hazel Carby, in *Race Men*, should not be forgotten. Black theological discourse must maintain an awareness of any tendency to discuss the black body strictly in terms of the black male body, as if this one signifier can be separated from others. Ontological blackness does not constitute an all-purpose designation in that it does not exhaust the full range of sociopolitical identifiers.[43] Otherwise, bodies are fixed and rigid, and this is lamentable in the same way the flattening effect of ontological blackness as definition of black bodies of importance or matter is lamentable. Furthermore, black theologians have often discussed the pleasures of the body strictly in terms of heterosexual orientation and in this way buttress a long history of homophobia (a form of essentialism) within black theological thinking and religious practice such as found in black churches. (I take up the topic of sex(uality) in chapter 4, and much of my discussion there is in response to Kelly Brown Douglas's intriguing work.[44])

Anderson's books and my own inclinations suggest identity works on the body (discursive and material), and the body informs identity. There is a process of exchange here, but one that does not always produce Anderson's "cultural fulfillment." To challenge existing theological assumptions regarding each case (e.g., gender, sexual orientation, and ontological blackness) requires a body that shifts and adjusts, thereby highlighting and confronting stultifying norms. It also requires ongoing diligence to make certain that both the discursive and the material body are recognized and addressed theologically.

African American life is a mosaic and should not mean that difference is the only marker of value, the only framework through which we work in the world. Instead, the mosaic should be understood as representing both difference and sameness as a creative tension.

The challenge for theology is to continuously question notions of identity and authenticity so as to make certain the complexities of embodiment are not compromised. I am ever mindful of Stuart Hall's warning that we must understand experience within the context of representation: "It is only through the way in which we represent and imagine ourselves that we come to know how we are constituted and who we are."[45] The body and embodiment become the controlling logic for the production of theological thought, and the body is recognized as being marked by more than blackness and as experiencing life as more than black. Blackness is only one of many patterns of identification that coat bodies and that are shaped by material bodies. Blackness' status as a marker of identity and a criterion for participation in the structures of community, must be continuously probed, questioned, and never allowed to shape to authoritatively the dynamics of embodiment.

The new shape of black theological thought should involve a more complex and suspicious application of the trope of blackness as defining or foundational theological category. Rather than the privileged position normally afforded to this category, attention to the complex body as physical and discursive reality entails recognition of the rather flat nature of life meaning gleaned from the historical workings of blackness (over against whiteness). For the doing of black theology, blackness cannot stand alone but must be interrogated always in connection to other life modifiers. Blackness is recognized in new black theological thought as much for what it does not tell us about African Americans, as for what it says about our interpretation and framing of a particular historical moment. So conceived, the *black* in black theology no longer points to an ontological certainty. The black in black theology connotes not the color of the people and the accompanying posture toward whiteness alone. It does not connote a particular lineage. Instead it is a flexible qualifier, easily exchanged for others such as "African American," and meant to suggest a particular mood or tone as opposed to ideological requirement. In this way it, the black in black theology, is maintained often through force of habit and tradition as opposed to some necessary epistemological agreement.

3

What to Make of Gendered Bodies?

Addressing the Male Problem

The task now is to interrogate theologically the ways in which black bodies have been defined as representative of the social system and its complex arrangement of life. I begin this process with a questioning of manhood and masculinity as the assumed representative framing of the black body: Why in black theology are the bodies usually black, male (chap. 3), and heterosexual (chap. 4)?

Much time has passed since the October 1995 gathering of African American men in Washington, DC, but much about the framing and defining of black bodies has remained the same over the years since that event.[1]

What distinguishes the Million Man March is the lack of agreement on its merit. Louis Farrakhan's call for movement toward responsibility—humaneness—was considered suspect because of media depictions.[2] Yet it is arguable that in the late twentieth century only some one of Minister Farrakhan's stature, like him or hate him, could have brought it about. With the dilemma of leadership continuously exposed by figures such as Cornel West, how many within African American communities could muster the movement of one million African American men?[3]

Farrakhan called for a physical movement to Washington, DC, on October 16, 1995, as a symbolic or metaphorical gesture denoting a changed sense of self, an embracing of responsibilities, in short a humanization process. This call seems in keeping with the historical agenda of the Nation of Islam, the religious organization developed by the Honorable Elijah Muhammad and currently led by Farrakhan. For example, Muhammad, in *Message to the Black Man in America*, describes the agenda that foreshadowed this movement to Washington:

We must begin at the cradle and teach our babies that they must do something for self. They must not be like we, their fathers, who look to the slave-makers' and slave-masters' children for all. We must teach our children now with an enthusiasm exceeding that which our slave-masters used in having our forefathers imbed the seed of dependency within us. We must stop the process of giving our brain power, labor and wealth to our slave-masters' children. We must eliminate the master-slave relationship. We must educate ourselves and our children into the rich power of knowledge which has elevated every people who have sought and used it. We must give the benefit of our knowledge to the elevation of our own people.[4]

This was, ideally, a call initiated by Farrakhan to humanization. Ideally, it had the intent of forging accountability and responsibility for one's actions and mistakes. And, ideally, it was to entail attitudinal movement away from harmful notions of masculinity that deflect one's responsibility to self, friends, family, and community. All of this was symbolized, placed within the metaphor of movement: away from harmful ways of being in the world, to Washington as site of change, and back to home with new ways of operating and renewed commitment to transforming the world. "I, from this day forward," participants were to recite, "will strive to improve myself spiritually, morally, mentally, socially, politically, and economically for the benefit of myself, my family, and my people." Commitment did not end with that line because those gathered also vowed to address their concerns in a more measured way, pledging that "that from this day forward, I will never raise my hand with a knife or a gun to beat, cut, or shoot any member of my family or any human being except in self-defense."[5] Whether effective or not, the march garnered the attention of the country and became fodder for Hollywood playback, including an offering from the filmmaker Spike Lee.

Spike Lee and Black Male Bodies

What follows is explicitly grounded in certain methodological considerations. I rely on a loose interpretation of the anthropologist Victor W. Turner's triadically structured ritual process of separation, liminal period, and reintegration as the framework for thinking through Spike Lee's film. In *Ritual Process*, Turner builds upon the ethnographer Arnold Van Gennep's original three-phase notion of ritual. In so doing, Turner suggests that the ritual process involves a movement or transition "in and out of time." That is, those participating in ritual activity involve themselves in a transforming process, consisting in the movement from a societal present (things as they are), into a period of ambiguity, and back into a reconstituted societal present (an existence premised upon new insight, abilities, and responsibilities). During the liminal or ambiguous period, society is recognized through hierarchies and structures, juxtaposed to some type of *communitas* (i.e., a system of relationships based upon equality and commonality). As Turner illustrates, this process is discernable in a variety of communities, an interplay between social existence and the possibility of better *communitas*.[6]

With all of its problems, the value of the Million Man March, the call to atonement, is found not in the DC gathering per se but in the *process* of getting there—the liminal period of alteration, presented in Spike Lee's *Get On the Bus*. This film captures the movement toward humanity, *communitas*, entailed in community building; as such, it serves as a symbol or sign for the marches' attempt to epistemologically and ontologically move black men in liberating directions. Although problematic in that Lee does not successfully move beyond some of the stereotypical depictions and provincial attitudes present in early work, it is still a tremendous effort, from initial financing arrangements through production. In a real way, the film jaggedly presents the often-uncomfortable complexity of African American life; it is quite clear over the two hours that all African American men *are not* the same. This community is far from monolithic and phobia free.

As the cast of characters begins to board the bus (Turner's moment of ritual separation) headed to the Million Man March, the complexity begins to surface. The need for humanization, or atonement as Farrakhan puts it, is unmistakable, and the bus ride presents the opportunity for transformation. Oddly enough, they gather in the parking lot of the First African Methodist Episcopal Church of Los Angeles, a church within the first black denomination in this country and a church historically committed to the uplift of African Americans. In addition to this symbolism, the passengers embark on a transforming journey aboard the "Spotted Owl" bus. We are later told that this owl represents, as do the black men within it, an endangered species. The colors of the bus are yellow, black, and green, which brings to mind Marcus Garvey's Pan-African flag and his efforts to instill within African Americans a sense of self-respect capable of sustaining positive and transforming actions.

Each participant seeks to ride into history, to be a part of something big, but they do this for a variety of reasons. Overarching all is a sense of divine destiny, of providence. This is of limited importance, however, for the participants. Sure, they pray, but for those who do (other than two Muslims and an elderly gentleman) it is an act of ceremony. This points, I believe, to the symbolic importance of religious organization and language; it provides a way of speaking to circumstances.

What are the circumstances motivating this journey? What are these men separating themselves from? What is the nature of their existence, their current and pressing realities? We begin answering these questions with two passengers, Evan Sr., and Evan Jr. (a.k.a "Smooth"). Evan Sr. is a father who gave life to a child he was ill equipped to care for; he spent much of his life running away, as many do, from his responsibilities. Evan Jr., his son, has been convicted of a misdemeanor and ordered by the judge bound, literally, to his father (by a chain) for seventy-two hours. Evan Sr. decides to take his son on this journey in order to present him with life options, a sense of accountability and responsibility for one's actions; underlying his agenda is a desire to bond with his son, to insert himself into his son's life, in order to atone for his misdeeds.

Two gay males board the bus, Kyle and Randall, also bound for the Million Man March. They are leaving a context in which it is detrimental to acknowledge publicly one's lifestyle and whom one loves. Kyle and Randall find that this heterosexism and homophobia impact the ways in which they respond to each other; yet both recognize these issues are intimately connected to race and class, and the march affords opportunity to respond to these issues in the company of other concerned African Americans. For them, this ride means a claiming of their space and rights within black America. But this will not be an easy journey, in part because of the aggressive homophobia of another passenger, Flip (Philip Carter), an actor from Los Angeles who, in vulgar ways, questions the right of "faggots" to ride the bus and participate in the march. The reasons for Flip's participation in the march are vague at best, but he does function as a ghetto gadfly, sparking conversation and touching ideological soft spots. In a more overt way, Flip represents the sense of homophobia earlier embodied in such figures as Eldridge Cleaver and others who presented the quest for manhood in macho terms.

Notions of homophobia are never sufficiently addressed, although reevaluation of African American manhood should also entail a rethinking of who men are "permitted" to love. The film's attempt to address this issue falls short: the resolution comes through a violent encounter between Flip and Kyle. Kyle, one is led to think, achieves respect and "manhood" for himself, and Randall through winning his physical fight with Flip. One problem is resolved only by creating another, that of black-on-black violence. This is a John Wayne-ish move, inappropriate for a community already on the verge of destruction because of externally imposed and internally enacted violence. Flip's comments are not limited to Kyle and Randall; he also addresses issues of bi-racial relationships, the racial and cultural sensibilities of bi-racial children, and colorism. Gary Rivers, a police officer from Los Angeles is the butt of Flip's remarks concerning racial purity.

Gary, on the other hand, is interested in contributing to progressive action that fosters a sense of accountability and responsibility for actions taken. Jamal, an orthodox Muslim and ex-gangbanger, desires participation in efforts toward unity and harmony within black communities; this is Allah's call on his life. Xavier ("X"), a UCLA student, brings his camcorder and tapes the interactions on the bus. He chronicles the events for us and it is often through his lens that the audience participates as voyeurs. Xavier invites the audience into the transformative conversations and, in this way, urges the viewers' own growth. The bus driver, George, is the conductor who negotiates the movement sought by all of these men. "Pop" or Jeremiah (the biblical imagery of the prophet) is the storyteller, the griot; he tells the history, points out moments of success, and criticizes failure. He is personally leaving a context of surrender to the status quo—a lifetime of opportunities sacrificed on the alter of illusionary security. Pop understands this as his opportunity to step out in an act of daring and growth. There are indeed others aboard the bus, but these named are by far the more significant characters, all seeking in some way to tackle social contexts marked by racism, classism, homophobia, colorism, black-white relations (e.g., black/Jewish interaction), and heterosexism.

Once the bus pulls out of the parking lot, the liminal period begins, a period of uncertainty and fluidity during which issues are rehearsed, bonds forged, ceremonies learned and enacted. Fears and hopes are expressed without regard to how that information might be used later. Suspicion and guardedness are suspended; issues are discussed and fixed using central elements of black oral tradition such as signifying and "the dozens." ("Signifying" involves verbal indirection; it blurs the figurative and the explicit meaning. The "dozens" is a verbal game of insults.) These men need to establish the agenda, to set the ground rules, to prepare for what will take place once Washington is reached. This liminal period is meant to be a purging process, a readying the self for transformation, for profound alteration—for *communitas*.

As part of this process, there is an effort to create homogeneity or a monolithic reality in which all black men on the bus agree as to the basic parameters of acceptable behavior. In the words of Victor Turner: "It is as though they are being reduced or ground down to a uniform condition to be fashioned anew and endowed with additional powers to enable them to cope with their new station in life."[7] On the surface, this might appear a useful tool, but it is a dangerous one. Take for example the exchange with a short-term passenger on the bus, Wendell Perry, a Lexus dealer from Memphis, Tennessee.

In Memphis, the "Spotted Owl" pulls into a rest area that allows for further discussion of white reaction to the Million Man March and, more specifically, Minister Farrakhan. As a result of heated conversations on the bus combined with some accurate and inaccurate depictions of Farrakhan, the Jewish bus driver George refuses to continue with his duties. Inside the restaurant, conversations develop regarding the agenda of the march and the status of Farrakhan as a leader of African Americans. Evan Sr. corrects many of the misperceptions, summing it up with the remark that pro-black feelings and desire for selfhood are not by nature anti-white feelings.

As they are preparing to board the bus, Wendell Perry asks for a ride to the march. His motive for attending, as he initially presents it, seems legitimate from the passengers' perspective. However, once the bus is moving again, Wendell shows himself to be a Republican who is contemptuous of "niggas," those African Americans whom he considers lazy, lacking in ambition, and economically wanting. He denies racism as a significant factor in the failure of many African Americans to achieve recognizable success. In an effort to create the consensus often present in the liminal phase, Wendell is thrown off the bus. Granted, many of his remarks are extremely offensive and suspect, but no more so than the rantings of Flip. Consensus is sought, but is it useful or even possible? Can an appreciation for diversity and difference develop through the suppression of uncomfortable difference? Is "left of center" the only ideological and political position for African Americans? These are just some of the questions posed by conversation on the bus: perhaps the only possible consensus is recognition of diverse opinion as grounded in the multiplicity of experiences. This philosophical stance, developed during the liminal period, provides the transformation necessary for reentering social space in fruitful ways.

This transformation must happen in an unlikely way because some never make it to the march. Jeremiah passes away, and the men close to Jeremiah spend their time in the hospital. Lee rightly points out that transformation did not center on physically gathering in Washington. In fact, the transformation must occur outside the speeches and greetings. It must occur during the journey, through the conversations, encounters, and moments of reflection housed on the many buses, in the planes, trains, and cars as folks encounter folks.

Farrakhan and the other organizers of the Million Man March envisioned an evaluation of black manhood, which was to promote renewed accountability and responsibility for the condition of African Americans. Was this achieved? Overt areas of problematic black male behavior were subtly critiqued as is evidenced in the response of travelers to the more overtly offensive remarks of Flip. Relationships between men and women that are healthy and nurturing are quickly promoted through Gary's remarks regarding his respectful relationship with his girlfriend, Jamal's relationship with his girlfriend, and George's relationship with his wife. Abuse and infidelity as markers of masculinity are denounced. Manhood within the film also requires responsibility for one's family, mentoring and guiding one's children constantly and consistently. Showing concern, compassion, and love openly and frequently are embraced. The transformation of the two Evans is a marker of this. Yet there is something ambiguous and spotty about the bus conversations and the questions generated; after all, only so much can be done in two hours.

The transformation might appear an act of atonement, much needed conversation between the "brothas," a restructuring of manhood, but it lacks perspective because it is devoid of critique by those who have suffered from the *mis*-construction of manhood—black women. Within the context of a closed and all-male exchange, such as that orchestrated by Farrakhan's Million Man March or filmed by Spike Lee, troubling dimensions of gender construction and their lived consequences go without interrogation. This is not the end of the story, however. The march and the film provide something of a heuristic, a framework by which to access the nature of the black body in other arenas. A similar dilemma might be said to exist within the context of black theological thought. While not providing full and systematic unpacking of the black male body as metaphor, the following section serves to question the perceived rightness of traditional theological thinking on the assumed black (male) body.

Questioning the 'Way Things Are'

For some time now, I have found the blues appealing. There is something about the aesthetics of that genre, but also something about the general worldview that is hauntingly tragic and attractive. In particular, Muddy Waters has captured me, particularly "Manish Boy," holding my attention many an evening. But what is this "manish boy"? Perhaps someone with hypersensitivity to the ways in which the body receives and gives pleasure?

> I'm a hoochie coochie man
> The line I shoot will never miss
> When I make love to a woman,
> she can't resist[8]

To be a "manish boy," I believe, is to be positioned between adulthood and childhood, moving between assertions of responsibility to expressions of a narrow focus on strong individual want. Yet it also involves an unfortunate attempt at invisibility, not of the body per se, but of the body's moral and ethical possibilities and obligations. It seeks to ignore, or render invisible, the male's obligation to move the body in ways that are ethically and morally sensitive and productive. Within the context of the blues, this perspective is most commonly and graphically presented with respect to the libido, the body as sexual. Regarding this, one finds Muddy Waters noting that,

> Now when I was a young boy, at the age of five
> My mother said I was gonna be the greatest man alive
> But now I'm a man, way past twenty-one
> Want you to believe me baby,
> I had lots of fun.[9]

While black males can legitimately claim oppression within the context of the United States, maleness has also entailed certain forms of privilege including a limited ability to render the body invisible in certain regards. Granted, practices such as profiling clearly indicate that the black (male) body is never completely free from observation; yet there remain ways in which the black male body can be moved through the world with a limited obligation to observe certain moral and ethical responsibilities, particularly with respect to interactions with black women. This ability to shadow human interactions involves invisibility.

I label this epistemological and ontological oddity, this type of invisibility, the "manish boy" phenomenon. It is this male relationship to the world that, at least in part, accounts for the positioning in negative ways of women with respect to themselves and community. Perhaps, in part, this is what Zora Neale Hurston meant when referring to black women as the "mules" of the world. And perhaps this ability to remain undetected is noticed and signified in the subtle brilliance of Alice Walker's "Mr." on so many occasions in *The Color Purple*: simply "Mr." as the identifier of Celie's husband.

In the first instance, Hurston, notes the manner in which the bodies of black women are "fixed" and understood in terms of service given (what Delores Williams might note as the metareality of surrogacy); while others, including black men to some degree, have bodies that are more ambiguous. Walker, who is well aware of Hurston's analysis of African American women's alterity, outlines the various ways in which even privilege within the context of discrimination (such as the benefits of maleness for racialized men) allows for the body to take on a "shadow" existence—to be somewhat ghostlike in that its "weight" is deniable. In both cases it seems clear that invisibility of the black male body allows for moral and ethical slippage. Aren't, for example, Walker's "Mr." from *The Color Purple* (sometimes Albert) and Hurston's "Tea Cake" (from *Their Eyes Were Watching God*) in this sense manish boys?

With this said, and in light of the Million Man March and Lee's film, as well as my training as a theologian, I cannot resist asking a question: What is the theological equivalent of the manish body? Are there ways in which this ability to disappear the black male body has shaped black theological discourse in particularly harmful ways? Put another way, has black (male) theological discourse acted in bad faith with respect to its moral and ethical outlook because black male theologians have conducted their work as "shadows," as bodies not bound by the regulations these same bodies forge in relationship to others? The obvious, and correct, answer is yes.

I ask these questions, and provide an answer in the affirmative, in large part because of implicit and explicit lessons I have learned from womanist scholarship.[10] Although this should be an obvious statement, womanist scholarship urged me to recognize that I have a body, and that this body is, in fact, gendered. In the same way that white privilege entails the ability of whites to think of only the "other" as being raced, male privilege (even in its limited form as experienced by black men) entails a similar option for "not-ness," or invisibility (a dimension of invisibility, I should like to say was ignored in Ralph Ellison's *Invisible Man*).[11] Such willful ignorance on my part did damage to my ability to theologize in complex ways; it also influenced my pedagogical options.

I made certain assumptions and embraced particular unacknowledged privileges that accompany the male body, such as an assumption that one is entitled to comfortably occupy "space." And with respect to pedagogy, whether I acknowledged it or not, my physical presence in the classroom sent nonwritten and nonverbal messages to my students. My body provided information that affected the manner in which my students received and processed the knowledge I attempted to impart. But I often ignored this reality.[12] With my first encounter of Alice Walker's definition of "womanist," I was challenged to recognize the means by which the unacknowledged assertion of the black male body affects the manner in which black women experience the world. My participation in and advancement of strategies of force impact the ways in which I understand myself and interact with others.

The gendering of bodies and the implications of the processes involved are difficult to change and difficult to resist, but this is not to say we have no recourse for thinking about these bodies in complex (and hopefully transformative) ways. While black (male) theological discourse has acknowledged and attempted to exorcise its more demonic (in the sense of Tillich's "life harming life") features, problems remain. Black theology has failed beyond a few exceptions to critique and offer an alternate to the hypermasculinity promoted in some Christian circles as a way of combating the destruction of the traditional model of familial existence.[13] By so doing, black theology fails to take advantage of an opportunity to extend its vision beyond an updated version of the cult of domesticity. There is no doubt that this epistemological stance fosters a theological posture that misreads African American communities and their needs, the nature of their oppression, in that it views these communities through a lens of heterosexual male-centered existence.

I am not suggesting the complete obliteration of maleness, if this were even possible. Rather I am suggesting that there must be ways to add complexity to it, and to place it in relationship with other modes of encounter with the world—to construct black bodies in ways that are not premised strictly on an epistemology of "maleness" and heterosexuality. In short, this is an effort to create bodies that run contrary to the existing process of normalization by which significant bodies are understood as male, middle-class, and heterosexual. By extension, this challenge to normalization on the discursive level must be matched by an appreciation of variation and difference with respect to how physical bodies approach and participate in the world.

Jacquelyn Grant's *White Women's Christ, Black Women's Jesus* and Delores Williams's *Sisters in the Wilderness*, both books written by theologians, required me to acknowledge the manner in which my very *be*-ing as a male entailed a certain language and grammar that in itself placed restrictions on my theologizing.[14] I am unwilling to say that my socially constructed and reified existence as "male" means a hopelessness with respect to my position as oppressed/ oppressor. Redemption is possible for even those who move through the world carrying the weight of the male body. Still, there is need for sensitivity to the ways in which the existence of the male body (my body) as coded, as symbol of the social system, involves a type of theological double-talk.

Womanist scholars, through the development of a complex and intellectually sophisticated theological methodology and theory of experience that is interdisciplinary in nature, have challenged traditional theological formulations. This critique highlighted the manner in which black theological discourse, dominated by males, entails the passive acceptance of privilege that does damage to efforts toward liberation. This damage involves the passive assumption that the black body is male.[15] That means a certain set of symbols, signs, and a fixed grammar shape theological perspective and argumentation. Womanists have convincingly demonstrated in black theology a failure to take seriously, to really take seriously in a way that changes deeply the manner by which scholarship is conducted, alternate modalities of experience: sexism, heterosexism, and the like.

In addition to the ways in which womanist scholarship has surfaced (through what I refer to as a hermeneutic of archeology) African American women's experience as theological sources or data, there is a more theoretically and methodologically centered consequence of womanist work.[16] This second theoretical and methodological challenge posed by womanist scholarship has pushed on me a growing awareness of the incomplete status of my theological formulations, through an effort to maintain the invisibility of my body.[17] If I am sensitive to the sociocultural, psychological, and political implications of my physical presence even in the ways in which I think and teach theology, it is likely that theological formulations will take on a more nuanced, a more complex, a "thicker" meaning.

Womanist existential sensibilities push theologians to entertain the possibility of transforming black theology into a proper body theology. In this way it moves in the direction of discourse genuinely concerned with the implications of existence (and meaning) present in the physical body and the body as metaphor, mining the body for its theological import. So doing involves the ability to construct theology that does not seek to avoid or ignore the body, but rather theology that is done through sustained contact with the body, again as metaphor and material. This seems the theological implication of the womanist appreciation for "roundness" highlighted in Alice Walker's definition of the term, the term appropriated by black women in religious studies during the mid-1980s. Such an understanding of theology's connection to the physical world holds intriguing potential for doing black theology in ways that push beyond its methodological provincialism and theoretical xenophobia. It is conceivable that black theological thought, following the *best* of the womanist tradition, will give the notion of liberation greater depth and epistemological balance in that it becomes a sense of free movement, which appreciates the flesh rather than simply attempting to ignore it or assume that only male bodies matter.[18] This entails the death of the manish boy and the birth of a more complex and more deeply connected human— one who appreciates, in Alice Walker's words, a yearning for "survival and wholeness of entire people, male and female."[19]

The remainder of this chapter extends beyond my personal engagement of womanist theology to explore possibilities of alternate theological thinking on the gendered body in light of womanist thought; but not this framework alone. I view womanist critiques of the nature and meaning of the gendered body in black theology through the conceptual principles offered by Foucault, sociology of the body, and theories of the material body.

Interrogating the Black Male Body

In both explicit and implicit ways, womanist theology has pushed for clarity concerning the scope of the problem and the mechanisms available for working through the problematics of gender. Womanists have wisely noted that a proper articulation and vision of social transformation as complex and productive relationships had to entail the exorcising of the black male body, the acknowledgement of its weight and presence, and the effort to render problematic assumptions concerning the knowledge and power that privilege male bodies, even males bodies stigmatized by race, in time and space. In its most pressing form, this realization meant knowing that it is not enough to acknowledge sexism as a dimension of oppression experienced within African American communities. Here I point to a perspective offered by Michel Foucault. While he references the fight for gay rights, the concept works in a variety of contexts relevant to this chapter. Foucault notes that the most pressing issue is not the acquisition of a limited range of rights and legal protections; rather, the fundamental dilemma revolves around the inadequacy of social relationships that inform and support patterns and frameworks of discrimination.[20]

The history of the body is permeated throughout by discourses of "truth" (e.g., "Men don't behave that way"; "'Man-up' and deal with it!") and ontologies of bodies as subjects in various times and spaces—both imposed and fortified by society and social groupings—and constituting to some extent a "soul" that shapes the body to particular patterns of expression and meaning.[21] Gender becomes an organizing principle and something with which physical bodies wrestle. It is responsible for the emergence of certain types of bodies as a matter of cultural production;[22] but it also serves as a real dimension of material bodies (as irreducible to cultural constructions vis-à-vis power).

The takeaway from Foucault's insights involves the need to recognize the manner in which the problematic nature of black masculine frameworks is tied to systems of knowledge and their accoutrement of dispersed power, which support these frameworks within the context of social relations. Within these frameworks, and in line with the norms of the social body, black masculinity becomes both problem and benefit for certain bodies. However, it also becomes important to remember that gender, as a framework of power, is not a stable cultural product, exerting a unified and unify force beyond the scope of question and critique from all angles. To the contrary, gender's utility and pitfalls are accessible as it is explored in relationships to embodiment and lived experience.[23] Attention to the joys of social relationships, and the manner in which these relationships involve discomfort and restriction related to localized moments and spaces of experience, proves helpful. The point is not to destroy gender as a category of analysis and as a form of power's impingement on material bodies, as if this were even feasible. Instead, the goal for black theological thought should be exposure of how gender (always in collaboration with other markers) frames our sense of the world and our experience of the world. This in turn allows development of approaches to life that lessen the negative impact of restrictive gender dynamics. I am mindful of Foucault's cautionary note regarding the nature and function of the power that shapes social relationships and self-perception. Power, he argues, cannot be circumvented completely, nor can it be "dissolved," because disciplines—methods of control related to power—that inform/shape bodies are not absolute. They can, however, be effective and difficult to identify as anything other than necessary and reasonable modalities of differentiation and ranking. These methods of control (techniques of socialization) for black bodies shifted during the course of American history as the relationship of black bodies to the social body was altered.[24]

Nonetheless, these methods were meant to produce and explain black bodies as laboring both discursively and physically for the welfare of others. In addition, these methods of control served to support and enforce social regulations based on difference. For example, the black male as *dangerous* made reasonable means of coercion to control the spaces occupied by black bodies. Black males were not to interact in "inappropriate ways" with whites, and they were not to engage white women in ways that could be considered sexual. Failure to follow these rules could result in death. The discourse of black females as exotic, sexually available or asexual "mammies" made utility of their bodies by whites (and black males to some degree) reasonable as a source of labor or pleasure.

Black bodies had to be easily observable, open to manipulation, and properly placed. In these various cases, the intentional aim was to shape, monitor, and arrange black bodies so as to affirm as "right" (or correct) the modes of identification and purpose that privileged normal (with respect to race, gender, class and so on) or, in other words, civilized bodies.[25] Connection and dependence marked the relationship between civilized bodies (white bodies) and stigmatized bodies, but while recognized on some level, this dependence was not relished.[26] As a consequence, black bodies were despised, not trusted, but deeply necessary and desired. And what is more, African Americans both embraced and fought this depiction of the discursive black body and the resulting perception and arrangement of physically black bodies in localized environments. This process of accept/fight involves tension between adherence to cultural norms and interrogation of these same norms in an effort to damage them. As an ongoing pattern, the instability of both stigmatized and civilized bodies makes this expressed conflict somewhat inevitable and politically charged.[27]

The intentional critique and the embrace by African Americans of the political structuring and arrangement of bodies was accomplished by means of celebration of a discourse of blackness (see chap. 2). In addition, there were centuries-old aggressive and passive attempts to overlap with the established rules of gender as represented, for example, through the "cult of domesticity," the "cult of true womanhood," shift in form (e.g., rejection of body image through body alteration).[28] One must also include here Afrocentric ideological frameworks affecting the aesthetics, labor, and placement of material bodies. Both discourses of normalized bodies and counterdiscourses aimed at overdetermined and highly visible (in terms of utility) black bodies and thus reinforced hegemonic images within the context of the assumed superiority of middle-class values and aspirations.[29] Both tend to fix the ways in which these bodies experience and respond to life as good members of the social body and also as a *dis-ease* within this same social body. Hence, "social circumstances" are arranged to control material bodies whether they are deemed male or female. The philosopher Susan Bordo points to a dimension of this reach of power structures: "The racist ideology and imagery that construct non-European 'races' as 'primitive,' 'savage,' sexually animalistic, and indeed more *bodily* than the white 'races,' extends to black women as well as black men."[30] These bodies, defined in gender terms that mean restriction and, in religious terms, deep metaphysical trouble, weigh down women.[31]

For women the tension of embodiment and the weight of the body has entailed a push to embrace structures of labor and relationship, objectification, and other modalities of alienation for the good of another individual or the group.[32] For men this process means representing masculinity through a range of body postures running from "Stagger Lee"–like rebels to the stooped-shouldered "yes men" and everything in-between. At other times, it means challenging the demands of the civilized male body. The cultural coding of gender pulls bodies in a variety of directions, attempting to mold them in various ways and for various purposes. For both black men and women, this double bind is complicated by the overlay of race and discourses of racial inferiority that also serve to shape and present bodies.[33]

I do not suggest that the gendered body is always a troubled or oppressed body. Gendering of bodies involves contact with positive and negative power structures that serve as mechanisms of interaction promoting both healthy and damaging relationship networks.[34] Furthermore, it is not the case that gender-based structures always place women as passive recipients of instruction and men as aggressive agents of domination. Following Foucault's line of reasoning on this point, power is not in this context simply defined as something exercised by someone over someone else. It is not possessed in this manner. It is a more pervasive arrangement of techniques, effused strategies and forces working in connection to various discourses. Men often have a greater reason to support dominant arrangements; there tends to be benefit for them because patriarchy is a significant discourse. Nonetheless, buying into and benefiting from the "male as center" discourse must be expressed in degrees because race, sexual orientation, and other factors affect levels of benefit.[35] Understood in this way, the arrangements of power and knowledge impinge (but perhaps unevenly) upon all bodies and also contain opportunities for struggle. Viewing gender (and other cultural marks on living bodies) in light of this posture toward the working of power and knowledge brings into view whiteness and other modalities of representation, which are typically left as invisible factors of meaning. Difference is not linear. Everybody/ every body is recognized as involved in the relationships of force that must be examined. There are no exceptions and no exemptions.

Prospect for Future Study

With respect to the shaping of a new black theological discourse (mode of thinking), this perspective on the nature and meaning of gender pushes for several considerations. First, sustained attention to cultural production, as a means of shaping and articulating material black bodies, is necessary. To the extent that black theology has engaged cultural production, it has done so under the assumption that cultural production is a raw material, which can be handled, arranged, and analyzed from a distance because it involves things distinctive from our bodies/our selves (e.g., songs and narratives).

Little thought was given to the ways that elements of culture are simply components of larger and more effusive strategies of power and truth connected to embodiment. As a result, the working perspective on gender with black theology has not sufficiently recognized the manner in which we are embedded in cultural production (as material bodies) and on some level formed by it (as discursive bodies).

Second, following this attention to the nature and meaning of cultural production, new black theological thinking will have to demonstrate a multidimensional perspective whereby a variety of culturally informed categories—race, gender, class, etc.—are held in tension and recognized as involving overlapping and related modes of determination and discipline. This multidimensional analysis entails more than acknowledgement of oppression as weblike or as the need for solidarity. More complexity of thought is necessary because perspective on gender as both a problematic and useful marker of social relationship is vital, but this perspective must always note the manner in which the "good" and "bad" of gender is best assessed on the ground, within particular and localized contexts. Technologies of discipline, seeking to foster docile bodies, make it difficult to transverse these various locations.

The privileging of epistemology as the structure of this solidarity may not be sufficient to alter the workings of power and knowledge. Ability to move easily between these various categories is not without its difficulties: although bodies are plastic, shifting, and changing, they do not do so easily and without constraint. The shifting nature of the body has to do with the manner in which it is penetrated by various technologies of power while also informing and challenging power/knowledge structures.[36]

Based on the nature of control and the power relations supported by them, new black theological thought simply seeks opportunities and means by which to "play these games of power with as little domination as possible."[37] Black theological discourse must accept this cautionary note: power and discourses of knowledge interact continually in ways that are both beneficial and detrimental to given individuals and groups at particular times. This is not to surrender to power dynamics but to recognize that individuals and communities struggle from within grids of power and are never able to step outside these arrangements. But unlike Foucault, new black theological thought understands this situation with respect to both discursive bodies and material bodies. Such recognition means comfort with the idea that struggle over the harmful dimensions of discourses of gender (and race) is perpetual and must involve recognition that any reworking of gendered dynamics of lived experience will undoubtedly create certain spaces of privilege and other spaces of pain. In short, new black theological discourse works within power relations to trouble power relations: there is no "outside" where one might organize a critique. Everything is within the context/arrangement of power.

In addition, these parameters of struggle are further complicated by the presence of physical bodies that experience themselves and others in ways that are often awkward, contradictory, and loaded with meaning not fully captured through language. Embodiment is an indispensable element that cannot be accounted for through discourse because the "lived body" is the nexus of culture and nature. As the philosopher Drew Leder remarks, "the lived body helps to constitute this world-as-experienced." Furthermore, "we cannot, understand the meaning and form of objects without reference to the bodily powers through which we engage them. . . . The lived body is not just one thing in the world, but a way in which the world comes to be."[38] The key is to keep bodies visible and flexible, to continually work to recognize variety and difference as important markers representing different types of bodies, to recognize the manner in which bodies are gendered, and to continually question the accepted range of body "types" (for example with respect to the manifestation of desire) whenever we become epistemologically comfortable.

Finally, framing this rather "nonliberationist" (at least as liberation is commonly pitched in liberation theologies) take is a feeling for life as an ongoing process of development and destruction, growth and decay, creativity and reification.[39] However, lurking on the edges of this thinking as *a consistent source of tension* remains an interest in the possibility of political practice more robust than Foucault can offer, and more certain than black humanism will (rightly) allow. New black theological thought does not resolve that tension, if a resolution is even desirable. It simply acknowledges this tension not as "good" or "bad" but simply as a component of thought (and practice) that gives greater challenge to the struggle for complex and robust life-meaning.

4

Sex(uality) and the
(Un)Doing of Bodies

Insights concerning gender, such as those marking chapter 3, serve to raise other questions because, as Foucault notes, power opens to new possibilities of subjectivity and ways by which to manage new efforts toward the subject.[1] There is an ongoing process of discovery as systems of meaning are recognized and embraced and/or challenged.[2] As a result we see/experience ourselves and are also seen/experienced in various ways. Knowing this brings to mind important questions. For example, a turn to Alice Walker in light of her definition of womanist sexuality begs questions both black and womanist theologians have tackled gingerly, but which merit much more attention.[3] What do we say theologically about the ways in which material bodies receive and give pleasure/desire? What do we say theologically about the ways in which discursive bodies are formed in discomfort with but as the visibility of pleasure/desire?

Embodied theological thought requires interrogation of sex and sexuality. My preference is to think of the two as linked, connected to a similar history of the body—a discourse of body expression and management. To accomplish this, I have on occasion made use of *sex(uality)* as a way to express the overlapping nature of the production and expression, and the manner in which flesh and discourse connect through the structure and mechanics of desire. While somewhat challenging at times, context in large part dictates usage of this term.

As noted in the introduction, with black theological thought, sex(uality) is often addressed as a political matter in the same way race and class have been discussed with regard to political space and in terms of individual and collective social identity. In this way the nature of sex(uality) is narrowed and assumed "proper" modalities of sex(uality) are used as a marker of one's position within the African American community. Alternative expressions are considered anti-community. For example, this is certainly one way to interpret the critique of homosexuality made by many African Americans. And, while I hold black theology and black religion in the form of black churches accountable for their less-than-inspiring approach to this dilemma, it is important to remember that both theology and religion contain borrowed sensibilities shaped over the course of centuries. Most noticeable of these borrowed sensibilities involves articulation of black sex(uality) in terms of a popular interrogation of the Cartesian dualism (mind/body) whereby ideas are privileged over the body. While this is an undeniably important point to note, a vital target of critique, there is so much more to say on the topic, so many other mechanisms at work with respect to the troubling nature and structuring of sex(uality) within black theological thought and black religion. Foucault, for one, helps to surface these other dimensions in terms of the underlying logics and technologies of self that inform the nature, meaning, and functioning of sex(uality).

When Bodies Become Flesh

Whereas many assumed a growing effort on the part of religious institutions and other structures of knowledge to quiet desire, to render invisible sexuality, Foucault argues just the opposite: new ways of monitoring the body serve to increase the visibility of sex(uality). It is discussed, according to Foucault, but this discourse is meant to monitor and confine the arrangements of sex(uality). The question becomes "the over-all 'discursive fact,' the way in which sex is 'put into discourse.'"[4]

In the sixteenth century the discourse of sexuality involved not restriction on speaking sexuality, not frameworks of silence on the subject, but rather more attention to and a greater preoccupation with the structures and practices of sex(uality). Religion and the structures of religious practice provided mechanisms for this increased attention to modalities of desire, although Foucault does not have in mind the religious structures and mechanism that dominate black Christianity or the American context in more general terms. The body and activities of the body were guided in this manner, whereby sexuality was monitored and articulated in ways that supported the "truth" (right ways) of experience as presented by religious communities and seconded to some extent by social understandings. As desire turned the body into flesh, the latter became the central point of concern: the location of sex(uality) as a problem and as the prime target of religion's guidance over sex. Although initially arranged within the context of religious community (e.g., the monastery), the practice of monitoring sex(uality) and a discourse on sex was extended and made applicable to all within the social body. The typical citizen, and not simply one who took vows of special obligation, was expected to be aware of and work to control the expression of desire.[5]

With time, Foucault suggests, this religiously based push for control was combined with other mechanisms whereby the monitoring of sex(uality) gained political, economic, and larger social significance. In short, there emerged "a policing of sex" that meant sex(uality) became not only something confessed but also something studied and analyzed for its impact on the "population (the large scale arrangement of humans)."[6] This new discursive work was not restricted to verbal language, although it grew in a variety of ways through the sciences. It was also present in the aesthetics and physical structures housing and guiding bodies. Both frameworks of concern—religious confession/guidance and socioeconomic/political monitoring—project sex(uality) as something potentially damaging if not controlled and expressed consistent with the "truths" embedded in the discourses of these two frameworks.

In the eighteenth and nineteenth centuries, pleasure and power reinforced one another and sought to foster bodies that had a certain look, abilities, commitments, and relationship to established social networks (e.g., class status).[7] So conceived, sex(uality) is not simply a biological "something," it is also a construction, a dimension of the culturally produced body, and it is framed by "bio-power"—the slippery relationship between the biological and political meant to shape and rehearse the tone and texture of life (e.g., happiness and health).[8] It is also the case that particular bodies, including women and criminals, were more scrutinized and arranged than others.[9] This intensified monitoring, combined with the general tension between body and mind, serve as an important point of consideration with respect to black sex(uality).

In light of the above and with some modification, Foucault provides a way of thinking about how the sexually "stigmatized" bodies are named, discussed, and controlled. A word related to the modification of Foucault's thinking, though: As noted earlier, the confessional central to Foucault's analysis has limited importance within the context of black Christianity. Instead of the confessional, pastoral counseling and testimonial service are where personal struggles are expressed in black Protestantism. Within these mechanisms of discourse and control there is not the same level of detailed discussion Foucault assumes as representative of the confessional (even when the confessional process is expanded or when its impact on the working classes is limited). On the other hand, in many black Christian communities God is the primary confessor, not the pastor; and the primary location of discussion is not the community but the private spaces of practice. What is more, God is also the focus of desire, both within the context of the discursive body and the material body. It is not uncommon to hear during testimonial services, for example, women refer to God as their lover, their husband, and so on. It is also not uncommon to hear men speak in rather submissive ways concerning their love of God through Christ. (The homoerotic implications of this stance are noted later in this chapter.) These frameworks of thought and practice are also tied to an assumption that proper Christian conduct affords something more important than what is gained for sex(uality).[10] Although an important condition of human experience of life, sex(uality) is implied to entail a dispensable dimension, if not a perpetually troubling dimension of human embodiment. This is because rejection of the sex(ual) self could result in greater spiritual knowledge and experience. In this regard, black Protestant Christianity by and large holds to what Foucault's outlines earlier in volume 2 of his *History of Sexuality*: a "moral devaluation" of sex in line with sacred teachings and authority meant to downplay desire and the sensual dimensions of human contact over against the lasting value of spirituality.[11] Desire has its proper functions, its acceptable practices. To give into desire, beyond the defined limits outlined by the faith community and its discourses of moral conduct, means the privileging of physical experience of life in line with fallen human nature, which is lodged within the confines of the physical body as prison of the soul.

As Foucault notes and as theologians have long argued, Augustine played a significant role in Western theologizing of desire and the body. The twist offered by Foucault, though, involves attention to the manner in which Augustine alters attention to monitoring of pleasure, to the controlling and redirecting of desire as expressed in the body through sex.[12] Producing a great deal of tension and anxiety, Christianity involves techniques of sex by which to monitor it (e.g., marriage) and limit its negative consequences.[13] This is not a strict denial of the self, but rather a strategy for developing a certain type of self, a normalized self that responds to the will of God.[14] The religious and the mundane were intimately connected, as the body was both exposed to and responsive to religious frameworks and sexual desire.[15] Structures of proper conduct, right thought, and approved speaking were necessary to maintain the proper posture and activities of bodies. And theology became a way of representing the interconnections or synergy between these various ways of living the "truth."

Foucault continues thinking through the connection between Christianity and the normalization of the self in volume 3 of his *History,* titled *The Care of the Self.* Moving attention to the structuring and practice of pleasure and desire, Foucault turns to the manner in which technologies of the self emerge and work with respect to caring for the self by enlivening connection of the self to the self, the self to others, and the self to institutions, as the title makes clear.[16] This care of the self or the cultivation of the self brings into connection the body and soul. In order to maintain the self, great effort had to be put into proper practices for the soul and for the body. The poor condition of one would harm the other. Both had to be controlled through strenuous ethics of pleasure and later desire. And, such organized restraint was meant to produce selves prepared and capable of participating in the structures and environments of sociopolitical, economic, and religious life.[17] The body was explained, monitored, and experienced in ways meant to produce the desired outcome—ethical subjects. What was at stake would increase through theological means to include the ultimate welfare or damnation of an eternal component of the self. In other words, failure to control oneself with respect to potential distractions and vices such as improper fulfillment of desire (outside the context of marriage) had existential and soteriological consequences.[18] Both exercise and exorcism were necessary: the former involved the practice of modes of restraint and control, and the latter involved the purging of desire for the sake of nonspiritually productive pleasure. It is true that fields of power change and the discourses girding them also change; yet it is also true that within the context of Christianity these changes over time have not ended discussion of sex(uality) and efforts to problematize the structures and outcomes of desire, whether with respect to relationship to self (e.g., masturbation) or with others (sexual intercourse, etc.).

The takeaway from this attention to Foucault is clear: discourses of sexuality and techniques of control have long influenced our thinking about and practice of desire. Hence, creation of greater spaces of "freedom" with respect to sex(uality) must involve recognition of the role of power/knowledge in the thinking, speaking, and practicing of sex(uality). All too often, as Bryan Turner points out, the discursive body reflected an assumption that the material body was "the location of corrupting appetite, of sinful desire and of private irrationality. It is the negation of the true self." Turner suggests this is only one of the placements of the body in that while a theological problem, it was also a sight of instruction and control as "an instructive site of moral purpose and intention."[19]

Black theology and womanist theology have challenged the privileging of mind over body and have interrogated certain scriptural passages, but they have not recognized that sex(uality) is constructed and experienced. The "truth" they seek to mine as the reconstituting of black sex(uality) is also a construct and open to interrogation and reworking. Put another way, one more polemical in tone and texture, the current state of black theological thought on issues such as sex(uality) is damning; it is at least a nonproductive rhetoric that is much louder than it is helpful. As Michael Dyson suggests, this theological thought is framed by a rather passive read of scripture and African American history whereby a limited range of options are viewed as "legitimate." All other perspectives and approaches are viewed as out of line with the dominant perspective on the liberative nature and freedom forging mechanics of black Christianity.[20] Resulting from this is a truncation of innovation through limited challenge to assumed rightness, and a narrow range of frames for social relationships (i.e., resistance). Undergirding these restrictions is the assumption that there is an objective and prehuman history "truth" capable of guiding thought/action, and that there is a static enemy to fight.[21] This perspective seeks to remove the authority of a particular discourse related to mind/body differentiations. It, fails, however, to address the manner in which black theological discourse imposes another field of authority through the confinement of ontological blackness as noted in chapter 2, the ontology of blackened gender presented in chapter 3, and the limiting structures of desire of concern in this chapter. Movement toward a new approach to black theological thought involves a challenge to these limitations. Of greater importance, it also involves recognition that the struggle against these limitations is multidirectional and harnessed to black male and female bodies as they are lodged in discourses and structures of desire and stigmatization.

Race-ing Sex(uality)

According to Foucault, political power as of the late nineteenth century was displayed through attention to racial categorization as a way to frame the dynamics of marriage, family, and proper offspring.[22] This connecting of race and sex(uality) overlying some of Foucault's discussion is brilliantly unpacked in Ann Stoler's discussion of race and sexuality within colonial contexts.[23] Stoler argues that the structure of colonial geographies was dependent not only on political discourse but also the identity formation made possible through technologies of desire control as well as the structures of race.[24] In a word, some of the bodies were black, all were gendered, and all were framed by desire. There was in the nineteenth century, Stoler remarks, "a racially erotic counterpoint" became an important mechanism in the construction of the normalized body and normalized sexual arrangements.[25] This linking of race and sex(uality) as structures of thought and practice served to buttress strategies of difference that enabled and justified the construction and use of black bodies within colonial enterprises in various geographies, including the Americas.[26]

"Whiteness," for example played a role in the structuring of the Americas that extended beyond its service as economic and political markers of valuable difference. It connected to a prior framing of desire that normalized white bodies as refined and controlled. By extension, American domination could caste black bodies as oversexed and savage.[27] The disturbing nature of blending these two types of bodies—refined and savage—through desire was met with legal force. "What George Frederickson has called the 'first clear-cut example of statutory racial discrimination' in the Virginia law of 1662," Stoler reflects, "fined 'interracial fornicators,' followed by a ban on all forms of interracial marriage in 1691."[28] Within the North American colonies representing a new religious geography and theological possibilities, through a placement of bodies in new spaces of existence, was an experiment related to the will of God that required preservation of the "chosen people."

The structures of force and discourses of chosen-ness required partnership with desire controls vis-à-vis discourses of sex(uality) and race. Put in place, consequently, were ways to monitor individuals and to arrange the practices and lived experiences of groups (i.e., "bio-power").[29] Black bodies were subjected to a range of technologies of force (up to and including death) meant to discipline them and render them docile (and plastic) as a way of maintaining the "truth" of prevailing life structures and orientations. These technologies also served to keep black bodies under surveillance and subject to the needs of the social body. Beyond the nineteenth century, as the story of John Grimes later in this chapter notes, this surveillance was an internal and external mechanism of docility; whites used it to arrange black bodies in time and space, and blacks used it to arrange black bodies (and, when possible, white ones as well) according to rules of normalized desire and approved relationships. Interactions framing and framed by discourses of race, gender, and sexuality were not unidirectional but, rather, involved crossed lines of contact and influence.[30] "Given the differences that race, class, gender, ethnicity, and so forth make to the determination of meaning," remarks Susan Bordo, "'reading' bodies becomes an extremely complex business."[31] To the extent framing of difference could hold and resist challenge, it made privileges for a select group of elites reasonable and justifiable. However, holding this framing in place over against resistance and internal shortcomings was difficult in that black bodies (discursive and physical) were both a problem of normalization and a requirement for normalization. The purity of the chosen people of North America (i.e., culturally and physically white) required the taint of race for justification of privilege and the structuring of desire and pleasure. However, the "wrong" types of contacts between normalized and stigmatized bodies could result in the harming (with respect to political abilities, social positioning, cultural currency, and economic opportunity) of the former. Anything other than supervised contact between black and white bodies resulted in challenge to the grounding of difference and produced problematic people.

Some members of the social body, as the story of Helga Crane later in this chapter suggests, held a "fictive" status that betrayed them as outside the rules of interaction and difference.[32] Identity tied to the formation of subjected selves often ran afield of ethical citizenry: Not all white bodies were white enough (i.e., without some sort of taint, whether economic, political, or physical) and not all black bodies were neatly categorized (e.g., the problem of miscegenation). Body image(s), whether individualized or arranged across a more expansive cultural geography, provide a penetrable structure for life definition and for engagement of life.[33] Bodies overlapped because they were constructed in relationship to unstable markers and shifting discourses. The social body, hence, contains within it sources of its refinement and its destruction: bodies can turn on themselves and body image(s) can distort. While body image(s) instruct by providing attention to aesthetics of presentation, comportment of the body, uses of the body, and other measures of how bodies should occupy space, these instructions can destroy through normalization.[34] Attention to black bodies and theological frameworks of embodiment must be mindful of these insights regarding the interplay between discourses of race, gender, and sex(uality).

The Shaping of Black Sex(uality)

The tension between religious devotion and physical pleasure is old, but it has been only intensified by the ramifications of a legacy of disregard for black bodies. Furthermore, it is deeply embedded in the practice and teachings of the Christian faith and at times tied to scientific pronouncements. The body, then, as a physical reality capable of receiving and giving sexual pleasure is recognized as "a highly restricted medium of expression," restricted by the larger social system.[35] An orgasm in a sense becomes a prime recognition of restriction in that it points to the body's goodness but also its profound limitations in that this release is a "little death." One might even consider the orgasm interpretable as sexual *communitas,* by which I mean the less pleasurable realities of social existence are suspended and overwhelmed by a joy that cannot be maintained long term.

In nineteenth-century America, some of those within scientific circles argued, "desire by itself 'disturbs and disorders all the functions of the system,'" and an orgasm "stimulated the 'convulsed heart' to drive blood 'in fearful congestion, to the principal viscera', damag[ed] all other organs."[36] The negative weight of science served to dampen, so to speak, the individual's relationship to her or his body. However, the dilemma is much older than pre-twentieth-century medical speculation. Such developments prior to the Modern Period were given theological power over bodies when, for example, one notes that Thomas Aquinas considered sexual desire dangerous to both one's spiritual development and one's physical body. This is not to say that sexual desire was by its very nature problematic. If this were the case, even sexual activity between spouses would be sinful. Rather than this, sexual desire was considered an interruption of one's energy and commitment to higher concerns and reason. Albeit mystics countered the preoccupation with reason theologically pushed by scholars such as Aquinas; their efforts to demonstrate the possibility of knowing God through (rather than in spite of) the body did not serve to foster a more general appreciation for the body and the sexual self. There remained a Cartesian privileging of the spirit over the body and its desire/needs.[37]

Within the context of Christianity, religion and sex(uality) were understood "as a binary opposition."[38] This, of course, stems from the manner in which the Christian faith placed in direct relationship the spirit of God and human flesh, most pronouncedly in the Christ Event. This, however, is a Christ who remains rather sexless. And what the followers of Christ through the centuries gather from this event is an understanding of the body as a reluctant and difficult partner for the spirit. The ethicist Emilie Townes, in a discussion of health and caring, puts it this way, "when we live out of an incarnational understanding that takes us out of the *dynamic* dualism we have of body *and* spirit, then we lapse into the *deadly* dualism that tells us that the body is inferior, if not evil, and must be transcended by the spirit of Jesus."[39] Recall the sentiment of the Apostle Paul paraphrased here: That which I would not do, I do.

The flesh fights the deeper desires of the spirit and in this way makes difficult meaningful connection to the divine. In a sense, those who are Christlike are required to overcome the flesh, to subdue its desires and pleasures for the sake of spiritual connection to the divine. One might say, "it is Augustine's fear and loathing of the sexual body that has determined the entire course of Christian history."[40] Later figures such as Martin Luther gave importance to sex within the context of marriage.[41] This, however, did not entail recognition of sex as good. Rather, it was seen, even if it did not produce children, as a necessary component of married life. Yet, like the Apostle Paul, Luther and other major figures in the Protestant denominations gave more weight to a spiritual existence over and above that of marriage.[42] Religious communities continue into the twenty-first century to teach, "a sexual code based on fear of the body and of sexuality, in understandings of sexual virtue as the repression of bodily desires by the force of the rationale will, on physicality, especially sexuality, as an obstacle to spirituality."[43]

In the early American colonies, Puritan sensibilities played an important role in the formation of conservative attitudes toward sex(uality), by which activities such as anal intercourse, for instance, were deemed great evils to be avoided without exception. While the rhetoric was strong, actual punishment for sodomy was rare. According to one source, "there were about twenty sodomy prosecutions in British North America, of which two ended in hanging, both in the seventeenth century. . . . Because sodomy convictions required proof of penetration and testimony of two witnesses, they were extremely difficult to prove."[44] A preoccupation with the unruly nature of the body and the dangerous nature of its desires and pleasures would spread in the colonies through the two Great Awakenings, the first in the 1700s and the second in the 1800s.

Christianity certainly did not invent this problematic relationship to sex(uality), but there were ways in which the Christian faith highlighted theologically in negative terms humans as sexual entities and gave believers the mission of undermining or undoing their sexual selves.

Christian faith's (along with secular authorities') regulation of sex(uality) eventually gave raise to new perspectives on the body and what is commonly referred to as "modern sexuality," marked by new ways of controlling and in some instances "denaturalizing" and discourse-enveloping sex(uality) and sexual life.[45] As "modern sexuality" develops, it does so with respect to growing notions of and perceptions of race and racial difference. That is to say, "imperial power is explicitly and implicitly linked with sexuality . . . imperial powers shaped cultural constructions of masculinity and femininity and how images of colonial peoples were gendered and sexualized."[46] It will be important to remember bodies are constructed, shaped, and positioned, and that much of this activity is sexed and deeply connected to matters of pleasure and pleasuring.

Within the framework of imperial developments and conquest in North America, the black body represented the physical world of work and pleasure, and also served as a prime symbol of chaos. In either case, in physical terms or as symbolic representation, those of African descent were something both appealing and repulsive. As an ontological and epistemological challenge, black bodies were controlled through relegation to subhuman status and the violent forms of control and linguistic determination that such an indictment allowed. Hence the individual African's activities and patterns of conduct were shaped by and served to reinforce the larger symbolic framework of society. It should be noted that interracial relationships in the New World occurred early and often. But physical intimacy did not mean that the "other"—those of African descent—held equal status with those of European descent. In fact, race and class distinctions were reinforced through theories of sex(uality): sexual restrictions and regulations. The enslaved (and free) person of African descent was named and "known." While understood as irrational and of lesser value, Africans in North America were sufficient fodder for slaveholder's erotic pathologies and the general sexual release of any white person who desired black flesh. Enslaved Africans in this sense, both men and women, became acceptable repositories for sexual desires and repulsions because subduing the racial other in the New World implied the ability to sexually have them. Black bodies were considered, in Foucaultian terms, "saturated with sex."[47] The genitals of the African, hence, were both threatening and desirable. So sexual and sexualized were they that sex became the prime marker of their reality and meaning from the perspective of pro-slavery whites. Through erotic imagination and sexual conquest of enslaved Africans (male and female), both sexual and racial difference were addressed and order maintained, with the added benefit of physical pleasure for the conqueror.

M. Shawn Copeland notes with great insight that "European and European American representative aesthetics scaled, identified, and labeled the bodies of black women as primitive, lascivious, and repugnant. This evaluation was at once religious and moral." That is to say, "it reflected both white Western Christianity's ambivalence toward the body, sex, as well as sexuality, and the impact of religion on what Kelly Brown Douglas refers to as the construction and 'management of sexual discourse,' thus fostering the 'domination and demonization of the different Other.'"[48] Put another way, during the period of slavery, those of African descent were painted as sexual savages who operated based on the satisfying of unnaturally strong desires. As a consequence, they were incapable of proper social relationships with whites and had to be controlled to avoid social chaos.[49] Interestingly enough, one mechanism of control was sexual contact. Linda Brent's *Incidents in the Life of a Slave Girl*, for example, speaks to the manner in which enslaved African women faced the threat of unwanted sexual contact with whites. She says the following, concerning her master's plans to make her his mistress:

> When my master said he was going to build a house for me, and that he could do it with little trouble and expense, I was in hopes something would happen to frustrate his scheme; but I soon heard that the house was actually begun. I vowed before my Maker that I would never enter it. I had rather toil on the plantation from dawn till dark; I had rather live and die in jail, than drag on, from day to day, through such a living death. I was determined that the master, whom I so hated and loathed, who had blighted the prospects of my youth, and made my life a desert, should not, after my long struggle with him, succeed at last in trampling his victim under his feet. I would do any thing, every thing, for the sake of defeating him. What *could* I do?[50]

Brent made an effort to maintain some control over her body and the pleasure it gave others. Yet, the system of slavery allowed little space for assertions of self. There was for those of African descent a feeling that one always stands the chance of losing oneself to others. One easily becomes an object to be manipulated for the satisfaction of others, which involves an ontological and existential slide into nothingness except for the pleasure one's body can give others.

Sex was a ritual through which white men, for instance, maintained the established social order, but for black women it was a terror to be escaped as best they could. Although Brent could not choose to avoid sexual contact, she could decide with whom to have such contact. This is a valuable move from her perspective because:

> to be an object of interest to a man who is not married, and who is not her master, is agreeable to the pride and feelings of a slave, if her miserable situation has left her any pride or sentiment. It seems less degrading to give one's self, than to submit to compulsion. There is something akin to

freedom in having a lover who has no control over you, except that which he gains by kindness and attachment.[51]

During the period of slavery, black flesh formed bodies that mattered in only a limited sense and for limited purposes, all revolving around the pleasuring of whites—economically, socially, and physically. The genitalia of these black bodies, then, was given extreme attention and importance over against the deeper ontological reality of blacks.[52]

Sex(uality) became a mode of regulation; in this way, Judith Butler remarks, sex(uality) served to not only control but also create bodies. In part through a discourse of sex(uality), whites developed a story or language of black being that had materiality and that "call[ed] into being" both a type of black body and a type of white body. This process entailed restrictions on the existence and movement of both types of bodies, and also the ability to recognize the ontological depth both might shadow.[53] This paradoxical activity of fondling and fixing involves both a process of construction (the making of these bodies) and de-construction (a perverting of meaning that might be associated with the subjects represented by those bodies).[54] In a sense, discourse of sex(uality) became ritualized annihilation—a controlling of bodies—that provided whites (and some blacks) with psychological and physical pleasure that was orgasmic (i.e., gratifying) on the level of the individual and the social.

After slavery, sexual aggression such as rape and sexual mutilation (e.g., castration during lynching) continued the process of sexualization as affirmation of the status quo. Frantz Fanon, from a colonial but related context, speaks to this preoccupation with black bodies as radically sexual when connecting the hatred of whites for blacks to sex(uality). He says, "since his [the white man's] ideal is an infinite virility, is there not a phenomenon of diminution in relation to the Negro, who is viewed as a penis symbol? Is the lynching of the Negro not a sexual revenge? We know how much of sexuality there is in all cruelties, tortures, beatings."[55] Through the physical destruction of black body parts that symbolized threat (and source of potential and often forbidden pleasure), sex(uality) provided another powerful means by which whites maintained control over people of color. As R. W. Connell remarks, "cultural hierarchies of bodies are robust."[56]

Controlling bodies had to entail regulation of sexual desire to the extent that sex(uality), acted out through flesh, had ramifications for all spaces occupied by (or denied to) these bodies. As we shall see, religion and theological discourse served as useful tools in sexually policing bodies because "while people struggle to find life and meaning in the relationships of the sofa beds of friends and lovers, systematic theology struggles to master and obliterate those meanings."[57]

The oppressive nature of life in the United States, combined with adherence to traditional Christian perceptions of the flesh and sex(uality), resulted in alienation from the body, particularly the body as erotic and sexual and even more so with respect to homosexuality and other modes of pleasuring the body outside established sexual norms. Judith Butler speaks to this when reflecting on the work of Hazel Carby. Carby remarks that the vulnerability of black women's bodies continues into the twentieth century, "including rape, because their bodies continued to be sites of conquest within white racism, then the psychic resistance to homosexuality and to a sexual life outside the parameters of the family must be read in part as a resistance to an endangering public exposure."[58] Race and sex(uality) mark each other, play off each other, and inform each other in the context of the United States.

Religious Reinforcement of Normalized Black Sex(uality)

For black churches, religious tradition/scriptures and the desire to gain for blacks recognition as morally and ethically meriting full inclusion in society generated participation in the prevailing attitudes towards sex(uality). Nonetheless, it is important to remember that an embrace of societal and religious sexual norms was both active (based on reading of and adherence to biblical tradition) and reactionary (based on a desire for social inclusion). This tension between race and sex(uality) is vividly and creatively described in literary depictions of black religiosity.

There is an uncomfortable sexual quality to the movements and language of many black religious practices and aesthetics. The writer Nella Larsen expresses just exactly how awkward or unwanted this sexual dimension can be.[59] Helga Crane, the protagonist in *Quicksand*, stumbles upon a religious meeting during a period of personal angst. While pleasurable on some level, Helga's encounter with black worship is also terrifying in that it momentarily mutates existing boundaries by reasserting the visibility of black bodies. Yet this occurs without there being a full escape from the hierarchal structures and norms of the social environment—the body as metaphor circumscribes the material body. It entails a movement forward by ritually moving back. Larsen describes Helga's experience this way:

Fascinated, Helga Crane watched until there crept upon her an indistinct horror of an unknown world. She felt herself in the presence of a nameless people, observing rites of a remote obscure origin. The faces of the men and women took on the aspect of a dim vision. "This," she whispered to herself, "is terrible. I must get out of here." but the horror held her. She remained motionless, watching, as if she lacked the strength to leave the place—foul, vile, and terrible, with its mixture of breaths, its contact of bodies, its conceited convulsions, all in wild appeal for a single soul. Her soul. And as Helga watched and listened, gradually a curious influence penetrated her; she felt an echo of the weird orgy resound in her own heart; she felt herself possessed by the same madness; she too felt a brutal desire to shout and to sling herself about.[60]

Helga is confronted with bodies that seem out of place, through their movement providing a corporeal theologizing of their meaning as an aesthetic quality.[61] These bodies within the religious context seem to defy the reified nature of their social construction. These bodies were supple, not flat nor rigid. They did not suggest discomfort with occupying space, but in fact demanded recognition of both their existential and transcendent importance. Here they move, and sway, demand space when the social mechanism of constraint would suggest their invisibility, yet they remain trapped in this constructed form.

In religious ecstasy, the bodies in this church seem like her own, but at the same time different: She did not move through time and space in the same manner, for the same purpose. It is true, one gathers from the sway and heightened bodily engagement with the sacred (re)presented in/by the women encountered, that the transcendent is experienced through/in the body in ways that promote a sense of the sacred as sensual and immanent.[62] Helga's body was sensual without the buffer effect of surrender to transcendent power. Helga was, as they put it, a "scarlet 'oman"[63]—sensual, sexual, and possessed of a body the women in church sought to exorcise.

Helga traveled north, south, and east to Europe; she moved across geography hoping to chart a new meaning for herself, a new framing of her body, but different physical territory betrayed similar mechanisms of meaning that rendered her body as metaphor the same in different places. This body as metaphor, as sociologists of the body remind us, informs the meaning and purpose of the physical body, and the reverse is also true.[64] In Denmark, this is made all too clear when Axel Olsen, who had proposed marriage to Helga, says the following: "'You know, Helga, you are a contradiction. . . . You have the warm impulsive nature of the women of Africa, but, my lovely, you have, I fear, the soul of a prostitute. You sell yourself to the highest buyer. I should of course be happy that it is I. And I am.'"[65] Perhaps in Olsen's words there is more than a hint of this doubled body: the form of Africa (i.e., body as metaphor) and the content of "America" (i.e., as material), complete with a sense of the blackened American body as commodity, which could be traded and consumed for the benefit of those with power. In this way, the body as metaphor, the "impulsive nature of the women of Africa," shapes the diasporic and material body as object for use.

Helga Crane was familiar (and at times uncomfortable) with the appeal of her body constructed as one dimensional and sexualized. This appeal, however, pulled her apart and created momentary epistemological and existential dissonance between her bodies—as symbol or metaphor it is restricted, and as material, her body blurs the line between two social worlds. Members of the "white" world who should disregard it, desire her body; and her flesh is questioned by the "black" world that should embrace it. This in part is the dilemma of the "tragic mulatto." But here in this church setting Helga is forced to see and be with other bodies, to know herself in/outside herself. And this realization was erotic. Later in the text, Helga's wrestling with moral evil through the rhetoric of theodicy does not escape the lure and sexualized nature of the body: she interrogates God and her life in light of the children she has and the child she will soon have: "Marriage that means children, to me. And why add more suffering to the world? Why add any more unwanted, tortured Negroes to America?"[66] The theodical silence with which the story ends allows readers to assume that Helga surrenders to the absurdity of theological formulation and Christian community for the sake of her extended flesh—her children. Helga wanted to leave, to rescue her body, and she held tight the assumption she would make plans once she felt better, the production and care of her children having taken so much from her body, had transformed her body by denying it the markers that once framed its sensuality and "place":

It was so easy and so pleasant to think about freedom and cities, about clothes and books, about the sweet mingled smell of Houbigant and cigarettes in softly lighted rooms filled with inconsequential chatter and laughter and sophisticated tuneless music. It was so hard to think out a feasible way of retrieving all these agreeable, desirable things. Just then. Later. When she got up. By and by. She must rest. Get strong. Sleep. Then, afterwards, she could work out some agreement. . . . And hardly had she left her bed and become able to walk again without pain, hardly had the children returned from the homes of the neighbors, when she began to have her fifth child.[67]

There are implications to the tension present in Helga Crane's life. Her experiences of attraction and repulsion regarding the sexualized qualities of human life are not simply a matter of Larsen exercising literary license. Rather, Helga's experience speaks to long-standing opposition between religious perceptions of the body and the sexual dimensions of human interaction that is also expressed in the work of James Baldwin.

Baldwin, near the end of *Go Tell It On the Mountain*, provides a scene that merges the religious and physical, psychological and emotional experiences framing the development of the protagonist John Grimes. John is on the floor of the Pentecostal Church he and his family attend, "wrestling" with the call of God and the demands of surrender to God's will. He has been "slain" by the Spirit. And while in this position, prostrate on the floor, John rehearses in his mind the tension between spirit and flesh, between the religious rhetoric and posture of his stepfather, a preacher—but "being a preacher ain't never stopped a nigger from doing his dirt"[68]—and the erotic activities that seem to run contrary to all things holy:

> And I *heard* you, all the nighttime long. I know what you do in the dark, black man, when you think the Devil's son's [John] asleep. I heard you spitting, and groaning, and choking—and I *seen* you, riding up and down, and going in and out. I ain't the Devil's son for nothing. . . . And I had you. I hate you. I don't care about your golden crown. I don't care about your long white robe. I seen you under the robe. I seen you![69]

There is something fundamental, intrinsic, in this tension between spirit and flesh that tortured John as he lay on the floor of that church. It was not simply that John wrestled with the sexual self within the context of a religious tradition that despised the generic human body. It was not just any body that was despised. It was his black body, a body condemned, according to certain interpretations of scripture, by God through Noah's son Ham and Ham's son, Canaan. It was his body, complete with its desires and sexual interests.

John, and many blacks, feel this assumed stain, and it is only intensified through a recognition of the body as sexualized, a sort of double condemnation.[70] Voices bombarded John, on the floor, framing harsh questions through indirect appeal to Genesis 9:

then the ironic voice, terrified, it seemed, of no depth, no darkness, demanded of John, scornfully, if he believed that he was cursed. All niggers had been cursed, the ironic voice reminded him, all niggers had come from this most undutiful of Noah's sons. How could John be cursed for having seen in a bathtub [John saw his father naked in the tub as alluded to in the quotation above] what another man—if that other man had ever lived—had seen ten thousand years ago, in an open tent?[71]

John seeing his father naked in the tub, and the epistemological link with Ham assumed in the above quotation, did not generate feelings of comfort with the sexual self. Rather, what stems from recognition of sexual potential for the religious person is a desire to reject or hide from the body. There is expressed during those long moments on the floor the difficulty of carrying one's flesh through this world, while searching for a way to heaven. This God that John wrestles with created flesh but seems to despise it and, what is more, seems to require followers to also despise those things the body yearns for. The theology and practice of John's church push toward dysfunction and sexual pathology in the form of "crosses" gladly carried by the righteous. As Michael Lynch notes in his analysis of Go Tell It On the Mountain, a "religious neurosis" marks the characters of the book. It is a neurosis through which "temporal happiness and spiritual redemption are seemingly impossible attainments—largely because," as Baldwin notes through the somewhat autobiographical character John Grimes, "they are seen as antithetical terms of a dichotomy."[72]

The body expresses its desires and needs regardless, although the strictures of the church, according to Baldwin's account, amplify either the rejection of sex(uality) or the lurid embrace of the same. As work on racial identity done by Anthony Appiah and Amy Gutman might suggest if applied to Baldwin's book, John's struggle for meaning expressed throughout the novel shows that identity (including the erotic self) is informed by a complex of perspectives and opinions, many of them forged through sensibilities made available by cultural organizations such as religion.[73] In this sense, one might say that the black church, in John's case a Pentecostal church, seeks to control sex(uality) through a process of enclosure whereby the adherent is cut off from her or his body and the larger world.[74] What results are "life scripts" giving shape to every aspect of movement through the world—social sensibilities, political perspectives, attitudes toward the sexual and erotic, and so on.[75] This strict mapping out of life is not unusual, as James Nelson remarks, because sex(uality) is believed to have a power that religion fears and seeks to monitor and restrict.[76]

Questioning of these life guidelines results in guilt and anxiety, which mar relationship to one's body and the bodies of others.[77] Such a situation is existentially and ontologically debilitating: Does such an arrangement entail life? Is this to live, to really live, to make one's mark on the world? To the contrary, movement through the world motivated by rejections of one's body—what one's body gives and enjoys—is to exist barely. In this way, the beauty of the black body, something Baldwin through John seeks to experience, is at best a hauntingly tragic beauty, something one must acknowledge and celebrate only in the darkened corners of one's mind and historical spaces, all the time aware that sexual "sin" leaves a deep and persistent stain. Pleasure within the context of such an anti-body religious environment yields something depressingly short of freedom from the terror of existence in an absurd world. As Vivian May remarks, "through John's transgressions, Baldwin indirectly portrays how fundamental the church has been in defining and controlling sexuality. Baldwin demonstrates that social and cultural pressures affect how we pursue and acquire the trappings of identity."[78]

In reflecting on the religious environment in which John struggles for life, Baldwin makes a theological shift, suggesting in soft tones that salvation need not entail the rejection of one's body. Rather, the ability to love oneself and others through erotic love is the marker of salvation.[79] This erotic quality is continuously pushed below the surface, but hinted at or teased through the sway of spirit possession or the knowing/unknowing moments of bodily contact, as the devout of God embrace at the end of a powerful service. But can spiritualized pleasure fulfill the ache of bodily desire? Baldwin left the church in order to find salvation so conceived. Yet, how does one—can one—secure salvation, as he understands it within the context of traditional religious community? Is the black church capable of embracing a more complex and inclusive notion of sex(uality) and sexual pleasure?[80]

These questions suggest a problematic method utilized within the context of black churches. This method, what Foucault might consider a "juridico-discursive method," entails relationship between power and sex as a matter of negation: power says no to certain formulations and practices in connection to a regulation of rules determining what is permissible. This "no" also emerges in connection to prohibitions and a "logic of censorship," which allows for the proper functioning of sex(uality) and the effort to suspend all other practices and conversations.[81] What results is formation of a discursive body in compliance with certain rules and regulations and the control of the physical body's practices: Helga and John feel in their bodies the workings of power as techniques of force tied to "truth," and they experience the monitoring of their desire as a consequence. This poses a challenge of thinking and *be*-ing for both authors and their characters. Also present is a significant challenge to and critique of theological thinking on restrictive modalities of self-care.

Thinking and Living Embodiment and Desire

Mindful of the above discussion, perhaps the most complete critique in black theological discourse of black churches on this score is found in Kelly Brown Douglas's *Sexuality and the Black Church* and *What's Faith Got To Do With It?*[82] In these texts Douglas argues that God's revelation has weighty consequences for an understanding of and appreciation for sex(uality) for individuals and within religious community.

Black churches may have encountered a warped theory of sex(uality) as part of "the White cultural assault upon [black] sexuality," but unlike other harmful ideologies received (e.g., inferiority of blacks) it was embraced and refined within the context of black community discourse as a nondiscourse, as a modality of control in that ideological penetration of sex(uality) affects one's total reality as historical being in that "sexuality implies one's very humanity."[83] (Again, the sexual ethics and norm of black churches are a result of an [re]active process.) Douglas seeks to balance this depiction of sex(uality) as reaction to white discourse with a sense of blacks as forging more positive and "healthy" notions of their sexual selves. In essence, Douglas argues that the exploitation and manipulation of black sex(uality) has harnessed black bodies, making and shaping them in ways that result in a discomfort on the part of blacks with their bodies and their sexual selves. In turn, black theological discourse responds with an immature rhetoric, which in no way resembles the more hearty discourse on socioeconomic realities, for instance. In a word, sex(uality) became a "taboo issue" for both black churches and black theology.[84]

Over the course of centuries, Douglas laments, the sex(uality) of blacks has been mutated and amplified in the popular imagination of the United States. This being the case, how then could blacks develop a discourse on sex(uality) that did *not* run the risk of being warped and used to buttress stereotypes that assume blacks are always thinking about sex? Rather than run the risk of having such a discussion backfire, blacks have preferred to avoid public discourse on sex(uality).[85] While one might see this as a problematic silence that supports homophobia and other difficult attitudes and perspectives, and one that feeds a continuing discomfort with black bodies, Douglas suggests that one might also see this as a "form of Black cultural resistance to the corrupting influences of White culture, or a survival strategy against White cultural attacks."[86]

I agree with Douglas's argument that sex(uality) is an essential component of theology as black religious expression, if the centrality of embodiment as the marker of human-divine relationship is to be maintained. Such is the case, and again I agree with Douglas, because "to manifest our loving relationship to God is to be in a loving relationship with God's creation," thereby rendering attitudes such as homophobia an act of bad faith, a break with "authentic Black faith."[87] There is merit to Douglas's analysis, although I would give greater emphasis to the active role blacks have played in promoting a warped depiction of sex(uality). But this is not the first issue blacks have failed to address adequately. The same was the case, for example, with sexism and classism. And the manner in which Cornel West links these various strands of oppression entails need for complex strategies of the subject that work on numerous levels. "I don't think that one can actually engage in serious talk about the fundamental transformation of American society . . ." says West, "without talking about hitting the various forms of evil across the board."[88] However, correctives have been offered with regard to ideological oversights (i.e., use of nongendered language, push for increased ordination for women in some churches, political challenges to and suggested economic correctives for class-based discrimination) while little attention has been given to troubling discourses of dominance, pleasure, and desire.

This much is clear: blacks in general and black religionists in particular have advocated harmful policies regarding sex(uality). Such policies are expressed, for instance, in the framing of rather conservative notions of femininity and masculinity as normative. In turn, these normative notions reinforce sexism through a restriction on the spaces in which women rightly operate (e.g., regulations against ordained ministry) and homophobia through an ideology of homosexuality as conspiracy against the black family. An effort to "safeguard" the black family against threat undoubtedly informs this conflict.[89] One example of this practice within religious circles must suffice here. I provide this statement elsewhere and again here because of the manner in which it frames the black church's complicity in promoting myopic gender arrangements. Reflecting on the appeal of a black church in Baltimore, a member said black men typically stay away from church because:

Sex(uality) | 91

the image of Christ is "wimpish" and encourages black men to "turn the other cheek" in response to racial injustice; that the traditions of "blond and blue-eyed" images of Christ reflect blacks' self-hatred and capitulation to white supremacy; that religious services are too emotionally driven because the churches are dominated by women, who "by nature" are emotional; and that, unlike the Nation of Islam, which among many unchurched men represents the essence of black manhood, black churches attract homosexuals.[90]

In response and as a way of attracting men to black churches, some promote an irresponsibly "muscular" message, one that enables overtly homophobic postures such as that presented by Goldie Phillips, a member of Bethel AME Church in Baltimore. He remarks that "Under Pastor Reid's charge, they cannot look at Christianity as sissified. . . . If they belong to this church and they've been studying under him for any time, it's impossible to view it like that. The brothers who come to church, they need to be touched, I mean physically touched. They need to know that they can maintain their macho manhood, but they can be touched."[91] This quotation raises an issue noted by Michael Dyson, who writes about an implied homoeroticism in Christianity. "Think, for instance," he writes, "of men claiming to love Jesus standing on their feet in fully enthralled ecstasy, emoting about their connection to a God who became flesh and dwelled among us, as a man. For men to publicly proclaim their intense, unsurpassed love for a God who became a man leaves the door open for homoerotic identification and communion within the liturgy of the black ecclesial universe."[92] How to think about this erotic moment within the context of a discourse on desire?

Even the metaphorical possibility of connection lurking in the shadows of surrender to Christ by males brings into play the "act of penetration" as a matter of activity and passivity—with Christ as dominant (active) and the surrendering Christian as passive.[93] For the male quoted and for many others surrender to Christ, even as a religious and spiritually expressed action, involves a moment of inferiority that renders the black male less than male in normalized terms. There is dissonance between the commitment to Christ and traditional projections of masculinity as aggressively heterosexual and always connected to the dominant partner in intimate encounters.[94] Viewing soteriology as a "game of mastery,"[95] all too many Christians have attempted to address this dilemma through silence on the issue, or through a reworking of Christ-encounter combined with a discourse of homophobia. Only by means of this move do they see a way to embrace Christ and maintain dominance as a marker of the self in relationship. It de-problematizes Christian commitment through a discourse of hypermasculinity whereby "care of the self" is linked to preservation of normative structures of erotic desire.

Such a perspective, wherever found, is problematic and should be challenged on every front. Douglas notes this, but attempts to maintain sympathy toward the manner in which blacks have fought for identity and integrity within an absurd social environment in ways that might counter efforts to hold blacks and their churches accountable and responsible for their problematic attitudes toward sex(uality). Without troubling the discourse of mastery, she writes, "the case supporting homophobia," for example, "in the Black community reveals homophobia almost as a misguided strategy for protecting Black lives and the integrity of Black sexuality, as a necessary position to safeguard Black life and freedom."[96] In her more recent work, Douglas does not stray in a significant way from this earlier paradigm.[97] Instead, in *What's Faith Got to Do with It?* Douglas targets the Cartesian dualism as the core problem for black sex(uality) to the extent black religious institutions have embraced it. While an important critique, it does not sufficiently trouble the manner in which discourses of desire function. She critiques the dualism of mind vs. body, but she does not sufficiently resist the normalization of bodies that serves to fix black bodies as stigmatized bodies. And, when this is given some soft treatment, Douglas, like most with black liberationist perspectives, does not tackle the problem in relationship to both the discursive and material body.

Black theological thought has maintained discourse on the proper expressions and purposes of sex(uality) heavily tied to procreation. In this way, black theological thought has assumed and reinforced some of the more problematic techniques of sex(uality) found within the Western discourse on and monitoring of sex(uality). It proposes what Foucault might call a "rigorous style" by which sex(uality) is controlled and moralized through restrictions on desire to a certain number of spaces dominated, of course, by marriage.[98] Consequently, bodily pleasure outside accepted modalities involves "sin" because it entails a misuse or abuse of the body. A problematic view of the body (racism and gender-based discrimination) is tied to problematic strategies of pleasure and desire (homophobia and heterosexism).

Underlying liberationists perspective on the problem of sex(uality) remains an assumption of the body as problem to solve, a Cartesian assumption that the body marks a limit,[99] in this case as a limit with respect to the soteriological claims based on biblical narrative and "kingdom of God" hopes of both "this-worldly" and "other-worldly" orientations. The substantive differences between these two orientations is not the location of God's promise to suffering humanity, but the need for a "new" body in order to embrace and benefit from this promise. Both find the material body a barrier. For the former, "this-worldly" orientation, the body is a barrier in that physical worries revolving around health impinge upon the articulation and practice of this promise. The latter finds the body limiting: it must be overcome in order to experience God's promise as non-earthbound reward. Consequently there is a failure to recognize the manner in which religion (and religious insight/ practice) is formed and articulated through and in the body as discursive instrument and as physical experience of life.[100] Highlighting a challenge to the discursive body, without a similar analysis of the "placement" of physical bodies normalization's play on technologies of race and sexuality, is treated in a myopic manner. The critique offered by Douglas is not grounded sufficiently in embodiment capable of resisting discourses and technologies of control, which are related to the cultural production of discursive bodies and the placement and utilization of physical bodies.

Black theological discourse has not wanted to address discourses of desire and control as related to the substance of lived experience. The effort has been to pull these two bodies apart and thus privilege discussion of the discursive body (a move not dissimilar from the disjoining of mind and body), at the same time avoiding the more uncomfortable and lived physical body. Even this move favored in black theological discourse has assumed sex(uality) is tied to bodies in a way suggesting what those bodies are, as opposed to perceiving sex(uality) as a description or normalization tacked on discursive bodies.[101] These, in effect, have given little attention to physical bodies and have truncated perceptions of the discursive body.

By both implicitly and explicitly celebrating the heterosexual norm, African Americans have reasserted a racial and sexual hierarchy that discounts some possibilities of desire and reinforces others as acceptable and community nurturing. Black theological thought on this topic has not sufficiently analyzed the plastic nature of discursive patterns and the ties of discourse to physical bodies. Fundamental questions have gone unasked: How does one resist modalities of desire control from within the structures of knowledge that promote those modalities of control? How does one resist modalities of desire control, particularly when their normalizing effects have had some benefit for black bodies? Instead, black theological thinking has assumed a strong challenge on one point, which would destroy that particular structuring of life and, as a consequence, would also trouble other mechanisms of domination. Furthermore, black theological thought has floundered because of an assumption that *all is difference* rather than having recognized a more textured and interactive relationship between difference and sameness in the framing and functioning of black bodies.[102]

While religious institutions such as black churches should work to elevate estrangement—to celebrate the body and the ways in which the body gives and receives sexual pleasure—they actually reinforce a troubling body-spirit dichotomy. This has been aided by black theological discourse's failure to note the manner in which it tends to offer ethical thought that stultifies relationship between lived sexual experience and the self. True, black theological thought serves to "modify" structures of self-development (connected to knowledge, relationships, and institutions) and resist certain types of power frameworks. But, unfortunately, this has not involved a fundamental challenge to the underpinning of normalized desire. Too often discourses of race and gender combine with a discourse of desire in ways that are reactive and offer a soft embrace of the dominate framing of sex(uality). Racial difference and sexual difference are worked out by negating the latter to safeguard the racial community. Black theological thought often addresses the structuring of desire as if it is the same discourse as that of race and/or gender: one "size" of resistance fits all.[103] These discourses are connected, overlapping, and dependent, but they are not identical in content and purpose.

It is not difficult to uncover the manner in which such a posture, even if a matter of survival, is far from effective; it fosters a rather limited theory of relationship in which only certain types of activities provide acceptable arrangements of pleasure. While this may entail "the safeguard[ing of] Black life and freedom," it does not really allow for the type of individual and group "cultural fulfillment," as Victor Anderson names liberation, that appreciates sexual difference as a part of the mosaic of black life.[104] That is to say, freedom is available only to those who love in a certain way because black sex(uality) is given fundamental dynamics that require adherence to normative frameworks in order to secure recognition and approval. This is the important point shadowing the rest of this chapter: A new take on black theological thought must work from the premise that difference is only one modality of analysis. Furthermore, it is necessary to understand that sex(uality) is one of the cultural assignments given to black bodies and one of the ways in which black bodies experience life. Such recognition should facilitate a way of viewing sex(uality) as indeterminate, as framed by discourse and open to a variety of experiences when embodied.

There is no need to argue over the ethical legitimacy of certain practice. Instead, black theological thought must provide alternate ways of framing and reading practices and perceptions not based on structures of normalization. The grammar of normalization—ethically "right" and "wrong"—should not be brought to bear on the expression of desire within the context of theological thought. The question for theological thinking is not what are acceptable practices. Instead, theologians should ask these questions as part of their work (and in light of the above discussion): Why do we feel and think the need to limit the range of practices of desire/pleasure? And to what extent does the framework of limitation actually reinforce strategies of discipline and surveillance tied to discourses of race and gender we believe we rejected decades ago?[105] I mean more than just actions, more than the "physical structure of the act or the status of those engaged in the act."[106]

Prospects for Future Study

Within new black theological thought, sex(uality) becomes more than what individuals and groups do with or to each other. It holds in creative tension actions that preoccupy the teachings of religious institutions and more fundamental dynamics that escape their attention. Again, new black theological thought is not concerned with wrestling over what is "sinful" and what isn't as a way of doing battle with judgments stemming from an attitude of "sexual moral minimalism,"[107] by which less sex and a tame sense of sex(uality) is more in keeping with the demands of the religious life. More important than this is a rethinking of the theological value of relationship in ways that affirm sex(uality) and desire/pleasure as expression of complex modalities of interaction. Rather than simply seeking to have certain sexual behaviors once despised included in the array of accepted and appreciated modalities of pleasuring, a new direction for black theological thought might entail an understanding of relationship(s) as a more fundamental or elemental attack on warping notions of the body and its encounters with itself and others. In this way one is able to encourage the growth of complex patterns of exchange, celebrating the ways in which the body gives and receives sexual and non-sexual pleasure through a variety of experiences.

If even earlier modalities of black theological thought urged the bringing of one's experiences to scripture and tradition, in what way is the restrictive discourse of sexuality justified? New black theological thought must recognize a "starting point in people's actions, or sexual acts without polarizing the social from the symbolic. It is from human sexuality that theology starts to search and understand the sacred, and not vice versa."[108] The body should have this type of importance because it is, for the black theist, metaphorically and physically the vessel through which God's gift of sex(uality) flows.

For the black nontheist it is the center of experience. The body becomes an important and vital mode of expressing love to the world.

The question for most involved in black theological discourse: Is it possible to "celebrate, affirm, and experience . . . sexuality fully" within the context of traditional black Christianity?[109] The embodied nature of the Christ Event guarantees that Christ had a penis.[110] Yet, recognition of this, regardless of countless works of art that ignore it, is not a major break with inadequate theological discourse on sex(uality). Certainly Jesus was sensual, but *how* sensual and in what ways? This issue is not so easily resolved by shouting "Jesus had a penis!" (In fact, this might create other problems.) The more radical question, in light of black theology's timidity, involves what he did with it? Was it erect? Did it serve as an outlet of personal pleasure, or pleasure for either men or women, or both? Through such questions we better gauge who Jesus was in human flesh, the divine housed in a body like ours. Such questions are uncomfortable, if not considered bad form, but is that a problematic thing for theological discourse? No, the troubling nature of these questions within the context of what is typically polite theologizing suggest a lack of attention to the embodied nature of sexuality.

For Christians such recognition with regard to Christ has been unspeakable. As consequences, the wholeness sought by black Christianity has been compromised through a rejection of certain dimensions of bodily experience. That is to say, "Christianity is an incarnational religion that claims to set captives free, it tells us it is a religion of liberation. Yet it underpins many of the restrictive practices that body politics expose."[111] Black theological thinking, if it is to correct its inadequate discourse on sex(uality), must "encourage people to express freedom and eroticize their equality."[112] This involves a new perspective on the part of black theologians by which they push themselves and religious communities to recognize and enjoy the ways bodies move in and through the world. It is also the case that more attention to a comparative approach to theological thinking would be of benefit to the extent that traditions such as the Afro-Brazilian Candomblé and Caribbean Santería have a much more embodied perspective on the fulfillment of desire. This is not to say these traditions are free from limiting discourses on sexual normalization. Rather, it is to suggest the manner in which pleasure and desire are framed existentially and metaphysically might serve as a point of instruction for black Christianity (and modalities of Islam in African American communities). Again, this shift in focus involves the need not to simply expand limitations on the structures and expressions of desire but rather a questioning of those limitations in light of the mechanisms of restriction we claim to resist.[113]

Part 2

Bodies in Motion

5

Bodies as the Site of Religious Struggle

A Musical Mapping

Movement through the world involves struggle, but how do we articulate theologically this struggle in ways that reflect the embodied experiences of a range of African Americans? It is my belief that popular culture—including musical expression—provides a useful framing of struggle as religious quest. Yet, in light of my concern with embodied theological thought, even this religiously understood notion of struggle must be "earthbound." That is to say, this struggle is known by and through the body, in the ways in which bodies occupy time and space, and chronicled in a variety of forms including musical production.

Here we mark a shift in focus.[1] Previous chapters explored the manner in which attention to the discursive body and the material body productively influence thinking on some of the more pressing issues within black theological discourses: race, gender, and sex(uality). This chapter and those following it are concerned with examining how the relationship between religion and the body (discursive body and material body) is lived. I begin this shift by discussing the living of religion as recourse against what is commonly referred to in black Christianity as the grammar of the demonic.

By demonic I mean not only negative forces found within Christian cosmology but also a more general reality of non-normative sources of influence and authority. One might also think of the demonic in this context as forces of restriction and domination, or strategies of existence that seek to penetrate bodies according to schemes not always known in clear and fixed ways. The penetration of bodies by these forces is often experienced in black Christianity as oppositional when these forces challenge prevailing normalization patterns. Within this framework of contact, the soul might be drawn as the node of identity housed in (and shaped by) the body. By extension the divine in this case entails normative sources of influence and authority. Both the demonic and the divine are often imagined and discussed as operating through nonhuman bodies and within the cracks of human history. This framing of the demonic, the divine, and the soul (within the fields of embodiment) will inform the following discussion in both implicit and explicit ways. By using the blues and rap music, which privilege the body not just as a source of lived experience but reject disembodied strategies, I reformulate traditional theological vocabulary and grammar through a turn to the chronicling of bodily experience.

Sensitivity to the "Unseen"—The Church and the Spirituals

Finally, be strong in the Lord, and in the power of his might.

Put on the whole armour of God, that you may be able to stand against the wiles of the devil.

For we wrestle not against flesh and but against principalities, against powers, against the rulers of the darkness of this world, against spiritual wickedness in high places.[2]

The imagery and assumed theo-existential truth of the quotation from Ephesians has explicitly and implicitly haunted and guided the ethical sensibilities of the dominant modality of African American religion in the United States (i.e., black Christian churches) for centuries. This should come as no surprise, considering the wealth of writings by scholars such as Allen Callahan, Theophus Smith, Vincent Wimbush, and Cain Hope Felder, all of whom have over the course of two decades presented the intersections between black Christianity and the biblical text.[3] As these scholars have noted, black Christianity has drawn its vocabulary and grammar, its imagery, symbolism, and posture toward the world from the rich stories that make up the Hebrew Bible and the New Testament. Perspectives on the complex nature and framework of human relationships are given their weight and content in large part from the workings of situations outlined in scripture—the "placement" of black bodies within the frameworks of the biblical world. In this regard, black Christianity, as the passage from Ephesians would suggest, presents life struggles as synergy between physical forces and nonphysical forces, between transcendent realities and mundane presences intertwined within the lived context of human history. Black Christianity in various forms portrays sensitivity to forces shaping material and historical developments. Beyond the Holy Spirit, the third division of the Trinity whose workings are unseen but felt, demonic influences working toward evil developments and positive angelic forces shape progressive and healthy developments. Both demonic and angelic forces struggle for the souls and historical arrangements of human history.

Jon Michael Spencer seems to suggest that personification of evil forces is a matter of tales centered on "Southern African-American cosmology" rather than a "theologiz[ing] formally about evil." According to Spencer, this mythologizing of evil in physical form is not restricted to folktales and early African American cosmology. Rather, both cosmologies and more formal church teachings often depicted evil in the same manner. Whereas Spencer tends to see such imagery and cosmological arrangements as more intimately connected to the South, perhaps because of his interest in the Delta blues, I suggest that notions of demonic influence on earth are not geographically bound.[4] Theological imagery and doctrinal assertions, in various regions of the United States, often speak to this arrangement of synergy between celestial and mundane forces. This is certainly the case within African American evangelical circles, where the rhetoric and perception of the workings of the world are most vividly expressed. The Church of God in Christ, for instance, the fastest growing Christian denomination in African American communities, says the following concerning the reality of angels and demons:

The Bible uses the term "angel" (a heavenly body) clearly and primarily to denote messengers or ambassadors of God with such scripture references as Revelations 4:5, which indicates their duty in heaven to praise God (Ps 103:20), to do God's will (Matt 18:10) and to behold his face. But since heaven must come down to earth, they also have a mission to earth. The Bible indicates that they accompanied God in the Creation, and also that they will accompany Christ in His return in Glory. . . . Demons denote unclean or evil spirits; they are sometimes called devils or demonic beings. They are evil spirits, belonging to the unseen or spiritual realm, embodied in human beings. The Old Testament refers to the prince of demons, sometimes called Satan (Adversary) or Devil, as having power and wisdom, taking the habitation of other forms such as the serpent (Gen 3:1). The New Testament speaks of the Devil as Tempter (Matt 4:3) and it goes on to tell the works of Satan, The Devil, and Demons as combating righteousness and good in any form, proving to be an adversary to the saints. Their chief power is exercised to destroy the mission of Jesus Christ. It can well be said that the Christian Church believes in Demons, Satan, and Devils. We believe in their power and purpose. We believe they can be subdued and conquered as in the commandment to the believer by Jesus. "In my name they shall cast out Satan and the work of the Devil and to resist him and then he will flee from you." (Mark 16:17).[5]

Not all historical black denominations provide strong statements concerning the reality of unseen forces influencing human existence. However, such commentary finds its way into black Christianity in modes not confined to the formal doctrinal creeds and official theological postures of particular denominations. Perspectives on demonic forces are also learned through interaction with popular culture. Paul Tillich's remark holds true in this case: "Religion is the substance of culture; and culture is the form of religion."[6] Regarding this, one is just as likely to find discussion of these invisible forces battling for influence in human history expressed in oft-called "sacred" and "secular" songs as in formal theology.

Long before the formation of independent African American churches in the eighteenth century, scholars such as John Lovell Jr. have argued for the existence of spirituals, and it is through this haunting music that enslaved Africans articulated their rudimentary religious sensibilities and theological assumptions.[7] Drawn from pieces of Christianity secured through church services with whites, bits of scripture presented and shaped into song in the work fields, slave quarters, and within the context of secret gatherings known as "hush arbor" meetings, these songs spoke of the slave's sense of a God present in the world, poised to bring about the redemption of the enslaved and the "righting" of the world. This God was understood to be loving, kind, just, and the author of history, seen as teleological in nature, both during the time of the biblical stories and the historical moment in which the slaves found themselves. This God was also understood to work through bodies, to manifest within experienced arrangements of time and space. In the words of one song: "Didn't my Lord deliver Daniel, deliver Daniel, deliver Daniel? And why not everyone?" Or,

> God is a God!
> God don't never change!
> God is a God
> An' He always will be God.[8]

God's plan for the fulfillment of human history, complete with its reframing of black life, is accomplished through the perfect blend of divinity and humanity in the form of the Christ Event. Drawing from stories of the activities and attitudes of Christ, along with a deep sensitivity to Christ's humble family context, enslaved Africans embraced him, drawing bold existential and ontological links between themselves and this representative of God on earth. They found in the material poverty surrounding his biblically rehearsed birth, and in the suffering that informed his raison d'être epistemological links and similarities to themselves. Enslaved Africans faced hardship and undeserved pain and, more to the point, their plight would be rectified through the workings of God in human history and would be "felt" in the body.

> Children, we shall be free
> When the Lord shall appear.
> Give ease to the sick, give sight to the blind,
> Enable the cripple to walk;
> He'll raise the dead from under the earth,
> And give them permission to talk.[9]

Such was the belief based on their take on scripture, what they considered the unchanged commitment of God to righteousness and the existence of Christ as the sign of God's connection to those who suffer unjustly. First, the Exodus of the children of Israel and, now during their time, they awaited a second exodus of God's "dark" children experiencing oppression in the Americas. The uniqueness of Christ is the perfect balance between transcendent forces or realities and physical presence represented through the God/man, Christ.

The absurdity of the slave system, with its Christian tendencies (e.g., theological justifications for enslavement, religious instruction as indoctrination), gave rise to a cartography of struggle bringing into play a host of forces, only some of them physical but all of them deeply important and felt. The Christ Event confronts the evil found in the world guided by the workings of Satan and his dominion, and enslaved Africans recognized it and noted it in song. In these spirituals, enslaved Christians spoke of the battle between good and evil, and noted their souls and their existential condition as the prize and the battlefield respectively. What is interesting is the manner in which this confrontation is not limited to discursive arrangements: one could not simply quote scripture or manipulate written texts in such a way as to gain the desired outcome. Rather, the materiality of the body had to be brought into play. The body had to feel or experience this struggle. The body had to *do* something. Its occupation of time and space; its posture in the world mattered greatly. In the words of one song:

> Kneel and pray, so the devil won't harm me
> Try my best for to serve the lord
> Kneel and pray, so the devil won't harm me
> Hallelujah.[10]

Juxtaposed to the work of the devil, the spirituals speak of the company of angels as a life affirming and heaven-assuring event:

> O, I'm going to march with the tallest angel
> O, yes, march with the tallest angel
> O, yes, march with the tallest angel
> When my work is done.[11]

Within the spirituals, proper human activity involves a push against demonic forces and an embrace of angelic forces—the assumption being the ultimate welfare of humanity is tied to the triumph of good over evil— the kingdom of God over Satan. Yet, in the blues such a distinction is not assumed.

Feeling the Demonic—The Blues

What is best for the individual (only limited attention is given to community) as outlined in the blues might entail a relationship with the devil, based on the biblical notions of this force, over against the Christian God. Such a willingness to entertain demonic forces might suggest one rationale for calling the blues the "devil's music" in that the music was conversant with Christian principles, grammar, and vocabulary, but showing a willingness to entertain forces Christians fear and fight. It is more complex than this, however. Traditional theological responses to the blues' posture toward the world are too myopic, too determined by strategies of scriptural duplication (i.e., assumption of scriptural and historical continuity).

Within the blues, solidly Christian wrestling with the demonic as agent by which the self is altered in ontologically and existentially problematic ways assumes certain outcomes based on counterknowledge and corresponding behavior. That is to say, one who resists demonic influence and lives in accordance with the normalizing claims of scripture secures a better existence in line with the will of God. Such a perspective on the structure of power relations and the potential for "care of the self" is indeed troubled in the blues and rap music. Picking sides was an assumption made, and the failure of blues artists to quickly and neatly demarcate "right" and "wrong" ethical/theological positions met with a backlash. Again, from the perspective of many, it had to be "devil music."

For some, this label covered all non-Christian orientations noted and often celebrated in the blues; hence, references to conjure or hoodoo—to the extent these were seen as related to "dark" forces—meant a negative depiction. Yet, more to the point, the label "devil music" also served to highlight the demonic forces acknowledged and at times courted by blues figures. This assertion runs contrary to the sense of the blues as deeply earthbound in ways that reject substantive attention to notions of transcendence. While true in rather significant respects—blues often reject theistic orientations and embrace humanistic principles—some strains even speak to the workings of spiritual forces, perhaps to signify Christian assumptions within African American communities or as a genuine acknowledgment of a spiritual realm, by presenting themselves in physical form.

> Devil's gonna git you,
> Devil's gonna git you,
> Oh, the devil's gonna git you,
> The way you're carryin' on.[12]

The blues is a musical form rooted in sensibilities and attitudes as old as those giving rise to the spirituals. The blues and spirituals recognize the same cartography of existence; both musical forms assume that we move through the world accompanied and influenced by unseen forces.

> Black ghost, black ghost, please stay away from my door
> Black ghost, black ghost, will you please stay away from my door
> Yeah you know you worry po' Lightnin' so now, I just can't sleep no
>   more.[13]

Yet, whereas the boundaries between these forces and their effectiveness in human life are clear and based on the Christian faith for those singing the spirituals, for those motivated by the blues, there is a more utilitarian approach, one that allows for flirtation with both angelic and demonic forces, depending on which might offer the most efficient assistance. The blues lack the certainty of a teleological arrangement of history that gives the Christian comfort; instead, the blues romance a comfort with paradox, with a blending of opposites, manipulated and celebrated by the cleaver within and through their bodies. The blues chronicler Robert Palmer captures this epistemological complexity. "Blues lyrics," writes Palmer, "could be light, mocking, risqué, or could deal forthrightly with the most highly charged subject matter—intimate details of love, sex, and desire; a fascination with travel for its own sake that was rooted in the years of black captivity; the hypocrisies and foibles of preachers and other upstanding folks; the fantastic and often disturbing imagery of dreams; the practice and tools of magic and conjury; aggressive impulses that had to be severely repressed in everyday life." He continues, "and in some blues, particularly the Delta Blues of Robert Johnson, an unabashed identification with the leader of the world's dark forces, the ultimate other."[14] This stance avoids an ethical or moral arrangement of activity and desire. The blues tend to embrace a crude pragmatic posture whereby the expressed need and want of the artist determines the utility of sources, such as demonic or angelic forces.

The sense of commonality found in the blues is premised on the widespread nature, the shared desire for advancement, for goods, for good feelings, for the stuff of life. "Powers and principalities" offering excess to the riches of life, regardless of their nature or disposition, are approached. In most cases loyalty is first to the individual, based on the interests and desires of the individual, and codified by any force capable of making those desires real. Perhaps flirting with this understanding suggest one of the reasons for the great blues singer Peetie Wheatstraw's labeling as the "Devil's Son-in-Law and the High Sheriff from Hell."[15]

I am aware of musicologist Jon Michael Spencer's critique of blues scholarship, which uncritically assumes the blues to have evil intentions, a certain reading of blues as "devil's music" in ways that simply reinforce stereotypical depictions of African Americans, and suggests a rather flat and reified notion of the nature and meaning of evil. I would agree with Spencer that the blues are not "evil" per se. There is nothing about the blues suggesting that it is intrinsically flawed; rather, the tension regarding the "non-godly" dimension of the blues seems an imposed paradoxical arrangement as opposed to being generated internally. In other words, the dilemma of commitments regarding blues and evil stems from a dominant Christian worldview projected unto the musical genre of the blues. Yet, even in saying this, I want to suspend Spencer's assumptions concerning the normative state of Christianity as the religious orientation of African Americans, and thereby avoid his rather flat depiction of evil's function in American religion and life. Applying this to musical talent in African American communities, while some gave thanks to God for their abilities (assuming God favored them with great talent as a gift) others spoke of a bargain with demonic forces as the source of their musical (and social) prowess.

The blues speak of life circumstances, the play and interaction of contrary forces both visible and invisible in ways of great discomfort to those singing the spirituals. There is, in the blues, no great fear of hell nor great yearning for heaven: the former can't be any worse than the oppression encountered, and the latter takes a back seat to the significance and feel of life's earthbound pleasures and desires. And both are connected already to the flesh they know and live. In fact, the existential conditions faced by the physical body at times trump other forces. One gets a sense of this in the following, playful words from "Too Poor to Die":

> Dream I met the devil
> He is waitin' at the gate . . .
> But he wouldn't move my body
> Less I grease his palm.[16]

The overlap between the workings of the physical body ("move my body less I grease his palm") and the discursive or cultural constructed body ("dream I met the devil") is present but signified. Ways in which this contact with the devil might serve to represent approaches to discipline are not thwarted through alternate discourse of linguistic resistance but through the body as uncontrollable substance. In a twist that brings into question normalizing structures presented as working through positive (God) or negative (the demonic) means are held at bay through nothing more than a willful materiality. The stigmatized body—the "greasy" body—exposes the limitations of normalization mechanisms.

For some blues artists there are no universal truths that must be observed across circumstances and time. There is, instead, relativity, a contextual orientation in place, allowing experience to determine epistemology. This is a shift away from the certainty of theological formulations, of transcendent values. It is not what James Cone had in mind when proclaiming the experiential nature of truth. For Cone, truth is singular (revolving around the Christ Event as the will of God) and lodged in a somewhat fixed epistemology.[17]

I take no moral stance here, no effort to judge the rhetoric and imagery of demonic forces in partnership or as foe; my concern is to simply suggest the rich and robust sense of operative forces pervading and influencing embodied human existence.[18] Whereas from the perspective of black Christians such associations were morally and ethically charged, I am more concerned with narrating the nature of this interaction. And few present a more vivid depiction of the embodied nature of religio-theological wrestling than the bluesman Robert Johnson.

Born in Mississippi, Robert Johnson is perhaps the blues artist most closely linked, as folktales would suggest, to demonic forces. The hardships of his early life—relocations and family disruptions—may have had something to do with his early interest in the blues, nurtured through the mentoring of Willie Brown, Charley Patton, and Son House in Robinsonville, Mississippi. During these early years, legend has it, Johnson's musical ability was of limited appeal, pale in comparison to the other musicians making their way through the Delta. All this changed after Johnson left the area for an uncertain period of time and returned, upon which his musical abilities were staggering. Historical accounts by scholars suggest that he went under the tutelage of another musician, practicing his craft, returning only when his abilities were at a high enough level. Yet even these musicians are said to have, at times, talked in terms of invisible forces and their influence. For many others the account more explicitly and directly involves unseen forces, the workings of demonic forces in the service of humans . . . for a price. By accounts provided by family members and friends, Johnson's new abilities resulted from selling his soul to the devil in exchange for unparalleled talent. Certain of his songs are pointed out as testimony to this exchange.[19] While some artists give visual depictions of the demonic, often portrayed consistent with negative color symbolism as a large black figure, Johnson gave no such attention to the appearance of the demonic. His concern simply revolved around the ability of such forces to impinge upon human existence. Johnson recognized the presence of such forces, invisible realities encroaching on his life:

> I got to keep moving, I got to keep moving
> Blues falling down like hail, blues falling down like hail
> Mmm, blues falling down like hail, blues falling down like hail
> And the day keeps on remindin' me, there's a hellhound on my trail
> Hellhound on my trail, hellhound on my trail.[20]

Or, the connection between Johnson and the devil as one of exchange is also present in shaded ways in the following lines:

Early this mornin'
when you knocked upon my door
Early this mornin', ooh
when you knocked upon my door
And I said, "Hello, Satan,
I believe it's time to go."[21]

Johnson alludes to the consequences of securing musical abilities from the devil: One must surrender one's soul, one's self to forces beyond one's control. Even this deal with invisible forces is only a temporary correction to fulfilling desire and want; after a period of time comes damnation. And much of the time prior to that outcome is spent anticipating the inevitable, literally *feeling* the pursuit by "hell hounds." The alternative for Johnson appears to be embodied movement (not simply alternation between discourses), unpredictable and constant movement:

I got ramblin', I got ramblin' on my mind.
I got ramblin', I got ramblin' all on my mind.[22]

Had Johnson simply worked hard, under the guidance of formidable musicians, absorbing lessons without distraction or competition? Or had he made a deal with evil forces? Even if the answer to the latter is no, he recognized the significance of such imagery for projecting a reputation as a "bad man," a formidable figure whose lived activities and music produced a deep gut reaction that both repelled and attracted listeners. One might absorb his sound, his language, and follow the movement of his material body, all the while uncomfortably comforted.

Death for such men, those blues performers familiar with the world of diverse forces, did not necessarily entail an end to all events. Rather it marked a transition, a movement to a new venue for activity, but one arranged in exchange for a liminal period of prowess. There is a sense of the tragic in this: life often remained difficult, albeit marked by recognition but not without its downside. They lived hard and died hard. In certain ways, even deals with the devil involved a signifying of such demonic forces in that at times bad men "ruled" hell through the maintenance of their self-centered and destructive ways. Or, in other cases, they joined the ranks of unseen forces and continued to move through human time and space – both the "deal" with demonic forces and its aftermath shrouded in mystery. Perhaps such awareness accounts for Robert Johnson's request for burial near the highway so that his evil spirit might continue to travel via the bus line. The need to hit the road, to traverse time and space, is not dampened by death:

> You may bury my body, ooh
> down by the highway side
> So my old evil spirit can catch a Greyhound bus and ride.[23]

Perhaps what Johnson alludes to here is the continued presence of his soul—the mechanism lodged in his music—that shaped perceptions of and engagements with the world's he described. While his physical body would end, he maintained a place in the frameworks of influence through his soul and modalities of identity formation it encouraged.

Deals with feared forces could only enhance his reputation; Johnson understood lyrics alone (many of which he borrowed from other artists) could not cement his success and musical legacy. Rather, the personae of the artist, the overall ethos of being (e.g., soul) surrounding him needed to entail the wiles of the trickster and dealings of the "bad man." In short, association, real or imagined, with demonic forces served the purpose. Even this affiliation, this connection to the demonic, served as a modality of resistance to staid and reified notions of morality and ethics tied to what these blues men considered the hypocrisy of the Christian faith. They, in dealing with the devil, signified the claims of the Christian faith (its doctrine, theology, and particularly its theodicies) to the sources of the good life in ways that centered on the validity of the desires and wants Christianity condemned roundly, such as sexual freedom, material goods, and revenge. In this way, Robert Johnson and other blues figures like him were involved in an inverted spiritual arrangement whereby the needs and wants of the physical body were given priority over what Christians considered the proper welfare of the soul.

This arrangement was not unique to blues figures; others within black communities sought help with life circumstances through despised forces since the often-denied desires of life were, in effect, due to the structural arrangements of slavery and continued discrimination. Despised black bodies sought assistance from and intertwined their existential and ontological substance with despised "dark" forces. By so doing, it is possible an effort was made to use metaphysical evil to battle the damage done by the sociopolitical and economic fallout of racism as demonic force: Evil negates evil, and the body is the terrain for this contest.

Rap Music and Living With the Demonic

The bad man, the rebellious figure, feared within African American Christianity and its musical expression (first the spirituals and then gospel music), and celebrated by certain blues figures, continues his flirtation with demonic realities within the form of certain "gangsta" rappers, or what we might call the "children of the blues." Such rap artists share many of the existential commitments and the moral sensibilities of the blues performers, and this includes a similar stance on lived synergy between demonic forces and rebellious humans.

While rap music in many cases tends to avoid a direct appeal to demonic forces for the development of musical abilities and other markers of success in a troubled world, rap is not devoid of references to sensitivity to the presence and workings of demonic forces. Yet, rather than joining league with them actively, some rappers simply work in ways that seem influenced by the tendencies and characteristics of the demonic, while others simply step through the world seeing the demonic lodged firmly around them. At the very least, some rap music indicates an awareness of a delicate balance between lived experiences influenced by the divine and by the demonic, pressed into a macabre worldview. This type of tortured existence, one hanging between an absurd world and the workings of invisible forces impinging upon human existence, marks, for example, the lyrics by the rapper Scarface.

Born Jordan Bradley on November 9, 1970, in Houston, Texas, Scarface made his early fame (or position as infamous) through the rap group The Ghetto Boys, whose lyrics spoke without remorse of the dark side of existence. These rappers presented themselves as predators determined to exercise their wants and desires without attention to moral and ethical consequences. They represented in graphic relief the uncontrolled ego impulse as total freedom, which had tortured the existentialists, and framed it all in terms of African American life as understood through Richard Wright's character Cross Damon. In their bodies they lived the signs of this "freedom," and in their conversation that structured an applicable system of conduct.[24]

In the early 1990s, Scarface expanded beyond The Ghetto Boys by initiating solo projects, but did not move beyond the articulation of a macabre worldview. In his solo albums produced since leaving the group, Scarface has continued along the path of existential angst, with a glimpse here and there into the world of "powers and principalities" that influence but are not synonymous with the arrangements of human history.[25] As blues artists note the manner in which evil can follow "bad men," as early as from birth, Scarface also presents himself as dogged by the demonic even before he is able to consciously choose sides: good or evil. He notes, in a fashion framed by materiality of thought and action:

> I don't remember much about being born.
> But I do remember this: I was conceived on February 10th.
> Complications detected in my early months of ballin',
> around my sonogram you could see the evil was swarmin'.[26]

In his lyrics, death is ever present, and in some instances Scarface dissects the details of life's surrender to death: "You start your journey into outer space. You see yourself in the light but you're still feeling outta place."[27] Scarface, like so many other rappers, makes an appeal to relationship with the divine as the best, last, outreach of humanity; but he also recognizes the tensions between the forces of "good" pushing for this sort of relationship and the demonic, which influences humans to behave in less than ethically mature ways. In other words, normalization is marked by multiplicity—numerous frameworks by which to construct and present the self. From his perspective, the existence of these two competing forces is real, oozing from every aspect of human existence in the 'hood. Death lurks around every corner, and the life of a gangsta requires recognition of this and a willingness to accept the negatively serendipitous nature of such a life. Think in terms of the lyrics to "Make Your Peace" in which Scarface frames the demonic in terms of an alternate world invisible to human eyes, but nonetheless real and felt to impinge upon the body by shaping the soul:

> I had a dream and seen a double sun,
> A different world was in the makin'
> The rule of this new world was Satan.[28]

Deals with demonic forces may not be as prevalent in rap, although 2Pac's verse to "Smile," on Scarface's *Untouchable*, directly addresses this arrangement, noting the perception, shadowing perhaps the legend of Robert Johnson, the acquisition of goods and prowess assumed to stem from unnatural arrangements:

> No fairy tales for this young black male
> Some see me stranded in this land of hell, jail, and crack sales

Hustlin' and heart be a nigga culture
Or the repercussions while bustin' on backstabbin' vultures
Sellin' my soul for material wishes, fast cars and bitches
Wishin' I live my life a legend, immortalized in pictures.[29]

In spite of these lyrics, on the whole rappers, including Scarface, do not generally suggest directly that one try to outmaneuver these demonic forces—although the traumas of experienced life might indeed suggest an evil presence producing harm and anxiety. (Rappers, like blues figures, *feel* the texture of human existence.) On the other hand, one should simply recognize their presence and their impact on life because such forces are everywhere, identifiable in the activities of neighbors and friends by the observant. In Scarface's words, "who the fuck is you gonna trust when your road dog is scheming? And every other corner, you're passin' a different demon."[30]

The world for some blues artists and some rappers is similar, involving an absurd arrangement of forces that one cannot completely control, but one that can embrace or signify in a multiplicity of ways. It is this perspective that such artists accept and articulate in their music, absorbing the paradox of life in a knowing way and with a somewhat defiant posture. They approach their bodies with/through their bodies; they experience life as they both resist and embrace its various structures.

Embodiment

The difficulty of moving through a world haunted by such forces is not limited to Scarface with his existential angst and metaphysical uncertainties. Artists such as Snoop Dogg also wrestle with the various forces present in the world. Born October 20, 1971, in Long Beach, California, to Beverly Broadus and Vernall Varnado, Snoop Dogg's (aka Calvin Broadus) life was marked by the deep concern and religious orientation of his mother and the absence of his father. Of the few things given to him by his father, Snoop Dogg remarks, was a love for music. This love, combined with talent and skills given by God, mark the emergence of a rap career in which he chronicled life circumstances, arrangements, and relationships within the context of a troubled environment. He notes, "In every rap I ever recorded, in the mad flow of every street-corner freestyle I ever represented, there was only one thing I wanted to get across: the way it is. Not the way I might want it to be. Not the way I think *you* might want it to be. But the way it *really* is, on the streets of the 'hoods of America, where life is lived out one day at a time, up against it, with no guarantees. . . . My raps describe what it's like to be a young black man in America today."[31]

Snoop Dogg's rap shares with the blues a deep sensitivity to the nature and flow of life, the manner in which human relationships of all sorts shift and change in a variety of ways. He, like blues artists before him, recognizes the dark corners of life, noting both the promise and struggle associated with lived human existence. His is an existentially driven reality, but one that is also sensitive to the presence of realities uncontrolled by human intention. And, the "bad man" is best equipped to maneuver through this troubled terrain. In his words, "there was a whole new class of hero coming up—the pimp and the outlaw, the thug and the gangster—and if you wanted to stay alive on the streets of Long Beach or Watts or Compton or anywhere else where the American Dream was falling apart and fading away, you better get with their program. It was the only game in town."[32] Like the bad men of the century before him, Snoop Dogg is not troubled by this philosophy of connection; rather, he sees it as simply a matter of fact and he embraces the paradox that is life—"bangin'" as a way of life: Stagger Lee reincarnated as a late twentieth-century gangbanger.[33]

While the often ethically questionable nature of some of his lyrics might suggest a paradox, Snoop Dogg views his musical history as teleological in nature, a purpose-driven development framed and orchestrated by a God who has provided him with talent and opportunity: "Just when you think you've got Him figured out, some blindside twist of fate makes you understand that you *can't* figure Him out. That's why He's God and you're whoever the hell you are. He calls the shots, makes the moves, and keeps it all in check."[34] He views his rap lyrics and music as a matter of ministry, a way of transforming life and regenerating relationships. From his perspective all of life (and death) are controlled by forces unseen but felt: " . . . most of the time, most of us don't sit around thinking on how God can snap our string any time He gets mad or bored or needs another angel in heaven or another demon in hell. Most of the time, if we're honest, we don't give a thought to any of that metaphysical shit."[35] Nonetheless, although he may not "give a thought to any of that metaphysical shit," such influences on human existence are real for him and do penetrate material bodies thereby shaping how they occupy time and space.

Increased sensitivity to the fragile nature and the complex arrangements of life came to Snoop Dogg, he recounts, when faced with the possibility of life behind bars without the possibility of parole. It was with the threat of freedom removed, of space reified, and time controlled by others that Snoop

Dogg's interest in metaphysical questions and concerns, the depths of existence, was sharpened. The visibility of disciplinary mechanisms shrouded in a discourse of correction marked his body and highlighted its vulnerabilities. He writes, "My guess is, we all wonder about the time we've got set out for us on the planet and what we're going to do with it before the clock stops ticking and they put us in the ground. . . . And that might be because, for those few, the reality of their life coming to a stone-cold stop is more than just some what-if trick their minds play on them. Every once in a while, a human being, no different from you or me, really does face down those odds, and when that happens, nothing is ever the same again."[36] Unlike Robert Johnson and numerous other blues performers, there is no hint of conjuration, of folk practices, at work in Snoop Dogg's tale, but the existence of "powers and principalities" seems just as felt, just as compelling.

There is rhetoric of responsibility and accountability—the acceptance of certain disciplinary arrangements—in the autobiographical voice of Snoop Dogg that one does not find in blues artists like Robert Johnson. Yet there is a paradox to life that resembles the depiction offered within so many blues tunes. Perhaps this paradox is even heightened in Snoop Dogg's story because the battle between the demonic and the divine is made that much more vivid and recognizable in the relationship of material bodies to material bodies.

On August 23, 1993, a man lay dead on the street, and Snoop Dogg and two others would be implicated. It is this tragic event, from which he was found innocent, that sparked his theological and existential reflection on and wrestling over deals with demonic forces as a framework for navigating the uncertainties of human (non)existence. As Robert Johnson hauntingly portrayed such a deal for talent in several blues tunes, Snoop graphically suggests a similar deal in exchange for continued life and prowess in "Murder Was the Case," a project spearheaded by Dr. Dre (with Snoop Dogg as one of several receiving writer's credit for the title track) and, according to some, the title track was loosely "tied" to the murder charge Snoop Dogg faced at the time of its release. In his autobiography, however, Snoop Dogg is less than enthusiastic about that project, seeing it as potentially distracting from *Doggystyle* ("Murder Was the Case" is also a track on *Doggystyle*).

While arguing the murder charge brought him closer to prayer and God, thereby recognizing the inability of humans to ultimately shape history and control visible and invisible forces, the lyrics suggest a world of forces at work. More important than an autobiographical authenticity to the lyrics, or the validity of seeing the piece as commentary on the trail, is the reflection on demonic vs. divine influence open to human use. In this fictional narrative of a near-death experience, shot, one assumes, due to jealousy over his success, Snoop encounters the various forces marking the lived geography of human existence, all attempting to gain control of his soul (readers will recall my thinking on the nature and meaning of the soul presented earlier in this chapter):

> My body temperature falls
> I'm shakin' and they breakin' tryin' to save the Dogg
> Pumpin' on my chest and I'm screamin'
> I stop breathin', damn I see demons
> Dear God, I wonder can ya save me.[37]

While based on Snoop Dogg's personal narrative of relationship to God, one would assume the deal struck in the track is with the divine. The storyline is not so clear, however, and the ethical system in large part leaves room to wonder (again, a multiplicity of normalizing forces). Is the voice he hears after praying that of God, or one of the demons he sees?

> I think it's too late for prayin', hold up
> A voice spoke to me and it slowly started sayin'
> "Bring your lifestyle to me I'll make it better"
> How long will I live?
> "Eternal life and forever"
> And will I be the G that I was?
> "I'll make your life better than you can imagine or even dreamed of."[38]

The life Snoop secures as a result of the deal with the unnamed force entails the material goods and control that might make Robert Johnson proud. It is one that does not mirror the more narrow and rigid moral and ethical outlooks generally associated with surrender to Christ, at least as typically presented by African American churches. Here, however, the theological and ethical message is muddied in that Snoop's behavior results in a prison sentence.

Is this punishment for not practicing more conservative Christian values, or is it simply the uncertain, perhaps double-crossing arrangements of a deal with the devil? Is it divine punishment or the end of one's "run" through life, similar to Robert Johnson's deal with the devil not preventing what legend calls a painful death? One might think about a prison sentence, using Foucault's process, as a mechanism of control whereby the body is captured, exposed, and reconstituted as consistent with the established normalized body.[39] He is made "anew," so to speak. The question is which normalized body, in line with which normalizing agent? Only Snoop knows; we are left to wonder with only a few certainties, one being the presence of both good and evil forces shaping and shifting the nature and substance of human existence as that existence is lived, not simply discussed. Chronicled in the examples of the blues and rap music is a battle with forces of restriction and domination, which takes place in the context of lived experience and is noted through feelings of fear, surrender, absurdity, and so forth.

Blues and rap music are drawn from a range of thinking and be-*ing* modalities that reflect (and distort) the dominant and Christian processes of self-care. As Michael Dyson observes, certain rap artists "are trying to confront the discontinuity between destiny and merit, between social evil and the contention that God is good."[40] Many critics of rap music promote the differences between themselves and what rap music represents. But there is also within these critics a bit of discomfort with the similarities found (those matters of sameness they disparately want to deny). Put another way, rap music and the blues speak to and represent layered possibilities of thought and practice, all of which are available to (and utilized by) the more solidly Christian. For the Christian, the *real* Christian, rap music and the blues remind them of the delicate grasp they have on their desired self: "There but for the grace of God go I." Phrased differently, the "grace" believed to distinguish the proclaimed Christian and the blues/rap artist is an act of generosity they do not control, and do not merit.

Prospects for Future Study

You "feel me?" No, do you *really* "feel me?"

Sensitivity to a world packed with both visible and invisible forces marks the lyrical content of African American forms of music such as the blues and rap. In both cases the more ethically and morally aggressive artist flirts with such forces, signifying them and partnering with them based on a deep sense of individualized need and desire. These forces penetrate, shape, and are reflected by material bodies as they move through a physical world.

Drawing from sources such as lyrical content offered by these artists, whether blues figures such as Robert Johnson or rappers such as Scarface and Snoop Dogg, allows an alternate framework for black theological thinking still marked by theological articulation of life premised on "powers and principalities," but in a way that is embodied and experienced through a multiplicity of arrangements. These "powers and principalities" are shown to represent forces (strategies that define and implement ethical sensibilities in line with the norm) seeking to penetrate bodies, to render them useful and recognizable within the context of particular hierarchies of purpose.

This new approach to black theological thought might not understand such forces as the New Testament writers or contemporary Christians might hope. Nonetheless, new black theological discourse articulates a world sensitive to the host of forces and realities impinging on life, shaping and transforming it, all the while ironically enriching it. All that is thought, spoken, and experienced is finally directed to and framed by the body. Consequently, embodiment remains the central vehicle for religious engagement and theologizing that experience. Traditional notions of cosmic forces are rendered earthbound by this new black theological discourse in that these forces (i.e., strategies) are historical matters inconceivable outside the context of human interactions. Granted, earlier formations of black theology were seldom concerned with spiritual forces in traditional terms, yet this new black theological discourse expresses another step because it understands these forces through and within the context of anthropology, not Christology.

I do not suggest that those discourses familiar to black Christianity are completely lost, or that new black theological discourse jettisons completely the vocabulary and grammar of black Christianity. Instead, this new discourse embraces certain elements and resists others. It, at times, signifies Christian discourse as nostalgic, as the stuff of docile bodies. Still, new black theological thought is not free from constraint: it maintains mechanisms of surveillance and monitoring through the stories of bodily activities it promotes and denies. (In black church circles this might be referenced as "witnessing.") It maintains the visibility of active bodies and rehearses the ways in which bodies are culturally restructured and how that process (always incomplete) "feels."[41] As a consequence, and this is key, new black theological discourse is never able to step completely outside the frameworks it challenges. It may celebrate the margins and work from the margins of the social body, but it is not free of the workings and demands of the social body.

Some might assume new black theological thought to be without strong normalizing value (read "resistant to accepted norms"), serving instead as a threat to the invaluable structuring of a good life. There, however, is a bit of irony found in such a critique. New black theological thought both embraces *and* challenges normalized existence. Within new black theological thought, the "truth," assumed to be embedded in Christian discourse, is exposed as fractured and lodged in an assortment of truths. Christian discourse is only one discourse.

Advocates of the liberationist impulse associated with earlier modalities of black theological discourse, and with institutional representations of that discourse (black churches), might privilege teleologically driven hopefulness in spite of sobering possibilities. Yet, new black theological thought should privilege the incomplete nature of this process of formation of the self because fissures and cracks in the process are noted and celebrated. This new shape promotes the fluidity of the demonic (as defined earlier) as well as the benefits and shortcomings of any relationship, whether with dominant normalizing forces or demonic (yet still normalizing) forces. It, then, suggests the demonic is not wholly escapable, nor is escape always desirable.

New black theological thought recognizes that whichever path chosen, whichever "technologies of self" and corresponding discourses embraced, the results shape and are shaped by the body. It, the body, is both the context and the content of this encounter. One might read in this way Johnson's deal with the devil, or Snoop Dogg's dream of an arrangement that provides wealth and power, all the while delaying death. In either case, there is a haunting and eerie narrative of the battle for human souls, played out through the presentation and practices of the body in time and space.

6

On the Redemption of Bodies

Chapter 5 highlighted the tension involved in the theological construction of the self in relationship to competing and overlapping forces of normalization. It pointed out the various possibilities of lived experience when penetrated and shaped by these forces. The process of engagement, or surrender, to these forces was outlined, but questions remain: What is the desired or projected outcome of this construction, this engagement? What is gained (or what is lost)? These questions frame the possibility of redemption, the topic for this chapter. Rather than discussing redemption within the context of traditional discourses of new meaning ripped from the limited in number but overdetermined slave narratives and other commonly tapped sources, I find intriguing the notions of religious experience and redemption referenced in certain modalities of rap music, but which are seldom allowed to influence and affect the theologian's work.

Hip-hop culture and rap music in particular emerged during a period of discursive shifts; it took shape within the tensions and fissures of sociopolitical relations.[1] Black consciousness and black aesthetics waned as dominant ideological orientations. Disillusionment with the limited impact of the civil rights movement increased. The religio-cultural dominance of the black church was called into question as an organizing life framework. And hip-hop offered a new discursive and aesthetic arrangement as well as new ways for bodies to defy time and space (think, for example, in terms of break dancing).[2] Rap music provided the language for these new possibilities.

As a late twentieth-century development, rap is important because it helps to frame some of the more pressing challenges confronting theological thinking. However, I am not concerned here with a general assessment of hip-hop culture or even rap music in particular.[3] Nor am I providing an analysis of rap music and religiosity in a general way. The purpose of this chapter is more focused. By examining the religious rhetoric and practices of rapper Tupac Shakur (see 2Pac, chap. 5), I expose the troubled relationship between religious language and perceived religiously motivated activity. The tensions and fissures present in the intersections of discourse and practice are brought to light, and in the process, this chapter offers an alternate means by which to access the framework of religious experience and redemption.

Drawing on Foucault, by redemption I mean outcomes of self-care that involve comfortable modalities of identity either consistent with or in opposition to the strategies of normalization. Connected to this is the notion of conversion as the process of realization—the process by which one is confronted with oneself (the limits, shortcomings, and possibilities of oneself) within a context of asserted norms. Rap music is used here as a problematic by which to encourage attention to prevailing theories of black religious experience, particularly as related to notions of redemption marked as normative within black theological discourse. In this way, theoretical and methodological challenges are posed to the manner in which the authenticity of African American religious commitment and experience are gauged and verified often in opposition to the (stigmatized) material body. Rap music, in this instance, pushes for a different read, one in which the "salvific" is determined through the structuring, practices, and uses of the lived body.

One might think of black religion as the quest for complex subjectivity, the urge toward a fuller sense of one's meaning and importance within the context of community. In this regard it should have something to do with how bodies are constructed, and how they occupy time and space vis-à-vis strategies of domination.[4] Thinking about religion and religious experience in this way allows for a tension between the two modes of the body—discursive and material—undergirding this book. Religion and religious experience so conceived involve response to dehumanizing forces (e.g., race-based discrimination, gender-based discrimination, and heterosexism) faced by African Americans across centuries of life in the Unites States. Over against what I suggest as intersections between the discursive and the material bodies *in unstable ways*, most theologically informed theories of conversion and black religious experience tend to highlight and privilege experience as explicitly marking a more *stable (teleological) transformation* that promotes new and firm postures toward the world.

Black Christianity and the Saved Life

Liberation approaches, which privilege the "stable," also tend to see life postures as contributing to a refined sense of one's ontological connections and resulting obligations. This is the basic meaning of black Christian proclamations of conversion and accompanying redemption as the emergence of the "new" person, one whose thought and practice are guided by a surrender to Christ-centered moral and ethical arrangements.

Religious experience and life so understood involves the affirmation of and attempt to perpetuate the substance of conversion/redemption as marked by (1) confrontation with one's spiritual and related mundane (such as moral missteps) shortcomings, (2) wrestling with old postures and perceptions over against possibilities of a new consciousness, and (3) new consciousness and related ways of being in the world.[5] Taking place within this context of conversion is a disassociation from the "secular," an epistemological tenderness resulting in an attempt to step lightly through the world, and in this way avoid its contaminates and thus provide a proper example of moral and ethical correctness.

One's newly recognized and accepted ontological significance and merit (i.e., revitalized image of God) is matched by a new posture toward the world in line with a community of the like-minded. In the words of the spiritual, "You say the Lord has set you free; you must be loving at God's command."[6] Through this posture, black Christian renderings of religious experience, again with particular attention to conversion, suggest that the weight of transformation revolves around both a new posture toward the world (e.g., an altered perspective on the manner in which bodies occupy time and space) and, more importantly, a set of rather reified ethical and moral norms drawn from a rather traditional read of the Hebrew Bible and the Christian Testament. "Therefore," the text begins, "if any man be in Christ, he is a new creature: old things are passed away; behold, all things are become new."[7]

In significant ways, religious experience involves the placement of certain bodies in new contexts, a new matrix of interactions, recognition, and exchange whereby bodies are both "in the world" but not "of the world." And a teleological perspective always guides this processing of history. Thick relationship with Christ, surrender to the plan and will of God (as black Christians might name it), involves a new experience of the body, one through which the body becomes an interactive vessel promoting and contributing to God's plan for humanity. This sense of encounter with the divine involves looking both forward and backward. "Black Christian eschatology," Cornel West suggests, "is anchored in the tragic realism of the Old Testament wisdom literature and the proclamation of a coming kingdom by Jesus Christ."[8] This turn in two directions but with a clear goal of advancing a progressive future is also the mark of "prophetic thought and action," the posture of Christianity at its best. This prophetic orientation, according to West "tries to keep alive certain elements of a tradition bequeathed to us from the past and revolutionary in that it attempts to project a vision and inspire a praxis that fundamentally transforms the prevailing status quo in light of the best of the tradition and the flawed yet significant achievements of the present order."[9]

The body continues to change over time, yet mundane and existential alterations are now viewed as holding secondary significance in light of transcendent connections to God through Christ. I am not suggesting that black Christianity (and by extension certain forms of black theological thought) is otherworldly in orientation. Few would suggest that such an orientation captures all the various layers of Christian thinking and practice in black communities. Rather, that black Christianity's take on eschatology and redemption holds a general perspective, which gives robust consideration to internal transition effecting external reality and not the other way around. One gets a sense of this hierarchy in the theodical formulations of black theological discourse by which the historically uncertain Christ Event and its impact become the litmus test for all interpretations of current and lived human history.[10] "And ultimately," West believes, "with the aid of divine intervention, suffering is overcome."[11]

In this respect, religious experience involves a re-envisioning of the body through an appreciation, tenuous as it may be, of the body while also seeking to place the physical in proper context. Never able to fully jettison the dualism of body vs. soul, black religious experience of the Christian variety involves a contestation won. The mundane, the physical body and its environ, are monitored and controlled to some extent by the mechanics of the soul force (i.e., the divine and its frameworks of normalization). Albeit a marriage of practices never perfected, there is a continual sensitivity to spiritual failure and its historically arranged ramifications, as well as a push toward "perfection" in one's behavior. Redemption necessitates this realization but also mandates ongoing effort. In this sense, redemption involves something of a utopian hope because "it breeds a defiant dissatisfaction with the present and encourages action."[12] What West and other thinkers who are committed to the "Black Christian Tradition" posit as the general ethos of the tradition downplays variation.

One might temper the feasibility of the above assertions based on the necessary commitment of the individual to think, speak, and live certain patterns of religious normalization. The sustainability of the drive toward new life is suspect and understood in a variety of ways within the numerous denominations and faith communities found within black communities. Denominations differ with respect to the emphasis placed on the ability of humans to live out "perfection" in one's commitment to Christ. Some, such as the Church of God in Christ, argue doctrinally for the possibility of a "clean" life through sanctification and the presence of the Holy Spirit as the internal guiding force or compass for life decisions and arrangements. The Church of God in Christ faith statement reads, "We believe in the sanctifying power of the Holy Spirit, by whose indwelling, the Christian is enabled to live a Holy and separated life in this present world."[13] Many Baptist churches and the African Methodist Episcopal Church, for example, tend toward more doctrinal flexibility concerning the manner in which conversion results in rigidly transformed life arrangements. For members of the National Baptist Convention, USA, Inc., the largest of the Baptist conventions, sanctification is a gradual process moving from how bodies are defined and spoken to how bodies live:

> We believe the Scriptures teach that Sanctification is the process by which, according to the will of God, we are made partakers of his holiness; that it is a progressive work; that it is begun in regeneration; and that it is carried on in the hearts of believers by the presence and power of the Holy Spirit, the Sealer and Comforter, in the continual use of the appointed means especially the word of God, self-examination, self-denial, watchfulness, and prayer.[14]

Those associated with the AME Church, the oldest and largest independent grouping of black Methodists in the country think of the perfecting of the self in these terms:

> Not every sin willingly committed after justification is the sin against the Holy Ghost, and unpardonable. Wherefore, the grant of repentance is not to be denied to such as fall into sin after justification. After we have received the Holy Ghost, we may depart from grace given, and fall into sin, and by the grace of God, rise again, and amend your lives. And therefore they are to be condemned who say they can do no more sin as long as they live here; or deny the place of forgiveness to such as truly repent.[15]

All seem to agree on a basic assumption that conversion involves, at the very least, a new epistemological posture toward and sensitivity to how one moves through the world. This is because religious experience, again conversion as a prime example, involves a perpetuated arrangement—a continual maneuvering—marking a tension between the draw of this world and the promise of better possibilities. It is a thick and multidimensional evolution.

It is safe to say that as a general strategy, black Christian perspectives on redemption involve both an individual and collective response to modes of being in the world, forsaking those modalities of existence perceived as limiting, and an embrace of life strategies and styles of the self believed to be productive and consistent with divine will (i.e., in line with the community's accepted norm). What is clear is an assumption that such movement is progressive and certain. Redemption presupposes an "end" to struggle because, in theodical terms, suffering is "a stepping-stone to liberation."[16] Premised on the Christ Event, black Christians often suggest disciplining the body gains life. How familiar are these words: "no cross, no crown"? Nestled in this synergy of loss and gain is an old practice of viewing individual and communal development in terms of patterns marked by periods of advancement and periods of destruction.

Wilson Jeremiah Moses notes this form of argument within black sociopolitical and religious thought.[17] In brief, African Americans during the modern period wrestled with the larger meaning behind (and stigmatizing assumptions drawn from) the development and decline of peoples and nations. Was a wildly optimistic view of history plausible, or was a pattern of growth and decline more feasible? What were the factors effecting such patterns? Were these patterns inevitable or the result of factors correctable? In particular, how might one understand the developing nation of the United States in light of these larger historical trends? And even more focused, how might one understand and shape the future of African Americans in light of what occurred to other peoples at other times and in other places? How might African Americans fight efforts to render them of limited historical value and to fix their bodies as inferior, when these efforts are grounded in assumptions of European progress and African savagery? Responding to the more damning elements and consequences of cycles of history meditations and discussions, some African Americans privileged "a historiography offering a rationale for decline as well as one that offered reassurances of progress" for peoples and nations.[18]

In light of Moses's genealogy of decline and progress discourses, I suggest a brief highlighting of the theological framing embedded in those discourses and tied to his presentation. This approach involves taking certain liberties and focusing on what are some of the undercurrents of Moses's discussion. The argument I put forward is more than plausible when one considers the traditional theological parameters of black Christianity (or Christianities) and the typical mapping of doctrinal orientations within the "Black Church."

Some may object to that particular terminology used here and elsewhere in the text as signifier for distinguishable religious orientations, preferring instead bulky but accurate naming of overlapping black Christian communities. In spite of such objections, the "Black Church" is a commonly used marker, never meant to suggest a monolithic, static, and unified religious geography. I, like others who use it, appreciate the multiplicity of black Christianities housing numerous theological perspectives. Yet there are common theological threads; hence, it seems reasonable to argue that black Christian responses to growth and decline of peoples (including but not limited to Africa) share a privileging of historiography centered on the salvific outcome of the Christ Event. In other words, the growth and/or decline of a nation (or an individual) is tied to the "claimed" position within salvation history made evident either by an embrace of redemption through Christ or a rejection of this gift from God. Whether perceived in literal terms or not, only this cosmic event lodged in human time and space, preachers and scholars argue, could smooth the edges of pessimistic uncertainty and secure the embodied integrity of African Americans.

The problems of human interaction were obvious and included the capture and arrangement of black physical bodies through subjection to the socioeconomic and cultural wants of others. However, black Christians quite often pointed out the stress points in this troubled history. They believed weaknesses in the fabric of historical movement suggested teleological development and a sustained sense of hopefulness in spite of the obviously absurd quality of life. "Racial vindication," to borrow a phrase from *Afrotopia*, required a movement of theological import tied to the epistemological and assumed existential meaning of the Christ Event embraced.[19] Christ's triumph over death spoke possibilities to those embroiled in the mess of Empire's underbelly. Redemption on the level of the individual and the collective was available because of God's self-sacrifice. And embrace of Christ, that surrender to the will of God, would result in redemption and the stripping away of destructive thought patterns and life practices.

Surrender of self to the will of God through Christ caused ontological and existential dissonance for the convert (the believer), and this made the process painful in a variety of ways (e.g., emotionally and socially). Even so, it was so very important because through this process, all things do indeed "become new" for the individual. And nations are redeemed and kept from utter destruction as a consequence. The time frame for wellness may be a matter of mystery, but for black Christians committed to the redemptive qualities of the Christ Event, it is inevitable—"new" bodies dwelling in righteous nations. As so many have been wont to say, "God is on the throne, and all is well."

This theological re-reading of human interactions widespread during the nineteenth century also served as underpinning for black Christian perspectives on redemption throughout the twentieth and into the twenty-first century.[20] Sociopolitical and cultural developments would alter the texture and tone of challenges to African American historical merit, but the function of theological readings of history remained a widely used counterargument. The logic of this theological stance, however, would receive a firm challenge from an unlikely source—rap artists such as Tupac Shakur.

Tupac Shakur and Lived Religious Experience

Michael Dyson rightly notes that much of the aesthetic and language of rap music involves the dynamics of death and dying.[21] While one might assume nihilism embedded in this peak into death/dying—and there is certainly some of this—there is also a more textured attention to the ontological and existential transformation emerging out of death both real and metaphor. Framed in terms of the purposes of this chapter, much in popular culture in general and rap music in particular bears out a sense of redemption born of conversion.[22] In this way the discourse(s) of rap music and the discourse(s) of black Christianity emerge out of a shared cultural framework and in relationship to bodies. Yet, these are not identical perspectives on conversion/ redemption in that there are ways in which black Christian perceptions are resisted and challenged by the sensibilities of rap music presented by the likes of Tupac Shakur.

Tupac Shakur's theological turn involves recognition that certain modalities of demise, of death, can produce life.[23] This much he borrows from normalized black Christian theology, but the nature of this life embodied in time and space differs in large part because the vehicles for feeling and absorbing experience differ. If black Christians speak redemption through the shout, Tupac suggests the proper sound of redemption is a deep and hypnotic moan. While appealing on some level, this moan is also frightful in that it points out the inconsistencies and shortcomings of our certainties. The moan brings attention to soft spots, weak points, and flexible areas within the structures of meaning believed firm and normative; the moan shakes the corners of our existence. It exposes our discursive bodies as open to compromise and reverberates through our material bodies. Shakur's sound calls to blues and to humanistic tendencies, and the Christian's sound calls to the spirituals and the theological proclivities of the spirituals.[24]

There are productive and destructive lessons found with and in Tupac, and I do not intend to romanticize or glorify the ways in which his thinking and living life limited the range of responses to our world. Instead, and mindful of Foucault's critique of liberation motifs and his thinking on activism as uncertain, I want to hold in tension the various expressions of embodiment represent by and acted out by Tupac.

Artists such as Shakur suggest an alternate way of marking and arranging religious experience. Conversion involves a more committed and uncompromising posture toward the world, a particular use of the body as material reality. Conversion connotes a shift in one's approach to the world that signals sensitivity to and *embrace of* one's presence. In this way conversion does not require a change in behavior or interest, but rather a deeper awareness of self, of one's value, and one's weight within the world. This is not the world as one imagines it but as it is with all its warts. Such thinking renders useless a typical black Christian pronouncement: "We are in the world, but not of it."

Such a shift in thinking acknowledges the manner in which Tupac Shakur frames his work: "my music is spiritual, if you listen to it. . . . It's all about emotion; it's all about life."[25] He projects the exposing and unpacking of the spiritual dimension of his existence in ways that, like black Christians, recognize the absurd nature of historical realities. He notes the difficulties of life, the ways in which socioeconomic and political arrangements—the real and raw nature of life—impinge upon efforts to survive, if not thrive: "You know they got me trapped in this prison of seclusion. Happiness, living on tha streets is a delusion."[26] Again, in both instances, for the Christian and for Tupac, the world represents a troubled and troubling location, an arrangement of tense relationships. The response to such a predicament differs in these two cases, however. Whereas for Christians transformation of such circumstances involves a conversion, a reconstruction of self, which resolves the world by problematizing engagement of the world, Tupac's response involves transformation of self into the "thug." In this way, conversion does not mean disengagement from the world or an effort to purge the si(g)ns of worldly involvements, but rather a more energetic engagement *with* the world. The trope "si(g)ns" here is a reference to an interconnected reality representing presence in the world—sign—and activity in the world over against normative sensibilities—sin.[27] So conceived, the thug does not reject the world. Instead, the mark of transformation entails an epistemological shift resulting in clearer vision concerning the possibilities embedded in the complexities of life. For Tupac, conversion as the marker of religious experience need not point beyond the world but to a greater recognition of the beauty within the grotesque, an alternate valuation of those things stigmatized or picked out for greater monitoring because of their differences.

Images of life and visions of existence promoted in rap, which run contrary to the dominant Christian ethos, "produce competing views of black selfhood and the moral visions they support." Furthermore, "if such visions of black selfhood imply a spiritual foundation, then a conception of God is not far away. It is easy enough to detect the divine in hip-hop communities that value traditional expressions of religious sentiment. But what of thug culture . . . ?"[28] The epistemological posture, existential entanglements, and ontological assumptions that guide traditional black Christian notions of conversion are not embraced by Tupac. The divine is embedded in the despised—or thug—modalities and aesthetic of life.

Conversion as implied in the lyrics and life of Tupac does not involve the docile body in the shape of the normalized ideal. The very presentation of his physical body, complete with its modifications in the form of tattoos, suggests resistance to this normalization. Instead the stigmatized body is given unapologetic visibility, and the monitoring of that body is turned on its head: surveillance meant to control becomes a source of defiance. Tupac becomes what would trouble Christian discourse and ethics most, and the title of his 1995 album would speak to this oppositional stance: *Me Against the World*. As Marcus Reeves notes, this album suggests an alternate discursive body through the texture and practices of the material body. In that album Tupac, according to Reeves, positions himself "as a hip-hop Christ figure, standing against the enemy and dying for the sins of his music and his generation. His concerns about mortality were just as much an expression of the spirituality developing inside this outlaw tempting fate."[29]

Even death (is Tupac *really* dead?) does not stop the challenge of his body in that the demise of the physical only heightens the appeal of his discursive body. Or as Dyson remarks, "the very assertion of one's authentic identity is a refusal to accept the conditions and limitations and aesthetic death that opponents seek to impose from outside one's spiritual and intellectual arc of expression." How does this work? Dyson continues, "the very act of art is a refusal to die."[30]

I might modify this statement and suggest that Tupac put in play a posture toward the world that challenged prevalent strategies for encounter with a socioeconomic and politically hostile geography; and he did this through the presentation of his body as religious trope. Other artists brought into question the logic of life in the United States and even signified typically American strategies of confinement and manipulation (e.g., prison), but there is something different about Tupac's challenge. Dyson speaks of this difference in terms of "the quality of heart and honesty of expression he brought to his craft. He possessed an emotional immediacy and psychic intimacy that are hard to fake, that are difficult to drum up or duplicate through sheer manipulation of tone, timber, wordplay, and so on."[31] His manipulation and reappropriation of American vocabulary and grammar promoted a certain type of life over against indifference/complacency as death.[32] However, there is more than this at stake, and more than one way to read stigmatized bodies.

As William Van Deburg notes "heroes and villains are the yin and yang of our cultural world," and the most telling of the late twentieth-century image(s) of the latter are found in hip-hop culture.[33] While maintaining the importance of critiquing the homophobia and misogyny within American expression in the form of rap music, I suggest that it is often difficult to determine who fits into each category. Social codes embedded in popular culture warn against dangerous figures, those who threaten the fabric of collective existence (collective to the extent irregularities and the limits of our joint covering are overlooked).[34] The dark figures posing the threat resist their construction as docile bodies, instead celebrating their marginality and making visible the blemishes on the social body. Tupac accomplished this posture toward the social body to some extent by troubling the comforts of the status quo through a restructuring of the culturally produced body and an imposition of the material body into restricted spaces. Is Tupac hero or villain? Was his outlining of the terms of conversion and redemption efficacious?

We must be concerned with more than Tupac's art as understood in terms of his corpus of musical production. In addition to this, it is essential to note the manner in which his (discursive and material) body came to symbolize both the worst cultural formations (e.g., misogyny and radical materialism) and awkward resistance of these very formations. Marcus Reeves's words shadow this understanding. "But beyond the bullets and mayhem," he writes, "Tupac's legacy was ultimately grounded as much in his prolific musical output as it was in his sensational life in the headlines."[35] Followers continue to listen to his music and attempt to mold themselves around the teachings of Tupac. His body becomes their body. The music itself convicts, and the lyrical images inform. His discursive formulations and his aesthetics of difference become a means of redemption. Or as Dyson puts it, "a secular theology of soteriology is joined to postindustrial urban missiology—since salvation is linked to the mission of the 'church' of true believers—and Tupac is articulated as the messianic figure at the heart of black urban existence." To extend the point, Dyson contends, "he is a ghetto saint, an urban messiah."[36] Dyson assumes within Tupac's work an irreverent but nonetheless recognizable theistic (if not Christian) theological mooring, and Tupac's use of Christian terminology is intended to invest the lyrics with ghetto meaning.

I am more inclined to view Tupac's theologizing as anthropological and humanistic, involving manipulation of Christian grammar/vocabulary in order to break them. ("I am become death, the Destroyer of worlds!"[37] Shaper of destruction and rebirth! The signs of his destiny written on his body!) Nonetheless, Dyson and I agree on the discursive and felt significance of Tupac's thinking for segments of the social body. To illustrate this point, one might note the manner in which those attached to Tupac perceive redemption—a new relationship to one's physical body wrapped in a rearticulation of the discursive body—coming through his physical and ephemeral presence in the world and the hint of his ongoing impingement on our thinking and experiencing of life. Whereas Jesus the Christ asks "Do you believe in me? Will you follow me?" Tupac asks "Do You *Feel* Me?" The differences between these questions are significant and imposing. CHUCH![38]

For the Christian, conversion amounts to a sustained push toward a Christ-like existence. This is also the case for Tupac, but it is the "Black Jesus, patron saint of thugs," who shapes life transformation vis-à-vis conversion. Such a religious move does not entail surrender to absurdity, a morphing into an unrecognizable connection to the absurd. Rather, the convert's posture toward the world involves the movement of the trickster, not the traditional Christ. The trickster recognizes and signifies life arrangements that trouble most, all the while pushing for a more vibrant existence that does not fear the world. Tupac, like the African American cultural figure of folktales, Br'er Rabbit, or the thug as convert, calls the roughness of the briar patch "home."[39] Like Br'er Rabbit, some rap artists signify and improvise in such a way as to make the difficulties of life and existential challenges spaces of relative comfort. They reject the ease of the docile body and instead maintain their roughness and stigmatization as useful beauty and uncomfortable visibility.

It is true that Tupac denounced "thug life" when interviewed in 1995 by *Vibe Magazine*, but isn't it possible that what he moved against is a certain formation of the thug, one that gave little attention to the deeper shades of existence?[40] Perhaps this is similar to the preacher and theologian Howard Thurman's rejection of the form and fashion of Christianity while committing himself to the religion of Jesus?[41] It might, then, be the case that Tupac rejects a modality of the thug that does not reflect authentic embrace of the ways of Black Jesus through embodiment. In Tupac's words:

All I can say is I always try to be a real nigga in my heart. Sometimes it's good, sometimes it's bad; but it's still us. It's never to hurt nobody. I'm not gonna take advantage of you or bully you. I'm on some underdog shit. And I truly believe I've been blessed by God, and God walks with me. Me and my niggas are on some Black Jesus shit. Not a new religion or anything, but the saint for thugs and gangstas—not killers and rapists, but thugs. When I say thugs, I mean niggas who don't have anything.[42]

Such a perspective is not void of moral and ethical sensibilities; rather, Tupac offers an alternative narrative or paradigmatic structure for conversion, one that embraces the world as the arena for proper existence. "I feel like Black Jesus is controlling me," said Tupac. "He's our saint that we pray to; that we look up to. Drug dealers, they sinning, right? But they'll be millionaires. How I got shot five times—only a saint, only Black Jesus, only a nigga that know where I'm coming from, could be, like, 'You know what? He's gonna end up doing some good.'"[43] Such a resolution mirrors the workings of the Black Jesus, rendering Tupac and those like him—thugs—followers of Jesus who, through their actions in the world, live out the precepts of their faith. As the lyrics to the aptly titled track "Blasphemy" attest: "They say Jesus is a kind man, well he should understand times in this crime land, my Thug nation."[44]

It is this Black Jesus, this icon of life in absurdity who provides the parameters of life, who monitors and informs life transformed:

In times of war we need somebody raw, rally the troops
Like a Saint that we can trust to help to carry us through
Black Jesus, hahahahaha
He's like a Saint that we can trust to help to carry us through
Black Jesus.[45]

There is no ontological revolution brought about through conversion. No, it involves a fuller sense of one's presence in the world, a realization of the complexities of one's movement through the world. In this respect it does not entail a new set of moral and ethical guidelines—no metaphysical realities revealed; no special status secured. To the contrary, conversion and religious life for Tupac involved a greater worldliness, and with this came a certain modality of accountability: "I play the cards I was given," Tupac wrote, "thank God I'm still livin.'"[46]

When interviewed in prison in April 1995, Tupac spoke to this worldly accountability: "The excuse maker in Tupac is dead. The vengeful Tupac is dead. The Tupac that would stand by and let dishonorable things happen is dead. God let me live [after being shot 5 times] for me to do something extremely extraordinary, and that's what I have to do."[47] Attention to a need for action within human history does not mean Tupac ignores notions of heaven.

> I shall not fear no man but God
> Though I walk through the valley of death
> I shed so many tears (if I should die before I wake)
> Please God walk with me (grab a nigga and take me to Heaven).[48]

While the existential and/or transcendent significance of God for Tupac is somewhat vague, particularly in light of his conceptualization of the Black Jesus, reflection on heaven does not replace a deep sensitivity and commitment to full encounters with the world, an emersion into the "stuff" of the world.[49] What is more, heaven does not entail of necessity a radical shift from the mechanisms of life on earth. In Tupac's words, "if I die, I wonder if Heaven got a ghetto."[50] The answer appears to be yes, in that the geography of heaven involves "no shortage on G's."[51]

Conversion involves a turn inward, an embrace of one's connections to both pleasant and repulsive dimensions of existential reality. This is certainly one way to interpret the illusions to the Black Jesus in Tupac's "Hail Mary." Conversion, a push toward the center of meaning and existence does not require a suspicion concerning life's joys and pains. There, consequently, is no need to epistemologically arrange one's existence in ways that problematize the body's continued longing for the mundane. Connection to the divine through the transformative tone of conversion and religious life means a more refined integration of one's self to the world: "And God said," remarks Tupac, "he should send his one begotten son to lead the wild into the ways of the man."[52]

Tupac never offers a defining moment during which the allegiance to the divine is initiated. There are clear moments of struggle that suggest the need for divine intervention; but there is no clear and abiding alteration of behavior marking a turn. Rather, there appears a hermeneutically arranged shift, a new perspective on the workings of life through which the presence of divine intention marks all life activities, regardless of whether they fit traditional frameworks of proper moral and ethical outlook.

Framing Embodied Me(an)ing

Traditional black Christians with their focused sense of conversion are, in comparison to Tupac, religious savants. They are gifted within a small range of religious activities—prayer, choir practice, and so on. Engagement with the world in other ways is more troubling, showing a somewhat limited flexibility and an awkwardly demonstrated ability to engage life existentially. Epistemology by way of traditional conversion, again in comparison, is limited in scope and poorly combined with worldly activities. Discussion of traditional black Christian conversion suggests an effort (while not always successful) to create "flat" realities, two-dimensional entities who see conflict between transcendence and the world, and then attempt to embrace the former while denouncing the latter. A clear sign of the traditional Christian convert as religious savant might be found in the troubled relationship between soul and body that marks the conversation and workings of the erotic within black Christian communions—an inability to foster synergy between the nurturing of the soul (or metaphysical concerns) and addressing mundane wants and desires.

In spite of how the above might be read, this chapter is not concerned with judging the "quality" of religious experience in traditional Christian modes in contrast to what is presented in rap music. On that score, there are various ways in which both groups would be found wanting. Both engage in the harming of individual and collective identity and meaning through practices of homophobia, sexism, and so on. We must be ever vigilant in our critique of these practices. The concern here is with the manner in which engagement with rap music urges attention to the theoretical assumptions that tend to guide notions of conversion, redemption, and religious life. For Tupac, conversion and redemption involve a hermeneutical shift, an alternate way of viewing the world whereby proper morality and ethics is premised on the "realness" or "authenticity" of one's actions and not the manner in which they fit neatly into doctrinal structures offered through socially structured modes.

We are left to make a decision: One can embrace the grammar and vocabulary of religious conversion/redemption/experience that privileges certain formations of Christian frameworks. Or, one can trouble traditional assumptions and perspectives, and press for evolving and useful ways to think through the complex nature of religious engagement as an embodied set of commitments and practices. I choose the latter. Black theological thought *should* be premised on the latter. And mindful of this, I suggest Tupac offers a corrective, or at least a challenge, to a rather staid religio-theological discussion of conversion/redemption/experience. More traditional formulations in black theological thought assume that conversion and redemption entail exposure to resources enabling a push beyond the troubling frameworks of oppressive life arrangements—an "over against" world paradigm. In this way the convert is expected to think and live in ways that model this in contrast to the world posture. For Tupac religious conversion involves an embrace of the world, and thereby a signifying of dehumanization through an embrace of the very thing despised: the body as flesh. This move resembles what the cultural critic Albert Murray means by "ritualistic counterstatement." Like the blues, a musical forebearer, rap as represented by figures such as Tupac Shakur involves not so much commiseration but affirmation. In Murray's words: "You discover that it [the blues] is a music of affirmation; it is not a music of commiseration. It's out of that affirmation that you get all of that elegance. . . . That kind of musical statement is a basic existential affirmation. And the musicians counterstate their problems; they counterstate the depression, despair, despondency, melancholia, and so forth. Blues music is a ritualistic counterstatement."[53]

The lack of engagement with rap music by most black theologians is not really a matter of musical taste. Rather, I believe this lack may stem from a discomfort with the privileging of embodied engagement of the world rap represents. (In this way, the reaction against rap music by black religious scholars is an extension of the discomfort black churches experienced when confronted with the gospel blues.) Troubled through the rap artist's alternate hermeneutical posture is a rigid determinism and focused range of "accepted" signs of religiosity as lived; rebuffed are efforts to define religious engagement in terms of formal commitments to an array of relationships that seek to jettison life lived within the world as it is; embraced is a commitment to a religious posture that accepts and works through mundane wants and needs, and views life not through a hermeneutic of escape. Life is arranged through a hermeneutic of style, whereby the movement of bodies in time and space as a matter of creative impulse and sensibilities has vital value and thus allows for a full range of life pursuits (e.g., being a thug). At stake through conversion is a marked shift in orientation in relationship to difference. This, however, does not assume the certainty of particular moral arrangements of difference.[54]

I am not suggesting accountability be discarded. Misogyny, unabated materialism, and so on remain problematic. The "saved" body as described by Tupac Shakur is not free of oppressive tendencies and postures. The presence of problematic attitudes and behaviors does not offer final judgment, the last best criteria, for assessing the nature and meaning of conversion; conversion and religious life involve change in posture that may not be fully realized in terms of output. Hence, oppressive postures and practices are to be challenged, and we must work to end them. But, perhaps, their continued impingement on life is not the final word.

Conversion as religious experience involves a push against reified and dwarfed life meaning. Nonetheless, the outcomes of this push are not so easily judged. What it means to have a proper sense of self, of one's "fullness" is not reified through talk of conversion but remains open to debate, framed by the particular existential-cultural context of the convert and the community of converts. This communal dimension is vital, yet it does not suggest a normalizing ethical stance. In each case there are recognized and constitutive aesthetics, practices, and beliefs. The convert's efforts to live a proper life may involve signification of dehumanization in ways that do limited damage to the mechanics of oppression. Such efforts speak to a more substantive yearning for more life meaning that does not simply rest in the workings of political-economic frameworks. Such frameworks, based on the nature of dehumanization in the United States, must play a role; they must be placed in context, within the framework of a more expansive quest. As Jeffrey O. G. Ogbar remarks, "many rap songs grapple with issues of contention in society, imploring listeners to assume higher levels of moral and spiritual consciousness, as well as social responsibility."[55]

One might raise questions concerning issues of authenticity and the significance of selective memory that plagues personal narrative and our ability to access such stories. For example, Tupac speaks of inner-city realities as the paradigmatic structure for his work and life, but his lived context as a wealthy artist involves existential arrangements only impacted by such gritty realities to the extent he chooses. I am not convinced that we, when speaking in terms of religious experience vis-à-vis conversion, can provide nonshifting and grounded responses. It is at this point the pragmatic alternative becomes useful: conversion and religious experience are "real" to the extent converts understand them as real. In this regard, religious conversion and consequent life involve modalities of performance and articulated postures toward the world, acted out on the cartography of physical existence.

Tupac Shakur critiques and jettisons notions of conversion and religious life that require adherence to staid moralism: liberation as being a process of movement *away from* something is rethought. Religious conversion indeed exposes the thick and often troubling dimensions of life without naïvely framed consolation and comfort. For example, simple critiques of sexism, racism, and the like become insufficient in that life experiences are not one-dimensional and do not point in a single direction. This is a posture foreign to many, and deeply troubling to most. But those in the rap world who embrace this posture might respond by signifying a popular scriptural reference: The ways of God are foolishness to humans. Or, drawing directly from scripture: "For it is written, I will destroy the wisdom of the wise, and will bring to nothing the understanding of the prudent."[56] Such a perspective, however, does not amount to moral relativism since religious conversion, for Tupac, includes an awareness of the dilemmas and dangers of their undertakings. I am not convinced rap artists such as Tupac offer only a modality of nihilism writ as good; in light of this, I believe that Nick De Genova raises an interesting point when saying, "gangster rap can be found to transcend the mere reflection of urban mayhem and enter into musical debate with these realities, without sinking into didacticism or flattening their complexity."[57]

Prospects for Future Study

Drawing on insights such as those in the preceding section, new black theological thought tends to force theoretical complexity and methodological comfort with tension. It promotes desire for a fuller sense of meaning through the felt reality of bodies, as they take up time and space, as they force their recognition. It is through this forced recognition—involving a certain hold on the world–that they express the renewal of self that marks religious life. Traditional Christian conversion and religious life noted in the first part of this chapter, often involves a dualism of vision, the gaze backward toward a spiritual legacy connecting the convert to God through Christ, and a gaze toward the future in which the Kin(g)dom of God is proven. But for new black theological thought the primary preoccupation is with the salvific nature of the present when properly understood and embraced. Here is a shift in religious aesthetics: the look and workings of the body, from clothing to tattoos, are recognized as vibrant, beautiful, and a mark of wholeness.

This type of black theological discourse is a terrain for the embodied articulation of religious struggle and conversion, and it forces a re-examination of the assumed mapping of religious engagement. It makes easier theological recognition of the historical nature of religion and the manner in which religious conversion and life are not worked out in tension-free spaces, purely nontroubled spaces, but rather within the midst of absurdity and angst, joy and happiness. Through attention to sources such as rap music, new black theological thought reframes the nature and meaning of religion in ways suggesting the presence of the religious across and within the very structures of human interaction.

Sacred space loses a rather singular meaning, and religious encounter comes to suggest sensitivity to the workings of life. Norms of religious engagement and analysis are disrupted, and noted is the manner in which they tend to narrow and reify a certain framing of the religious. In so doing, theology is seen for its dependence on the creativity of human engagement with the world, and it is forced to trace its work through the messy arrangements of life—venturing into venues once held suspect.

7

Bodies in the World

The discussion in chapter 6 is a useful interrogation of embodied religious experience in the form of conversion and redemption, yet it leaves untapped an important area in that it does not sufficiently *place* black bodies and their redemption within the context of the larger natural environment. Humans are a part of the web of life, connected in profound ways to the world. And none have spoken the truth of this connection with more power and passion than Alice Walker. In her novel *The Color Purple*, she has Shug speak these words: "But one day when I was sitting quiet and feeling like a motherless child, which I was, it come to me: that feeling of being part of everything, not separate at all. I knew that if I cut a tree, my arm would bleed."[1] The human body exists within a framework of mutual dependence that must be addressed theologically. In light of some rather pressing questions, not the least of which is premised on the truth of this interconnectedness, is this: How should we understand and *feel* natural disasters?

The redemption theme at the center of chapter 6 continues in this chapter, but here it addresses the relationship of humanity to the earth that is often referenced in terms of "recovery stories."[2] When these stories, drawn from the Hebrew Bible, are held in tension in an overlapping fashion, the basic structure of humanity's relationship to the natural environment resembles shifts between decline and growth, progress and struggle.[3] The thread linking these various moments of engagement—whether one privileges decline or growth—is the nature and meaning of connection between bodies and the space they occupy.[4] And whether framed in terms of domination over nature or as respect-filled relationship to nature, this interaction surfaces ideological arranged issues of race, gender, and class.[5] While environmental history engages a variety of issues and questions, here I am particularly concerned with the connections between black bodies and thought on and action within nature.[6] Through a brief discussion, proper context is provided for the more focused theological analysis of recent disasters in the southern United States.

The Meaning of Nature

For more than a few centuries, efforts to reinvest the earth with religiously significant meaning have been underway.[7] But there have been various angles and dimensions to this project, and some have concerned the relationship of white bodies to troubling black bodies, and both to an earth in flux. The connections were clear in that North America was understood "as the site of natural resources, Africa as the sources of enslaved human resources."[8] In addition to the somewhat apparent racial component to this reinvestment project, there were gender dimensions just as prevalent in that the earth was understood metaphorically as female substance to be dominated by male power. The Bible provided a framework for this discourse, particularly the book of Genesis and its depiction of materiality as flawed but redeemable. Drawing from this process of renewal, religious conversation about the natural environment (of which we are a part) tends toward a theologizing grounded in doctrine of God and soteriology. As the song goes:

> Work ye, then, while yet 'tis day,
> Work ye Christians, while ye may,
> Work for all that's great and good,
> Working for your daily food.
> Working whilst the golden hours,
> Health, and strength, and youth are yours.[9]

Undergirding this project of redemption was an assumption that carving the United States out of the new land was a matter of divine right, a moment of divine will lodged literally in the physical earth. The language is nuanced in contemporary conversation with, in most cases, a less explicitly theologically contrived retelling of the story. Nonetheless, this country still tends to think of itself as privileged, based on a divine economy of attention that marks "Americans" (read citizens of the United States) as a special group, one on which God smiles and grants certain socioeconomic and political arrangements and reach not granted to others. From the Puritans on, this framework—eventually buttressed by supposedly scientific advances—has marked the ontological posture of the United States. To the extent the new "chosen" labored in the New World (and forced labor from enslaved Africans), it was to make evident the privilege and rights to land and its benefits. This perspective and its particular system of ethics and morals guided the shaping of geography and have framed national epistemology. As William Cronon notes, "the way we describe and understand that world is so entangled with our own values and assumptions that the two can never be fully separated." That is to say, "what we mean when we use the word 'nature,'" he notes, "says as much about ourselves as about the things we label with the word."[10] The links between human nature and nonhuman nature are clear to Carolyn Merchant, who writes with respect to the struggle marking the early United States that "the taming of external nature was intimately linked to the taming of internal nature. The civilizing process not only removed wild beasts from the pastoral lands of the garden; it suppressed the wild animal in men."[11] However, with respect to the particular link between black bodies and nature within the context of oppression, a general discomfort with the threat (but also allure) of the wilderness became a convenient framing for what black bodies meant to the United States.[12] There was at least an odd naturalist posture holding up white supremacist linking of bodies and nature. Like nature, black bodies—whether male or female—represented a "contested terrain."[13]

For socioeconomic, political, and religious purposes black bodies were constructed in opposition to cultural refinement. Black bodies in this way were projected as more closely linked to the materiality of nature: the dark corners of the environment *not* under the control of human will. Besides this discursive confinement, black physical bodies were typically perceived as resembling in aesthetic appearance those things held dangerous and uncontrolled.[14] Both black female and black male bodies encountered this type of framing and confinement to a space for the "uncivilized." Perhaps this determination to link black male and female bodies to the land stemmed from an unspoken and perhaps subconscious recognition, through the mirror of nature as unstable, that the social arrangements privileging whites bodies were subject to destruction at any moment.

Naturalizing Black Bodies

Black bodies, male and female, were vital in that they provided the physical force needed to claim and render docile the land. Hence, whatever the underlying rationale, the power of the imposed symbolism meant efforts to end the stranglehold of slavery and thus expose and destroy the structures of Jim Crow regulations; it would indeed require some attention to negative associations. Abolition and the ongoing struggle for full citizenship and equal status in the body politic had to play on the repositioning of black bodies in ways that connected them to the assumed value of white bodies. Over time as views on nature moved away from casting as danger, efforts to rethink and reposition black bodies would also be framed in terms of necessary partnerships between all humans and all nonhuman forms of life.[15] As the continuing need for justice strategies suggests, these approaches to the changed thinking about and actions toward black bodies have produced less than ideal results. Nature remains a contested topic and space, and many black bodies continue to feel the world an uncomfortable place. Both black bodies and the larger framework of nature continue to be foreign to some extent.

As the frontier vanished and urbanization marked the felt experience of bodies, recovery rhetoric would lose its importance and power. The association of black (male and female) bodies with wildness codified in nature would shift as other modalities of difference gained in popularity. In spite of the predominance of black bodies occupying southern geography, the Great Migration moved most African Americans into urban centers in both the North and the South. With time, lack of contact with the natural environment came to mark lived experience for both black and white urban dwellers. Black bodies, then, were not viewed as connected to uncontrolled nature but rather were arranged within the framework of nature's decay. One might think of this in terms of environmental racism,[16] and the manner in which black bodies are exposed in high numbers to the destructive fallout from human manipulation of nature.

"Ghetto" (in contrast to "Eden") becomes the terminology for demise as civilization turns on itself and black bodies are somehow seen as both sign and cause of this loss.[17] "Sublime nature," writes Merchant, "was now white and benign; the nature of cities black and malign."[18] Put differently, compromise of the natural environment by spaces of human construction and disregard relates to the oppression of stigmatized black bodies. And in recent years the resulting and precarious relationship of black bodies to the natural environment has been highlighted through natural disasters. While some prefer the terminology "natural disturbances," I doubt those most intimately touched by these occurrences would refer to or experience them as simple "disturbances." Black bodies, as a function of race, gender, and class, represent and feel the outcome of natural disasters as deeply connected to issues of justice.[19]

When the Wind Blows Hard: A Personal Note

My experience with conditions created by hurricanes is minor in comparison to that of some. However, I want to begin this section with a few thoughts on the hurricane named Ike that "kissed" Texas in 2008. I share this story because it informs my perspective on the nature and meaning of natural disasters as theological challenge.

It was dark and it was rainin',
You could hear that howlin' wind.
It was dark and it was rainin'
You could hear that howlin' wind.[20]

Before moving to Houston in 2004, I assumed the heat could be countered with ease, in part by means of an emotional and psychological acceptance of some discomfort as a component of Houston summers. And this mental adjustment could be combined with quick and strategic movements outdoors and then back into the comfort of cool shelter. In terms of more severe weather, I assumed one could outrun a hurricane. (Houstonians and others in hurricane-prone areas have learned that when large numbers of people try to outrun bad weather using a limited number of routes, no one goes anywhere.)

So imagine the knowing smile that crossed my face when I first encountered the words of William Cronon as he described a sign he saw on a U-Haul truck when making his way from Wisconsin to California. "It showed a crude map of California inside a circle with a diagonal line slashed across it. Beneath this image were written these words," . . . and this is the kicker, so to speak:

The California Dream:
Earthquakes
Fire
Floods
Mudslides
Riots
Recession
Crowding
Traffic Jams
Smog
We're Going Home to Texas![21]

"We're going home to Texas!" the sign said, going back to a geography that does not impinge upon human bodies through the force of earthquakes and mudslides. But, although the sign does not note it, Texas is a space where bodies feel the effects of hard rain and strong wind, of hurricanes like the one that hit Houston in September 2008.

Considering what happened in the coastal communities and the images of destruction shown by television stations and in print, my situation can be viewed as a matter of minimal damage. As far as hurricanes go, I was somewhat fortunate. I had a relatively undamaged and safe place to call "home," and it continues to hold pleasant reminders of pre-hurricane life. But even so, for what seems a rather long period of time, circumstances have changed; life has a different rhythm.

> In the storm's path lies one of the nation's largest concentration of oil refineries, the Johnson Space Center, the resorts on Galveston Island and Houston's downtown of skyscrapers. More than four million people live in Houston and its suburbs.[22]

It was a little after 9 p.m. on Monday, September 15, post-hurricane time, when I starting handwriting these thoughts in the dim light offered by my small, but cherished, flashlight. Completing it would have to wait until I could reach my campus office and enjoy the often underappreciated pleasure of electricity and a computer. But tonight, there is no electricity and no running water (and there would not be in my home for some two weeks). Still, I can sit in somewhat comfortable surroundings, looking out the window at the Houston downtown skyline and the flickering red and blue lights of police cars racing to catch those breaking the 9 p.m. Houston curfew. James Taylor sings softly in the background with as much clarity as my small battery operated AM/FM radio can muster. In classic form, he urges listeners to "shower the people you love with love." Shower . . . love. I think many of those listening would actually settle at this moment for the ability to simply take a hot shower.

This is life, post–Hurricane Ike, complete with its heightened sensitivity to both the large and small moments of our fragile existence. There is a great deal of time and little to occupy that time after dark, plenty of time to think and run through the countless "what if" scenarios.

> Granted, there weren't the thousands of shirt-waving souls stranded on Galveston's rooftops as we saw in the aftermath of Hurricane Katrina, but nevertheless, Hurricane Ike signaled the end of a storied American city as we knew it.[23]

Thoughts of the flood water running down city streets, the massive destruction of Galveston and other coastal towns, the terror on the faces of those seeking some relief, all push me to ask a question: If there is a God, where is God when such horrible things are happening? This is not simply a question generated by my own discomfort, or even the discomfort of my neighbors across the Gulf Coast. One need only think of the disasters that have occurred across the globe in recent months. Again, if there is a God, where is God when such things happen? This question, typically labeled by theologians "the problem of evil" and explored using the rubric of theodicy (i.e., "what can one say about divine justice in light of human suffering in the world?") comes naturally to a theologian. But really, it is the sort of question asked on a much larger scale: Why . . . ? Why this suffering caused by disasters such as six-hundred-mile-wide Hurricane Ike?

There is good news and bad news on this front. The good news first: Whether couched in a statement of faith and belief, or framed as a "secular" critique of religious commitment, in a country with "In God We Trust" stamped on our currency raising this question just seems a natural first response. The problem of natural and moral evil phrased in terms of theodicy has a long history and numerous traditional expressions. Even asking the question, theologically venting so to speak, provides some relief. In fundamental ways the question implies the large and deep question of life, of human existence, of our "purpose" and "meaning" in the world. It can be a theological way of assessment, redirection, and a starting point for "getting ourselves together."

Now the bad news: theodicy tends to be no more than theological throat clearing. It is an endless maze in that, according to scholars like theologian Terrence Tilley, there is no way to provide a satisfactory response on the long term.[24]

Some years ago, John Hick, a philosopher of religion, offered a study of various ways in which evil is addressed theologically. Careful readers of that text, *Evil and the God of Love,* will note the holes in the various arguments but will also appreciate the marked and desperate need to make sense of the unthinkable.[25] For centuries Christian scholars and ministers have wrestled with the justice of God in light of human suffering, but ultimately their responses fall short. Few in the general public would accept the idea of a demonic god as the backbone of Christianity. Some are willing to reflect on this theological issue and suggest that moral evil is a matter of human will and human misconduct: We are destroying the environment and creating conditions ripe for greater and greater storm activity and the like. Yet this response, while giving humans a swift kick, still begs the question: Where is God in all this? Is there a God to talk about in light of this suffering?

Even more acceptable for many is the idea of a limited God, a God who respects human free will and works in human affairs through persuasion rather than power to force certain developments and actions. However, when interrogated sufficiently, even this response leaves us thinking, if not speaking: Of what real benefit is a limited God? If God cannot or will not do the heavy lifting necessary to move humanity along (often against our collective will it seems), what's the point of speaking about God? What, then, does God do that we cannot do if we really try?

Addressing evil through the framework of theodicy does not achieve much in the long run. Yet, like moral evil, the type of suffering generated by natural disasters demands attention from those who consider themselves religious.

Such traumatic and lingering events require a response that shows in some way, shape, and form the inner workings of one's commitments that are either framed as a matter of religious conviction or moral orientation. That is to say, these events are embodied and require an embodied response. If this is true of Hurricane Ike, a relatively minor occurrence on the scale of hurricanes, should not the images of death, bodily discomfort, and compromise drawn from Hurricane Katrina urge an even stronger turn in theologizing?

Embodied Disaster

Natural disasters of Hurricane Katrina's magnitude call into question theological aesthetics as related to the geography of divine manifestation; earth subdued and rendered beautiful through an economy of utility and productivity is ripped apart and rendered unproductive.

> Hurricane Katrina made landfall on the Gulf Coast, destroying lives, leveling homes and leaving thousands of survivors with the same story: We lost everything.[26]

From the eighteenth century on, American perceptions of the natural environment were laced with growing perception of the land as reflecting the beauty of the divine, as having profound aesthetic value and cosmic connections even in its destructiveness. The workings of nature—in all manifestations—were viewed as religiously significant.[27] This, of course, was easier to embrace in thought than within the context of discomfort, fear, and uncertainty produced through embodied contact with an angry sky. The face of God is hard for most to locate in the aftermath of such events—in the sewage, the destroyed humans, the crippled industries, and so on. Indeed, the aftermath of natural disasters like Hurricane Katrina lacks the aesthetic qualities many find necessary when mapping religious life and its ramifications.

For the theologically minded, the first effort to address environmental trauma involves theodicy in order to address massive and what appears to be indiscriminate destruction in terms of divine righteousness and moral justice. In its most crude and troubling form, this response to the theodical question (i.e., what can we say about divine justice in light of human suffering in the world) seeks to project the problem as one of sin, of theological anthropology, of human shortcomings. Such a posture often results in the theologically narrowminded arguing that those who suffered the effects of a hurricane, for example the one that destroyed much of New Orleans, do so because of failure to follow the dictates of God. In the case of Katrina and New Orleans, this assumes, no doubt, that voodoo offends the Christian God and this God also views sexual gratification with moral outrage. A prime example of this response is easily drawn from the religious rhetoric of Michael Marcavage, the director of *Repent America,* an evangelical organization committed to the transformation of American life through adherence to a rather strict and conservative reading of scripture. Marcavage argues that while we should pray for those effected by Hurricane Katrina, we should recognize the destruction of New Orleans as divine punishment for a permissive social ethos, which embraces and celebrates what *Repent America* understands as problematic life styles. On its website, for example, is an article containing these words from Marcavage, "Although the loss of lives is deeply saddening, this act of God destroyed a wicked city," he vents. "From 'Girls Gone Wild' to 'Southern Decadence,' New Orleans was a city that had its doors wide open to the public celebration of sin. From the devastation may a city full of righteousness emerge."[28]

This is theological nonsense. What marks this theodical response to Hurricane Katrina is a matter of distortion, of manipulation through which the challenge of scripture is forgotten: God makes it to rain on the just and unjust, so scripture says. Weather patterns do not provide a way of distinguishing between the two. The flood and destruction of human life noted in the story of Noah in the Judeo-Christian tradition entails, as a matter of mythology, a situation one is hard-pressed to see mirrored in the natural disasters that have shocked the modern world. There is an element of divine indifference left unexamined in theodical work such as noted above.

> If it keeps on rainin', levee's goin' to break
> And the water gonna come in, have no place to stay.[29]

Others look at such tragedy through the lens of theodicy and provide a comforting, yet incomplete, response that revolves around an individualized need for proper perspective on the arena of God's love and compassion. For example, according to Billy Graham, the spiritually sensitive ultimately appeal to mystery with respect to the nature and meaning of natural disaster. "I can recall walking through the aftermath of hurricanes in Florida and South Carolina, and a typhoon in India that killed tens of thousands, and earthquakes in California and Guatemala, and every time I have asked 'Why?' Job in the Bible asked the same question thousands of years ago, and his only answer was that God's ways are often beyond our understanding, and yet He is sovereign and He can still be trusted. The Bible says evil is a mystery. Someday we will understand, but not now."[30] For Graham this does no permanent damage to God's integrity because "God knows what we are going through, and He still loves us and cares about us. In the midst of suffering and tragedy we can turn to Him for the comfort and help we need. Times like this will make us react in one of two ways: Either we will become bitter and angry—or we will realize our need of God and turn to Him in faith and trust, even if we don't understand."[31] While comforting on some level in that the basic attributes of God are undamaged, although perhaps weakened (Is God really all powerful, or just committed to the good and working *with us* to achieve it?) and humanity's relationship to the universe remains intact, such a response is not enough. Appeal to a metaphysical principle or a relationship to a divine reality that privileges spirit over body serves merely to further trouble the body dilemma. The problem is simply shrouded in mystery. This type of theological move does little to address the dimensions of natural disaster revolving around the resulting absurdity of physical time and space.

To Feel the Angry Earth

Natural disasters are not addressed best as theodical matters. Such analysis, particularly when combined with conservative political leanings as in the case of *Repent America,* masks (whether consciously or unconsciously matters little) what I would consider the more relevant and productive questions. Even those who propose theodicy-formulated responses that seek to point out what good humans accomplish in light of such misery—a redemptive suffering-type approach—seldom highlight the large structural issues that would benefit from religio-theological analysis.

The large, systemic concerns are those on which we should concentrate, and we should do so beyond the limitations of theodical argumentation and reflection. In this regard, theodical responses to natural disaster are a dead end. As David Jacobson reflects, "we can perceive the world and frame it, but only in material terms."[32] Material terms. Corporeality. I think it wise to draft on this thinking and highlight materiality, during the process of embodied theologizing. When one considers both the geography of devastation and the economy of assistance for recovery, Hurricane Katrina pointed out issues highlighting the geography of racism and classism as well as a twisting of the environment through global warming, property taxes, and shifting notions of geographic "flight." What is pointed out is not a theological anthropology of sin punished through movements of nature. Instead, it speaks to the consequences of troubled socioeconomic and political arrangements, and how they are born out in the location and conditions of human habitats.

Through natural disaster we learn the manner in which governmental (local, state, and federal) "responses" to trauma point out shortsighted policies and procedures regarding the natural environment. We learn through careful attention to what bodies say and do in light of the circumstances confronting them. Furthermore, such situations of environmental trauma are not the consequence of intrinsic flaws, unless we now categorize accidents of birth, such as race, into a certain class as intrinsic flaws. Rather they point to human sinfulness in a radically other way: destruction of the environment and the narrowing of healthy life options. Natural disasters expose the uneven playing field and lay bare the structures of injustice and discrimination that define the formation of life options. In this respect, ecological and social ethics trump theodicy as a tool of analysis. Natural disasters such as Hurricane Katrina are an issue of cartography in two respects: (1) the human construction of boundaries to mark space is disrupted if not destroyed, and (2) in the wake of such disaster another mapping is exposed, the layout of human life options, and the restrictions of more productive modes of citizenship and public existence are shown with all their inconsistencies and long-established inequalities.

It is a matter of justice-based responses to trauma, rather than attempts to theologize changes to the natural environment in ways that circumscribe conversation to traditional notions of theological anthropology and doctrine of God. I am not suggesting a "we can't know the mind of God" response so common in many modalities of the "prosperity gospel" advocated by figures such as Joel Osteen of Lakewood Church in Houston, Texas. Confrontation with such trauma, based on the "prosperity gospel," tends to be theologically weak since its concern is built around an individualization of the American dream that seeks advancement without a questioning of the structures that define and shape our very understanding of success. Yet, liberation theologians and ethicists, when at their best, do indeed recognize the inadequate nature of theological platforms that neglect a complex arrangement of relationship. "Strong theological censure of human injustice as well as concern for the nonhuman world," according to Garth Baker-Fletcher, "is needed." Furthermore, "without such censure one suspects that ecological concern could become an abstract exercise of those detached from and unconcerned about genuine human oppression."[33] That is to say, proper attention to the natural environment and vigilant struggle against social injustice both require recognition of multiplicity—the connections between the human and the non-human.

A hermeneutic of environmental racism/classism and ecological/social ethics might provide a useful mode of analysis for natural disasters. And, the posture for this type of critical analysis—one that opens us to freedom determined processes and modalities of transformation—might benefit from strands of humanism that appreciate the integrity of human life within the context of a larger concern for the natural environment. This does not require a rejection of the God concept in all cases, but rather a willingness to concentrate on the shared concern across traditions for proper human conduct in the world. Hence, the call for some attention to certain strands of humanist thought does not require conversion to humanism; instead, it encourages a highlighting of the anthropological dimension found in all religious traditions in African American communities. But even this dimension can be framed in terms of the metaphors of familiar texts. One might appeal, for example, to an analogy involving relationship between the evacuated/displaced and the Jesus of the New Testament without a "place to lay his head": "Foxes have holes, and the birds of the air have nests; but the Son of man hath not where to lay his head" (Matt 8:20; Lk 9:58, KJV). With this analogy in mind, several of the principles of humanism prove helpful, whether one is a theist or an atheist . . . or somewhere in between:

- a strong commitment to both individual and social transformation.
- a controlled optimism that recognizes both human potential and human destructive tendencies.[34]

By means of these principles, the "religious" are encouraged to concentrate on the application of theological and religious principles to healing, while giving greater attention to the forms of inequality and levels and rates of recovery. One of the benefits of these principles is the manner in which they give high regard, theo-religious primacy, to the physical body and the manner in which it is placed in time and space.

Humanists like Alice Walker argue that such regard for the texture of life must include recognition of humanity as a part of the natural environment, resulting in an epistemological and ontological link between all that is. The womanist (and process-thought influenced) scholar Karen Baker-Fletcher speaks in theological terms about this ontological synergy. "It is necessary to move beyond the notion that 'man' is supposed to 'dominate' the earth rather than love it as we love our own bodies. . . . [T]his vital step toward liberation is interlocked with steps that resist the interlocking oppressions of patriarchy, classism, racism, and homophobia."[35] Disruption of the natural environment, disasters increased and strengthened by means of human deeds and misdeeds, all raise questions concerning human failure to love, and love deeply, creation. Such a posture points to a rejection of traditional notions of stewardship—those which allow humans to dominant the environment and which prevent modes of conduct in the face of disaster—that allow for health and wholeness through a recognition of human need and the integrity of nature. The connections between human life and the health of the larger environment are vital, but they are fragile when notions of human progress and development go unchecked.

While Baker-Fletcher frames the ethical dimensions of this mutuality within the context of the Christ Event, embodied perspectives avoid notions of transcendence as paradigmatic. Both operate out of an ethic of belonging, but an embodied perspective is more firmly grounded in human obligations and appreciations for complex and nurturing relationships. By grounding its work within the realm of human endeavor, the embodied posture avoids the theodical considerations that ultimately arise in Christ-based approaches to world health and harmony. That is to say,

> a wildness, a free, natural growth, is therefore part of all that lives. Like the waters, the wind, and the groaning of the earth when it quakes, it frightens us with its fury, its ability to turn and stir into storminess and seeming chaos. Such freedom is necessary for life. New life can emerge from the wreckage of nature's storms.[36]

Life becomes recognized for its fluidity; hence disaster is understood as a part of life.

Liberal theologians argue that natural disasters should be considered "wild" as opposed to being framed in the traditional dichotomy of "good" vs. "evil." Yet the way in which the effects of this wildness are described with respect to human life suggest a more charged understanding.[37] Framing this wildness in the context of human life as destructive certainly places it within the context of the dichotomy Baker-Fletcher seeks to avoid: "It [wildness] provides life and sustenance but can also bring destruction to human life and civilization in the form of tornadoes, hurricanes, mad dogs, floods. Ultimately, it is necessary for our survival."[38] In short, destruction by natural forces is a vital reality because "sometimes the force of nature creates natural disasters and suffering. But God is still present in the midst of it all."[39] For Baker-Fletcher destruction is a part of God's work in the world, pointing to the power of God, that divine force that revives and reveals. In the hurricane, according to this perspective, is manifestation of *mysterium tremendum*. How can such an understanding of disaster, couched in the Christ Event, not generate theodical anxiety?

Prospects for Future Study

The shape of new black theological thought shifts away from preoccupation with Christology and theodicy as the proper framing for discussions of natural disasters, and this involves a reluctance to speak of "evil" in any traditional way. This new modality of black theological thought avoids attempts to think through natural disasters in light of the doctrine of God. Again, when faced with natural disaster, the response takes place by means of a hermeneutic and a system of ethics, premised on a deep desire for wellness, for wholeness. Accordingly, proper and responsible living entails synergy between the various components of the natural world, an ethic of "green" whereby the preservation and celebration of the earth becomes essential conduct. Not only is oppression structurally weblike in nature, life is also intimately intertwined and mutually dependent. Intimate connections between various layers of life remain vital, complex, "thick," evolving, and serve as the operating paradigm of existence. Behavior in relationship to the earth is judged not only by the activity of individuals but also by the collective movement of humanity against the integrity of the environment.

Nurturing this connection between humanity and the environment is in fact religious; it has something to do with the quest for complex subjectivity that is by definition the nature of religion.[40] In connection to the rest of the natural environment, we make meaning and gain a greater sense of our place in the world. In this way, gauging of one's religiosity is just as easily accessed through ritualized connection to the earth—e.g., a walk through the woods, recycling, and responsible use of energy—as through more traditional moments of institutionally structured worship. The push for greater spaces of liberty and opportunity must involve not only human communities but also the welfare of the larger environment.

However, even these statements of relationship between humanity and earth must be continuously interrogated. There are ways in which black theological thought should trouble the assumed centrality of humanity within the natural environment. Suspended, then, is the assumption that humanity is a favored creature with more inherent value. That is to say, as relatively recent inhabitants of this earth we must trouble the development of human communities as being of necessity the best measure of liberation. New black theological discourse lingers over the question of how to best access freedom by holding in tension humanity and the larger environment.[41] It raises uncomfortable questions and seeks to explore them in light of embodiment: What does it mean to do theology in a context in which humanity may be a relatively short-term development? How does one frame theological discourse and a sense of history if humanity is not the central story of life on earth but is instead a secondary character? What is the significance or purpose of theology if humanity might in fact be a problem for the earth, one the earth is rightly seeking to purge?

Mindful of this economy of life, disaster should raise a question first: Has this event resulted from a failure on the part of humans to remember and act in accordance with a deep connection to all life? Has an imbalance due to human manipulation of the earth (e.g., global warming), premised on a disregard for mutuality, contributed to this devastation of life? What can be done to correct this imbalance, to address the immediate concerns but to do so in ways that allow for a fullness of human life and the integrity of life in more general terms? The challenge is to respond to the immediate demands of disaster in ways that hold in creative tension sensitivity to the larger issues of justice exposed by the disruptive force of the earth's elements. By so doing we acknowledge the awesome power of the world and our humble place on the planet.

We begin to recognize the nature and meaning of our existence in flesh and as part of a vulnerable earth. Attention to the theological ramifications and connotations of natural disasters brings to the forefront the theological weight of the body's occupation of time and space, its connections to and dependence upon the earth. And such a turn to the experience of embodiment—body as material—marks the posture of new black theological thought.

Notes

NOTES TO THE PREFACE

1. Anthony B. Pinn, *Why, Lord? Suffering and Evil in Black Theology* (New York: Continuum, 1995).

2. William R. Jones, *Is God a White Racist?: A Preamble to Black Theology* (Boston: Beacon Press, 1996 [1973]).

3. For an example of this misread, see Jualynne Dodson's review in *North Star: A Journal of African American Religious History* 5, no. 2 (Spring 2001) http://northstar.vassar.edu/volume4/pinn.html. Dodson gives no attention to the theological purposes of the book as outlined in the introduction and the final chapter. I also address common misreading of this book and my other work in Pinn, *Understanding and Transforming the Black Church* (Eugene, OR: Cascade Books, 2010).

4. Anthony B. Pinn, *Terror and Triumph: The Nature of Black Religion* (Minneapolis: Fortress Press, 2003); Charles Long, *Significations: Signs, Symbols, and Images in the Interpretation of Religion*, 2nd ed. (Denver: The Davies Group, 2004).

5. See for example, James Noel's review of *Terror and Triumph* in *Journal of Religion* 84 (January 2004): 155–57.

6. See Pinn, *African American Humanist Principles: Living and Thinking Like the Children of Nimrod* (New York: Palgrave Macmillan, 2004); Pinn, *Noise and Spirit: The Religious and Spiritual Sensibilities of Rap Music* (New York: New York University Press, 2003).

7. Houston A. Baker Jr., *Afro-American Poetics: Revisions of Harlem and the Black Aesthetic* (Madison, WI: University of Wisconsin Press, 1988), 13.

8. Nicholas Davey, "The Hermeneutics of Seeing," in *Interpreting Visual Culture: Explorations in the Hermeneutics of the Visual*, ed. Ian Heywood and Barry Sandywell, 25 (New York: Routledge, 1999).

9. Pinn, *Terror and Triumph*, 192.

10. I understand that my argument naturally raises the need for application: what is the look of theology so conceived. Here, I mean to point simply in the direction of a formal, embodied theology. The book on which I am currently working, *In the Language of Nimrod: Toward a Black Humanist Theology* (Oxford University Press), is an effort to develop an embodied theology along these lines.

11. One sees this in Emilie Townes's work on issues of health and the environment. See, for example, Townes, *Breaking the Fine Rain of Death: African American Health Issues and A Womanist Ethic of Care* (Eugene, OR: Wipf and Stock Publishers, 2006); Emilie Townes and Stephanie Mitchem, eds., *Faith, Health, and Healing in African American Life*

(Westport, CT: Praeger, 2008); Traci West, *Wounds of the Spirit: Black Women, Violence, and Resistance Ethics* (New York: New York University Press, 1999); Traci West, *Disruptive Christian Ethics: When Racism and Women's Lives Matter* (Louisville, KY: Westminster John Knox Press, 2006). Furthermore, the manner in which embodiment is addressed in the work of theologians such as Kelly Brown Douglas is discussed in various chapters in *Embodiment*.

12. The most widely noted example of this is Victor Anderson's *Beyond Ontological Blackness* (New York: Continuum, 1995). Readers, however, should also see Cornel West, *Prophesy Deliverance!: An Afro-American Revolutionary Christianity*, (Louisville, KY: Westminster John Knox, 2002 [1982]). For the manner in which ontological blackness plays out in black theology, see James Cone, *A Black Theology of Liberation*, Twentieth Anniversary Edition (Maryknoll, NY: Orbis Books, 1990 [1986]); Dwight Hopkins, *Being Human: Race, Culture, and Religion* (Minneapolis: Fortress Press, 2005); J. Deotis Roberts, *Liberation and Reconciliation: A Black Theology*, rev. ed. (Maryknoll, NY: Orbis Books, 1994); James Evans, *We Have Been Believers: An African-American Systematic Theology* (Minneapolis: Fortress Press, 1992). It is interesting to read these texts in light of Hazel Carby's *Race Men* (Cambridge, MA: Harvard University Press, 2000).

13. Eddie Glaude notes such concerns in *In a Shade of Blue: Pragmatism and the Politics of Black America* (Chicago: University of Chicago Press, 2008).

14. A few examples are James Nelson, *Body Theology* (Louisville, KY: Westminster John Knox Press, 1992), and Lisa Isherwood and Elizabeth Stuart, *Introducing Body Theology* (Sheffield: Sheffield Academic Press, 1998).

15. This is a play on the framing of his work Foucault offers in 1978, when asked about the proper framing and his identity as an academic. He argued that he was not a "theorist," but rather that he was better represented as an "experimenter." See Jeremy R. Carrette, *Foucault and Religion: Spirituality Corporality and Political Spirituality* (New York: Routledge, 2000), 8.

16. M. Shawn Copeland, *Enfleshing Freedom: Body, Race, and Being* (Minneapolis: Fortress Press, 2009), 1.

NOTES TO THE INTRODUCTION

1. In this sense, black theology is linked to liberal religion as neo-orthodoxy without mimicking their worst expects. For an interesting study of liberal theology and neo-orthodox theologies see: Gary Dorrien, *The Making of American Liberal Theology*, vols. 1–3 (Louisville: Westminster John Knox Press, 2001–06).

2. Monica Coleman, *Making a Way Out of No Way: A Womanist Theology* (Minneapolis: Fortress Press, 2008).

3. J. Cameron Carter, *Race: A Theological Introduction* (New York: Oxford University Press, 2008).

4. See James Cone's early work *Black Theology of Liberation* and *Black Theology and Black Power* (Maryknoll, NY: Orbis Books, 1997).

5. Gayraud Wilmore, *Black Religion and Black Radicalism: An Interpretation of the Religious History of African Americans*, 3rd ed. (Maryknoll, NY: Orbis Books, 1998); Cecil Cone, *Identity Crisis in Black Theology* (Nashville: AME Church, 1975). While this agenda has been Cornel West's challenge to black theology for several decades, it is perhaps must

clearly articulated in *Prophesy Deliverance!* These texts, and others written during the first several decades of black theology, challenged its religious-cultural history and historiography as well as its sociopolitical and economic perspectives.

6. Katie Cannon, *Black Womanist Ethics* (Atlanta: Scholars Press, 1988); Jacquelyn Grant, *White Women's Christ and Black Women's Jesus: Feminist Christology and Womanist Response* (Atlanta: Scholars Press, 1989); Delores Williams, *Sisters in the Wilderness: The Challenge of Womanist God-Talk* (Maryknoll, NY: Orbis Books, 1995). In addition to these texts, readers should take note of James Cone and Gayraud Wilmore, *Black Theology: A Documentary History*, vols. 1–2 (Maryknoll, NY: Orbis Books, 1979/1993), especially the section related to womanist thought for early critiques of black theology.

7. Kelly Brown Douglas writings come closest to the formulation of an embodied theology. Douglas not only brings into black and womanist theologies a concern with the mind/body split, but she seeks to move beyond it. See K. B. Douglas, *Sexuality and the Black Church: A Womanist Perspective* (Maryknoll, NY: Orbis Books, 1999); *What's Faith Got to Do With It? Black Bodies/Christian Souls* (Maryknoll, NY: Orbis Books, 2005). For a more general sense of body theology, see, for example: Marcella Althaus-Reid, *Indecent Theology: Theological Perversions in Sex, Gender and Politics* (New York: Routledge, 2000); Nelson, *Body Theology*; Isherwood, *Introducing Body Theology*.

8. Susan Hekman, "Material Bodies," in *Body and Flesh: A Philosophical Reader*, ed. Donn Welton, 62 (Malden, MA: Blackwell, 1998).

9. The idea of thinking about racism and blackness in this way is drawn from John Colapinto, "Brain Games," *New Yorker*, May 11, 2009.

10. Antonio Damasio, *The Feeling of What Happens: Body and Emotion in the Making of Consciousness* (New York: Harvest Books, 1999), 145.

11. See M. Shawn Copeland, "Body Representation, and Black Religious Discourse," in *Intimate Matters: A History of Sexuality in America*, ed. John D'Emilio and Estelle B. Freedman (New York: Harper and Row, 1988). Copeland's *Enfleshing Freedom: Body, Race, and Being* (Minneapolis: Fortress Press, 2009) addresses this issue.

12. I am indebted to a variety of sources for this understanding of the body, including Mary Douglas, *Natural Symbols: Explorations in Cosmology*, 2nd ed. (New York: Routledge, 1996). Also see Bryan S. Turner, *The Body and Society: Explorations in Social Theory* (New York: Blackwell, 1984); Simon J. Williams and Gillian Bendelow. *The Lived Body: Sociological Themes, Embodied Issues* (New York: Routledge, 1998); Erving Goffman, *The Presentation of Self in Everyday Life* (Garden City, NY: Doubleday, Anchor Books, 1959); Goffman, *Stigma: Notes on the Management of Spoiled Identity* (Englewood Cliffs, NJ: Prentice Hall; New York: Touchstone Books, 1986); Sarah Nettleton and Jonathan Watson, *The Body in Everyday Life* (New York: Routledge, 1998).

13. Paul Rabinow describes these three phases as "re-examination of knowledge," "the conditions of knowledge," and "the knowing subject." See Rabinow, introduction to *Ethics: Subjectivity and Truth* by Michel Foucault (New York: The New Press, 1997), xi; Alec McHoul and Wendy Grace, introduction to *A Foucault Primer: Discourse, Power and the Subject* (New York: New York University Press, 1993).

14. Michel Foucault, *The Archeology of Knowledge* (New York: Routledge, 1972 [1969]).15. Michel Foucault, *Discipline and Punish: The Birth of the Prison* (New York: Vintage Books, 1979); Foucault, *The History of Sexuality: An Introduction* (New York: Vintage Books, 1978).

16. McHoul and Grace, *Foucault Primer*, 74.

17. David Bohm, *On Dialogue* (New York: Routledge, 1996).

18. Bohm's notion of fragmentation as an outcome of thought is helpful in understanding the problematic of the discursive black body. This constructed body, an exercise of thought and language, entails a process of disassociation, of breaking the whole of black identity and meaning into distinguished and disconnected pieces. See Bohm, *On Dialogue*.

19. James Cone, *The Spirituals and the Blues* (Maryknoll, NY: Orbis Books, 1972).

20. See Foucault, *Ethics*.

21. Some black theologians may read my perspective as hopeless or overly pessimistic. It seems to me, however, a failure of their work involves the overprescribed moralizing against rather than faint social analysis. I would suggest the ethical stance hinted above stems reasonably from an understanding of the body as unstable, pointing to a variety of possibilities and meaning. Hence, any effort to "rescue" black bodies must be sensitive to this instability and the uncertainties of strategy involved.

22. Bohm, *On Dialogue*.

23. Ibid., 9.

24. McHoul and Grace, *Foucault Prime*, 19–21.

25. Here I appeal to a version of Bohm's concern with truth, meaning, and the dangers of fragmentation as a problematic mode of thinking. See Bohm, *On Dialogue*, 27, 30, 43, 56, 59–60, 61, 78, 103.

26. Ibid., 103.

27. Susan Bordo is concerned with the manner in which only attention to the "real" body, the material body can allow for the type of progressive politics necessary for promoting struggle against oppression. Quoted in Susan Hekman, "Material Bodies," in Welton, *Body and Flesh*, 62.

28. Judith Butler provides a response to this critique of the discursive body in *Bodies That Matter: On the Discursive Limits of Sex* (New York: Routledge, 1993).

29. Susan Bordo, "Bringing Body to Theory," in Welton, *Body and Flesh*, 89.

30. Ibid., 89.

31. Susan Bordo, *Unbearable Weight: Feminism, Western Culture, and the Body* (Berkeley: University of California Press, 1993), 16.

32. Carol Bigwood, "Renaturalizing the Body (with the Help of Merleau-Ponty)," in Welton, *Body and Flesh*, 103. Judith Butler raises concerns regarding the potential for the development of "metaphysical foundationalism" if the material body is understood to exist prior to culture. However, Bordo and Bigwood do not suggest such an arrangement. Both argue that the material body is embedded in culture, but that attention to the cultural production of bodies through discourse does not capture fully the nature of the body and does not allow for full engagement with the problems facing oppressed groups. In addition, in the two articles cited here, both Bordo and Bigwood suggest that the privileging of culture and thought over nature and material can result in a foundationalism by suggesting a metaphysical privileging of culture.

33. Williams and Bendelow, introduction to *Lived Body*, 1.

34. B. S. Turner, *Body and Society*, 8. 41, 49.

35. Williams and Bendelow, *Lived Body*, 35.

36. B. S. Turner, *Body and Society*, 54.

37. Williams and Bendelow, *Lived Body*, 77.

38. Gail Weiss, *Body Image: Embodiment as Intercorporeality* (New York: Routledge, 1999), 3.

39. Williams and Bendelow, *Lived Body,* 8.

40. Douglas, *Natural Symbols.*

41. B. S. Turner, *Body and Society,* 188.

42. Bordo, "Bringing Body to Theory," in Welton, 92, 94.

43. Bohm, *On Dialogue,* 61.

44. Margaret Lock and Judith Farquhar, introduction to *Beyond the Body Proper: Reading the Anthropology of Material Life* (Durham: Duke University Press, 2007), 2.

45. In making this argument, I draw on a variety of disciplines, including liberation theology, sociology of the body, and philosophy of art.

46. The words of novelist Shiva Naipaul in *Love and Death in a Hot Country* (New York: Penguin Books, 1985) have profound theological merit: "The Gods ooze out of the pores like sweat." In this sense theology done in light of the body and its religious-theological weight is a type of "body-talk."

47. See, for example, Tricia Rose, *Black Noise: Rap Music and Black Culture in Contemporary America* (Middletown, CT: Wesleyan University Press, 1994); T. Sharpley-Whiting, *Pimps Up, Ho's Down: Hip Hop's Hold on Young Black Women* (New York: New York University Press, 2008); Margarita Simon, "Untapped Resources: An Interpretation of Female Rap Lyrics on Religion and the Erotic Through a Hermeneutic of Life Meaning." This essay appears in a special issue of *Culture and Religion,* "Hip Hop and Religion," Vol. 10, Issue 1 (March 2009): 86–96.

48. K. B. Douglas, *Sexuality and the Black Church*; K. B. Douglas, *What's Faith Got to Do With It? Black Bodies/Christian Souls* (Maryknoll, NY: Orbis Books, 2005).

49. Some might assume this book is simply my attempt to sneak humanism into theological discourse by removing black theology's concern with the transcendent, replacing it with the human body. They might see this as a version of the common take on humanism: "the human is the measure of all things." Theology is certainly done within a particular historical-cultural context—materialistic to a certain extent—and the theologian undoubtedly brings something of his or herself to the process of doing theology. This much is true. What I offer in these pages is not a backhanded humanism, notwithstanding reference to humanism in a few of the chapters.

50. Additional work on an embodied black theology must be done, including fuller attention to theoretical underpinning and more systematic attention to a grounded theory of the body within the context of African American religion. I address this subject in several ongoing projects: *In the Language of Nimrod: Toward an African American Humanist Theology* (to be published by Oxford University Press) and *Black Religion and Aesthetics: Religious Thought and Life in African and the African Diaspora* (New York: Palgrave Macmillan, 2009).

51. Some might argue that the presidency of Barack Obama changes the nature and content of black theology through a reframing of race. As many have noted, however, the election of the first black president has not changed the nature and meaning of race and the impact of racism on life in the United States. The challenges remain the same, and black theology has not fundamentally changed as a consequence of this election. It is certainly the case that there is much to discuss about President Obama's impact on politics and race relationship, but his "racialized" body does not alternate the basic

concerns of black theology. I address the impact of President Obama on long-standing issues of importance to theological and religious studies in a series of articles written for *Religion Dispatches* (see ReligionDispatches.com); some of those articles also appear in *Understanding and Transforming the Black Church* (Eugene, OR: Cascade Books, 2010). Also see "Jimmy Carter: Animosity towards Barack Obama is due to Racism," http://www.guardian.co.uk/world/2009/Sept/16/jimmy-carter-racism-barack-obama, November 2. 2009.

NOTES TO CHAPTER 1

1. This chapter is a significantly expanded version of the essay published as "Blessed Irreverence: What Black Theology Can Learn from the Visual Arts," in *The Subjective Eye: Essays in Culture, Religion, and Gender* , ed. Richard Valentasis (Eugene, OR: Pickwick Publications, 2006): 310–20. Used by permission of Wipf and Stock Publishers.

2. Ann Branaman, "Goffman's Social Theory," in *The Goffman Reader,* ed. Charles Lemert and Ann Branaman, xlvii, lxxiv–lxxv, 73 (Malden, MA: Blackwell, 1997). Also see Goffman, *Stigma.*

3. Nettleton and Watson, *Body in Everyday Life,* 2.

4. Jeremy Carrette, "Beyond Theology and Sexuality: Foucault, the Self and the Que(e) rying of Monotheistic Truth," in *Michel Foucault and Theology: The Politics of Religious Experience,* ed. James Bernauer and Jeremy Carrette, 228 (Burlington, VT: Ashgate, 2004), 228.

5. Foucault, *Discipline and Punish,* 11.

6. Ibid., 16.

7. Ibid., 25.

8. Ibid., 109.

9. Ibid., 29.

10. Mary Abbe, "Modern and Muslim," *Star Tribune* (Minneapolis), February 28, 2003, E20.

11. Ibid.

12. Ibid.

13. I make this statement in relationship to Foucault's work on technologies of the self. See Luther H. Martin, Huck Gutman, Patrick H. Hutton, eds. *Technologies of the Self: A Seminar with Michel Foucault* (Amherst: University of Massachusetts Press, 1988); Weiss, *Body Images,* 3–5.

14. Martin et al., *Technologies of the Self,* 10. Foucault makes this remark in describing his role as an intellectual. It, however, rings true with respect to the function of this photographic image and the "state" of the women presented.

15. Cresddia J. Heyes, *Self-Transformations: Foucault, Ethics, and Normalized Bodies* (New York: Oxford University Press, 2007), 4.

16. Ibid., 5–8.

17. Williams and Bendelow. *Lived Body,* 28.

18. Foucault, *Discipline and Punish,* 187.

19. Martin et al., *Technologies of the Self,* 11–18.

20. Goffman, *Stigma.* Gwendolyn S. O'Neal provides an interesting reading of African American religion in the form of black Christianity through Goffman's concept of the

stigma. See O'Neal, "The African American Church, It's Sacred Cosmos and Dress," in *Religion, Dress and the Body*, ed. Linda Arthur, 117–34 (New York: Berg, 1999).

21. Martin et al., *Technologies of the Self*, 45.

22. It would be interesting to "read" fully the marked bodies through the work of Susan Bordo's *Unbearable Weight*; Bordo, *Twilight Zones: The Hidden Life of Cultural Images from Plato to O. J.* (Berkeley: University of California Press, 1999).

23. I draw from and I am indebted conceptually to Marcella Althaus-Reid. See Althaus-Reid, *Indecent Theology*.

24. Terence S. Turner, "The Social Skin," in Welton, *Body and Flesh*, 83.

25. Arthur, introduction to *Religion, Dress and the Body*, 2–3.

26. B. S. Turner, *Body and Society*, 173–74.

27. See Foucault, *Ethics*, 262–84.

28. Weiss, *Body Image*, 5–6.

29. This should be not read to mean Foucault had no interest in issues of gender and race. Rather, it is more accurate to say that Foucault's interest in race, for example, involves attention to the historical development of a discourse of race. Furthermore, Foucault's interest in gender and sexual preference is also played out in terms of discourse and with focused concern with the manner in which these discourses influence and affect power relationships. See Ann Laura Stoler, *Race and the Education of Desire: Foucault's History of Sexuality and the Colonial Order of Things* (Durham, NC: Duke University Press, 1995).

30. Foucault, *The History of Sexuality*, vol. 3, *The Care of the Self* (New York: Vintage Books, 1988).

31. Bordo, "Bringing Body to Theory," in Welton, *Body and Flesh*, 95.

32. See Pinn, *Terror and Triumph*, chaps. 7 and 8. While *Terror and Triumph* frames much of what guides this particular chapter, my concern here extends chaps. 7 and 8 by offering more focused attention to the conceptual significance of art by linking it more directly to notions of the body and the doing of theology.

33. Arthur C. Danto, *The Philosophical Disenfranchisement of Art* (New York: Columbia University Press, 1986), 103.

34. Nelson, *Body Theology*, 43.

35. Arthur C. Danto, *The Body/Body Problem: Selected Essays* (Berkeley: University of California Press, 1999), x.

36. Williams and Bendelow, introduction to *Lived Body*, 7–9.

37. For examples of my work related to these functions of art/aesthetics see: *Terror and Triumph*, chaps. 6, 8; Pinn, "Sweaty Bodies in a Circle: Thoughts on the Subtle Dimensions of Black Religion as Protest," in *Black Theology: An International Journal* 4, no. 1 (2006): 11–26; Pinn's review essay of *How Race Is Made*, by Mark Smith; *Being Human*, by Dwight Hopkins; *What's Faith Got to Do With It?*, by Kelly Brown Douglas; and *Colored Pictures*, by Michael Harris, *Religious Studies Review* 33, no. 1 (January 2007): 1–8.

38. Arthur C. Danto, *Philosophizing Art: Selected Essays* (Berkeley: University of California Press, 1999), 59.

39. David Morgan, *Visual Piety: A History and Theory of Popular Religious Images* (Berkeley: University of California, 1999); Morgan, *The Sacred Gaze: Religious Visual Culture in Theory and Practice* (Berkeley: University of California Press, 2005).

40. Danto, *Philosophizing Art*, 132.

41. Francis V. O'Connor, *Jackson Pollock* (New York: Museum of Modern Art, 1967), 73.

42. Ibid., 40.

43. Ibid..

44. Ibid., 55.

45. See Danto, *After the End of Art*, 117–32.

46. Jonathan Weinberg, *Ambition and Love in Modern American Art* (New Haven: Yale University Press, 2001), 31.

47. Ibid., 49.

48. I was fortunate to experience prime examples of both styles of art at the National Museum of Modern Art, Georges Pompidou Center, Paris, and the Tate Modern, London, England.

49. Weinberg, *Ambition* and *Love*, 215.

50. Danto, *Philosophizing Art*, 68. One could point to the "readymade" work of Marcel DuChamp for what it says about the nature of art. And, while DuChamp's *Fountain* and other challenges to the aesthetic preoccupations dominating the art world gained attention in New York, it is the pop art of Andy Warhol and others that the questioning of art, its nature and meaning, is most vividly expressed. See Danto, *Philosophizing Art*, 72–73.

51. Kyneston McShine, ed., *Andy Warhol: A Retrospective*, 441, quoted in Danto, *Philosophizing Art*, 74.

52. Andy Warhol's *Diaries*, 8 October 1984, 606, quoted in Weinberg, *Ambition* and *Love*, 238.

53. I have in mind Paul Tillich's understanding of the erotic. As I have described it elsewhere, Tillich understands eros as a force that gives shape to human ingenuity and expression on a variety of fronts and in a variety of forms. It is libidinal and, as a result, concerned with physical pleasure, but it is more than this. It is also concerned with the beautiful in far-reaching terms and the desire to create relationships saturated with this beauty. See Alexander C. Irwin, *E.R.O.S Toward the World: Paul Tillich and the Theology of the Erotic* (Minneapolis: Fortress Press, 1991), 1, 5, 6. Also see, for example, Paul Tillich, *Love, Power, and Justice: Ontological Analyses and Ethical Applications* (New York: Oxford University Press, 1954).

54. Weinberg, *Ambition and Love*, 212.

55. See Mary Douglas, *Purity and Danger: An Analysis of the Concepts of Pollution and Taboo* (New York: Ark, 1966).

56. Danto, *Philosophizing Art*, 73, 74. While intriguing, I must emphasize what I propose here is not reducible to the playfulness with sex and sexuality as evident in Andy Warhol's work such as "Jean-Michel Basquiat, 1984," or the images of Marilyn Monroe. Or one might consider the images in *A Rake's Progress* set designs developed by David Hockney during the 1960s and modeled after William Hogarth's *A Rake's Progress* of the 1700s.

57. Davey, "The Hermeneutics of Seeing," in Heywood and Sandywell, *Interpreting Visual Culture*, 4, 8.

58. Arthur C. Danto, *After the End of Art: Contemporary Art and the Pale of History* (Princeton: Princeton University Press, 1997), 98.

59. Sharon F. Patton, "Memory and Metaphor: The Art of Romare Bearden, 1940–1987" In *Memory and Metaphor: The Art of Romare Bearden, 1940–1987*, ed. Mary Schmidt Campbell, Sharon F. Patton, and Kinshasha Lonwill (New York: Oxford University Press, 1991), 70.

60. Davey, "The Hermeneutics of Seeing," in Heywood and Sandywell, *Interpreting Visual Culture*, 22.

61. Danto, *After the End of Art*, 77.

62. I find Arthur Danto's philosophy of art convincing on this point. In addition to the books listed in previous notes, also see Danto, *Philosophical Disenfranchisement of Art* ; Danto, *The Transfiguration of the Commonplace: A Philosophy of Art* (Cambridge, MA: Harvard University Press, 1981).

63. Frantz Fanon, *Black Skin, White Masks* (New York: Grove Press, 1967), 82, 84.

64. As Linda Arthur remarks, "we wear our identities on our bodies and our bodies are used by religions to virtually communicate world views." Arthur, *Religion, Dress, and the Body*, 6.

65. Much of the function of Christianity and the scope of theology revolves around practices and thoughts necessary for salvation, metaphysically understood. Black theology, however, and certain strands of black Christianity, are much more earthbound. Yet their relationship to the body and to embodiment demonstrates a similar discipline, a similar effort to hide if not damage the body.

66. Religion loses its seating above and beyond mundane activities and practices within the social body; and instead it is intimately connected to the body as a "social practice." Carrette, *Foucault and Religion*, 110.

67. The modality of theological thinking suggested here does not require rejection of the God concept; rather, it necessitates centering the body and interrogation of religio-theological assumptions. This can take place from within a variety of religious orientations.

NOTES TO CHAPTER 2

1. This chapter is a significantly expanded version of the essay first published as "Black Is, Black Ain't": Victor Anderson, African American Theological Thought, and Identity," *Dialog: A Journal of Theology* 43, no. 1 (Spring 2004): 54–62.

2. Italics added. W. E. B. Du Bois, "The Forethought," in *The Souls of Black Folk* (New York: Vintage Books, 1990), 3.

3. Butler, *Bodies that Matter*.

4. Du Bois, *Souls of Black Folk*, 8–9.

5. Foucault, *History of Sexuality*, vol. 3; Martin et al., *Technologies of the Self*.

6. Foucault, *History of Sexuality*, vol. 3, 25.

7. Du Bois, *Souls of Black Folk*. I begin working through this notion of "soul" in Du Bois' writing in "Charting Du Bois' Souls: Thoughts on 'Veiled' Bodies, Celebratory Skepticism, and the Study of Religion," in *The Souls of W. E. B. Du Bois: New Essays and Reflections*, ed. Edward Blum and Jason Young, 69–84 (Macon, GA: Mercer University Press, 2009). My attention to this subject in the current volume entails more significant attention to the body—its nature and meaning—than is present in that earlier work on Du Bois.

8. Du Bois, *Souls of Black Folk*, 7.

9. Ibid., 3.

10. Shawn Michelle Smith, *Photography on the Color Line: W. E. B. Du Bois, Race, and Visual Culture* (Durham, NC: Duke University Press, 2004), 32.

11. Ibid., 33.

12. This discussion on the perception of black bodies is presented in chapter 3 with respect to issues of gender.

13. Stoler, *Race and the Education of Desire*, 8.

14. Ibid., 8.

15. S. M. Smith, *Photography on the Color Line*, 44. Also see Russ Castronovo, *Beautiful Democracy: Aesthetics and Anarchy in a Global Era* (Chicago: University of Chicago Press, 2007).

16. Robert F. Reid-Pharr, *Conjugal Union: The Body, the House, and the Black American* (New York: Oxford University Press, 1999), 5–6. While the nature and meaning of blackness may vary over time, I believe this attention to corporeality as access point to deep meaning is also a viable way to *David Walker's Appeal* as well as the physical taking of ontological freedom *qua* Frederick Douglass vs. Covey, as found in Douglass's autobiography. See: Frederick Douglass, *Autobiographies: Narrative of the Life of Frederick Douglass, an American Slave/My Bondage and My Freedom/Life and Times of Frederick Douglass* (New York: Library of America, 1994); David Walker, *David Walker's Appeal, in Four Articles; Together with a Preamble, to the Coloured Citizens of the World, but in Particular, and very Expressly to Those of the United States of America* (New York: Farrar, Straus and Giroux, 1995 [1829]). I would not limit this to blackness as associated with male bodies. The struggle for/over black bodies also takes place within the context of gender as is played out, for example, in the work of Sojourner Truth, Maria Stewart, Anna J. Cooper, and Pauli Murray. See: Patricia C. McKissack, *Sojourner Truth, Ain't I a Woman* (New York: Scholastic, 1994); Marilyn Richardson, ed., *Maria W. Stewart: America's First Black Woman Political Writers* (Bloomington: Indiana University Press, 1987); Anna J. Cooper, *A Voice from the South* (New York: Oxford University Press, 1990); Pauli Murray, *Pauli Murray: The Autobiography of a Black Activist, Feminist, Lawyer, Priest and Poet* (Knoxville: University of Tennessee Press, 1989).

17. Susan Bordo, "Bringing Body to Theory," in Welton, *Body and Flesh*, 89.

18. Readers would do well to consider my argument in connection to J. Cameron Carter's ambitious treatment of race. See Carter, *Race: A Theological Introduction* (New York: Oxford University Press, 2008). His argument and intent vary in significant ways from what I seek to accomplish here, and as a result I do not directly engage his work, although I write in awareness of his concerns and formulations.

19. Statement by the National Committee of Black Churchmen, June 13, 1969, in *Black Theology: A Documentary History, 1966–1979*, ed. James H. Cone and Gayraud S. Wilmore, 101 (Maryknoll, NY: Orbis Books, 1979).

20. Cecil Wayne Cone, *The Identity Crisis in Black Theology* (Nashville: African Methodist Episcopal Church, 1975), 142.

21. Albert Cleage's *The Black Messiah* (Trenton, NJ: Africa World Press, 1989) provided a highly charged reading of the blackness of Jesus as historical and physiological reality.

22. J. H. Cone, *Black Theology of Liberation*, 120.

23. See Maxine Leeds Craig, *Ain't I a Beauty Queen? Black Women, Beauty, and the Politics of Race* (New York: Oxford University Press, 2002), chap. 2.

24. Anderson, *Beyond Ontological Blackness*; Anderson, *Creative Exchange: A Constructive Theology of African American Religious Experience* (Minneapolis: Fortress Press, 2008).

25. For information on womanist scholarship, see Katie Cannon, *Black Womanist Ethics* (Atlanta: Scholars Press, 1998); Grant, *White Women's Christ and Black Women's Jesus*; D.

Williams, *Sisters in the Wilderness*; Emilie Townes, ed., *A Troubling in My Soul: Womanist Perspectives on Evil and Suffering* (Maryknoll, NY: Orbis Books, 1993); Diana L. Hayes, *And Still We Rise: An Introduction to Black Liberation Theology* (New York: Paulist Press, 1996).

26. See Anderson, *Beyond Ontological Blackness*, sec. 3.

27. Ibid., 54; citing Immanuel Kant's *Observations on the Feeling of the Beautiful and Sublime*. trans. John T. Goldthwait (Berkeley: University of California Press, 1960), 110.

28. Anderson, *Beyond Ontological Blackness*, 14.

29. Ibid., 11.

30. Anderson, *Creative Exchange*, 8.

31. Ibid., 10.

32. Ibid., 11.

33. Anderson, *Beyond Ontological Blackness*, 49 (hereafter cited in text).

34. Anderson, *Creative Exchange*, 31.

35. A small amount of the material that follows was also used to frame my humanist theology briefly outlined in "Toward Black Humanist Studies, Part 1: Theological Discourse Reconceived," in Pinn, *African American Humanist Principles*, chap. 8. There are connections between the claims made in this chapter concerning identity and embodiment and what I purpose in my humanist theology. I am currently working on a book project that in part argues my African American humanist theology as the first embodied theology produced as a form of black theology. The book is titled *In the Language of Nimrod: Toward an African American Humanist Theology* (Oxford University Press).

36. A move away from pre-language ideas of religious experience (nonbody as material thinking) open religion to investigation, even by those who understand themselves as religiously "other." The benefit of this thinking is that it avoids the external vs. internal criticism argument used by many in black theology to discount certain types of criticism. Their argument has traditionally been that the Christ Event is the central claim of black theology and only those who recognize the centrality of this event can provide an internal critique. A careful read of black theological texts will demonstrate that only internal critiques are responded to in substantial ways. Paula Cooey's discussion of religious experience in relation to the body is extremely helpful. Her analysis of Wayne Proudfoot's work informs my thought on this issue. See Paula M. Cooey, *Religious Imagination and the Body: A Feminist Analysis* (New York: Oxford University Press, 1994). For examples of this internal vs. external critique and the subtle consequences of this dichotomy, see the debate between James Cone and William Jones (particularly Cone's response as outlined in *God of the Oppressed* [New York: Seabury Press, 1975]. Also see Major Jones, *The Color of G.O.D.* [Macon, GA: Mercer, 1987]. Dwight Hopkins demonstrates this tendency in *Introducing Black Theology of Liberation* [Maryknoll, NY: Orbis Books, 1999] in that the work of Wilmore (*Black Religion and Black Radicalism*) and Long (*Significations*) do not significantly impact the black theology project's methodological framework and content.

37. The following works are helpful in developing this perspective: Aldo Gargani, "Religious Experience as Event and Interpretation," in *Religion*, ed. Jacques Derrida and Gianni Vattimo, 111–35 (Stanford: Stanford University Press, 1998). I also see this perspective as related to common understandings of Michel Foucault's take on religion. See for an example, see "Prologue to a confession of the Flesh," in *Religion and Culture: Michel Foucault,* ed. Jeremy R. Carrette, 1–47 (New York: Routledge, 1999).

38. Victor Anderson speaks to similar concerns in *Beyond Ontological Blackness* and *Creative Exchange*.

39. Popular culture provides a hint of how this might be queried through the question "You feel me?" On one level the questioner is concerned with an ability to understand the ideas and concerns as wrapped in language, but I cannot help but also recognize the undertone associated with the question, the manner in which it depends on the realm of material contact—feeling—for its force.

40. I am grateful to Paula Cooey for this definition of essentialism.

41. See Foucault's discussion of discipline and its intents in *Disciplines and Punish*.

42. Concerning the Nation of Islam on this, see Elijah Muhammad, *Message to the Blackman in America* (Chicago: Muhammad's Temple No. 2, 1965) and Elijah Muhammad, *Our Savior has Arrived* (Newport News, VA: United Brothers Communications Systems, n.d.); Robert Birt, "Existence, Identity, and Liberation," in *Existence in Black: An Anthology of Black Existential Philosophy*, ed. Lewis R. Gordon, 212 (New York: Routledge, 1997).

43. Carby, *Race Men* (Cambridge. MA: Harvard University Press, 1999); Judith Butler, *Gender Trouble: Feminism and the Subversion of Identity*, (New York: Routledge, 1990), 29.

44. K. B. Douglas, *Sexuality and the Black Church; What's Faith Got to Do With It?* Also see Horace Griffin, *Their Own Received Them Not: African American Lesbians and Gays in the Black Church* (Cleveland, OH: Pilgrim Press, 2006); James Cone and Gayraud Wilmore, *Black Theology: A Documentary History*, chaps. 11, 27; E. L. Kornegay Jr., "Queering Black Homophobia: Black Theology as a Sexual Discourse of Transformation," *Theology and Sexuality* 11, no. 1 (2004): 299–51; Anthony B. Pinn and Dwight Hopkins, eds., *Loving the Body: Black Religious Studies and the Erotic* (New York: Palgrave, 2004).

45. Stuart Hall, "What is This 'Black' in Black Popular Culture?" In *Black Popular Culture*, ed. Michele Wallace and Gina Dent, 29 (Seattle: Bay Press, 1992).

NOTES TO CHAPTER 3

1. This chapter greatly expanded and somewhat reconceived discussions first published as: "Keep on Keepin' On": Reflections on 'Get On the Bus' and the Language of Movement," in *Voices on the Future: Black Religion After the Million Man March*, ed. Garth Kasimu Baker-Fletcher (Maryknoll, NY: Orbis Books, 1998) and "What's The Theological Equivalent of a 'Manish Boy'? Learning a Lesson from Womanist Scholarship," in *Deeper Shades of Purple: Womanism in Religion and Society*, ed. Stacey Floyd-Thomas, 275–81 (New York: New York University Press, 2006).

2. The Million Women's March took place on October 25, 1997.

3. Henry Louis Gates Jr., *Thirteen Ways Of Looking at a Black Man* (New York: Random House, 1997), 145.

4. The Honorable Elijah Muhammad, "Help Self: What Must Be Done With The Negroes?" 57, in *Message to the Black Man in America* (Chicago: The Final Call Inc., 1965).

5. Kim Martin Sadler, ed., *Atonement: The Million Man March* (Cleveland: Pilgrim Press, 1996), xvii.

6. Victor Turner, *The Ritual Process: Structure and Anti-Structure* (Ithaca, NY: Cornell University Press, 1969), 96. While Turner provides three ways of understanding the term, I reference it as an often short-lived period marked by a sense of mutuality and connection.

7. Ibid., 95.

8. Muddy Waters, "Manish Boy," *Blues Straight Ahead*.

9. Ibid.

10. I refer to formal engagement through conferences and reading (and teaching as best I can) womanist scholarship, as well as the gracious ways in which womanist scholars such as Katie Geneva Cannon, Cheryl Kirk-Duggan, and Stacey Floyd-Thomas have shared their insights and critique through more informal conversations.

11. Ralph Ellison, *Invisible Man*, (New York: Vintage Books, 1995).

12. For my thoughts on pedagogy as it relates to the body, see Pinn, *African American Humanist Principles*, chap. 9.

13. Dwight Hopkins's recent work, an example of which is in *Loving the Body: Black Religious Studies and the Erotic*, ed. Anthony Pinn and Dwight Hopkins (New York: Palgrave Macmillan, 2004), seeks a new sense of masculinity.

14. Grant, *White Women's Christ*; D. Williams, *Sisters in the Wilderness*.

15. See G. M. Gonzalez, "Of Property: On 'Captive' 'Bodies,' Hidden 'Flesh,' and Colonization," in *Existence in Black: An Anthology of Black Existential Philosophy*, ed. Lewis R. Gordon (New York: Routledge, 1997); and Toni Morrison, "The Site of Memory" in *Out There: Marginalization and Contemporary Cultures*, ed. Russell Ferguson et al., (Cambridge, MA: MIT Press, 1990).

16. In addition to the Delores Williams's text already noted, good examples of this attention to black women's experience as theological sources include: Katie Geneva Cannon, *Womanist Ethics*; Karen Baker-Fletcher, *A Singing Something*; Emile Townes, *Ida B. Wells*; Marcia Riggs, *With a Steady Beat*; Cheryl Townsend Gilkes, *If It Wasn't for the Women: Black Women's Experience and Womanist Culture in Church and Community* (Maryknoll, NY: Orbis Books, 2000).

17. See my text on theory of black religion, *Terror and Triumph* for one of my more substantive attempts to wrestle with this issue. It is an effort to develop an understanding of black religion's nature and meaning through continued awareness of the manner in which black bodies carry and shape perceptions of the world and our relationship to the world.

18. This is not to say that womanist scholarship is without its own shortcomings. I do not want to romanticize womanist work; it has its own issues, when one considers that the debate between Cheryl Sanders and other womanists in the 1980s remains significant (see "Roundtable on Christian Ethics and Theology in Womanist Perspective," *Journal of Feminist Studies in Religion* 5 [Fall 1989]). Yet, within the context of this short essay, I have in mind the limitations of black theological discourse pointed out by first-generation womanist thinkers, such as Jacquelyn Grant, as well as women who predate the formal development of womanist theology, such as Pauli Murray (see Cone and Wilmore, *Black Theology*). Within the context of black theology, Victor Anderson points out this problem with respect to the limiting effect of ontological blackness for a sense of "cultural fulfillment," which does require surrender of one's individual inclinations for the sake of blackness as the community unifier. See Anderson, *Beyond Ontological Blackness*.

19. Alice Walker, "Womanist," in *In Search of Our Mothers' Gardens: Womanist Prose* (New York: Harcourt Brace Jovanovich, 1983).

20. Foucault, *Ethics*, xxxvii.

21. Ibid., 291.

22. Butler, *Bodies that Matter*.

23. Bordo, *Unbearable Weight*, 217–18.

24. Foucault, *Discipline and Punish*, 136–38, 223.

25. Chris Shilling, *The Body and Social Theory*, (Thousand Oaks, CA: Sage Publications, 1993), 131–51.

26. Ibid., 141.

27. Ibid., *Body and Social Theory*, 146–47; Bordo, *Unbearable Weight*, 17.

28. Bordo, "'Material Girl': The Effacements of Postmodern Culture," in Bordo, *Unbearable Weigh*, 245–75.

29. Weiss, *Body Images*, 100. Also see Mike Featherstone, "The Body in Consumer Culture," in *The Body: Social Process and Cultural Theory*, ed. Mike Featherstone, Mike Hepworth, and Bryan S. Turner, 170–96 (Thousand Oaks, CA: Sage Publications, 1991). For interesting examples of how this has played out within the context of black body aesthetics, see Craig, *Ain't I a Beauty Queen?*; Shane White and Graham White, *Stylin': African American Expressive Culture from Its Beginnings to the Zoot Suit* (Ithaca, NY: Cornell University Press, 1998); Paula Black, *The Beauty Industry: Gender, Culture, Pleasure* (New York: Routledge, 2004); Gilkes, *If It Wasn't for the Women*, chap. 10; Emilie Townes, *Womanist Ethics and the Cultural Production of Evil* (New York: Palgrave Macmillan, 2006).

30. Bordo, *Unbearable Weight*, 9.

31. Ibid., 5.

32. Examples include Alice Walker, *Meridian* (New York: Harvest Books, 2003); Walker, *Possessing the Secret of Joy: A Novel* (New York: New Press, 2008); Toni Morrison, *The Bluest Eye* (New York: Knopf, 1003); Morrison, *Paradise* (New York: Plume, 1999); Zora Neale Hurston, *Their Eyes Were Watching God* (New York: Harper Perennial Modern Classics, 2006).

33. "Double-bind" as defined by Susan Bordo in *The Male Body: A New Look at Men in Public and Private* (New York: Farrar, Straus and Giroux, 1999), 242–51.

34. B. S. Turner, *Body and Society*, 233, 246; Williams and Bendelow, *Lived Body*, 118.

35. Bordo, *Unbearable Weight*, 29.

36. Susan Bordo provides an interesting discussion of shifts with respect to the presentation of the male body, whereby it becomes open to visual consumption as objects of the gaze. See Bordo, *Male Body*), 168–225.

37. Foucault, *Ethics*, 298.

38. Drew Leder, "A Tale of Two Bodies: The Cartesian Corpse and the Lived Body," in Welton, *Body and Flesh*, 123.

39. Damasio, *Feeling of What Happens*, 144.

NOTES TO CHAPTER 4

1. This chapter is an expanded version of an essay first published as "Nimrod's Children Have Bodies: Humanist Sensibilities, Black Theology, and Sex(uality)," in Pinn, *African American Humanist Principles*, 83–97. Reproduced by permission of Palgrave Macmillan.

2. See Martin et al., *Technologies of the Self*.

3. "Also: A woman who loves other women, sexually and/or nonsexually. . . . Sometimes loves individual men, sexually and/or nonsexually." Walker, *In Search of Our Mothers' Gardens* , xi.

4. Foucault, *History of Sexuality,* vol. 1, 11.

5. Ibid., 18–23.

6. Ibid., 25.

7. Ibid., 37–48, 122–26.

8. Ibid., 139–45.

9. Ibid., 105; Foucault, *History of Sexuality*, vol. 2, *The Use of Pleasure* (New York: Vintage Books, 1990), 253.

10. Foucault, *History of Sexuality*, vol. 2, 20.

11. Ibid., 42.

12. Ibid., 253–54.

13. Ibid., 138, 151–83. As Elizabeth Clark notes, even marriage did not fear individuals from a concern with the consequences of lived desire. It was expected, Clark remarks, that within marriage sex would be a matter of nature and scriptural purposes and not a consequence of desire (hence pleasure). See E. A. Clark, "Foucault, the Fathers and Sex," in Bernauer and Carrette, 39–56.

14. Foucault, *History of Sexuality*, vol. 2, 253.

15. Carrette, "Beyond Theology and Sexuality," in Bernauer and Carrette, *Michel Foucault and Theology*, 217.

16. Foucault, *History of Sexuality*, vol. 3, 43–47.

17. Ibid., 56–57, 65, 94–95.

18. Martin et al., *Technologies of the Self*, 20–22.

19. B. S. Turner, *Body and Society*, 8, 81–82, 163; Foucault, *Ethics*, 285.

20. Michael Eric Dyson, "Homotextualities: The Bible, Sexual Ethics, and the Theology of Homoeroticism," in Dyson, *Open Mike: Reflections on Philosophy, Race, Sex, Culture and Religion* (New York: Basic Civitas Books, 2003), 360–84.

21. Foucault, *History*, vol. 1, 98–103.

22. Ibid, 149.

23. Stoler's concern with discourses of race and sexuality as they related to the structures of empire within the colonial period does not concern this chapter. Rather, I am interested in the connecting of these two discourses as having theological potential for restructuring the normalization strategies that both implicitly and explicitly inform black theological thought.

24. Stoler, *Race and the Education of Desire*, 4–5.

25. Ibid., 6.

26. Ibid., 10. Stoler is primarily concerned with the Dutch colonies but acknowledges that the function of discourses of race and sexuality in those colonies relates to experiences elsewhere: Dutch colonial experience can serve as a "touchstone for wider claims"; Bordo, *Male Body*, 247–53.

27. Stoler, *Race and the Education of Desire*, 123–24.

28. Ibid, 41.

29. Ibid, 33.

30. Ibid., 199.

31. Bordo, *Unbearable Weigh*, 24.

32. Stoler, *Race and the Education of Desire*, 183; Weiss, *Body Image*, 29.

33. Weiss, *Body Images*, 66.

34. Bordo, *Unbearable Weight*, 165–212.

35. M. Douglas, *Natural Symbols*, 22, 69, 71.

36. Peter Gardella, *Innocent Ecstasy: How Christianity Gave America an Ethic of Sexual Pleasure* (New York: Oxford University Press, 1985), 57.

37. See Meery E. Wiesner-Hauls, *Christianity and Sexuality in the Early Modern World: Regulating Desire, Reforming Practice* (New York: Routledge, 2000), 43–44.

38. Ann-Janine Morey, *Religion and Sexuality in American Literature* (New York: Cambridge University Press, 1992), 1.

39. Townes, *Breaking the Fine Rain of Death*, 174.

40. Morey, *Religion and Sexuality in American Literature*, 26.

41. See Foucault, *History of Sexuality*, vol. 3.

42. David M. Carr, *The Erotic Word: Sexuality, Spirituality, and the Bible* (New York: Oxford University Press, 2003), 7.

43. Christine E. Gudorf, *Body, Sex, and Pleasure: Reconstructing Christian Sexual Ethics* (Cleveland, OH: Pilgrim Press, 1994), 2–3.

44. Wiesner-Hauls, *Christianity and Sexuality*, 238–39.

45. Ibid., 2, 3, 5, 6.

46. Ibid., 9.

47. Pat Caplan, ed., introduction to *The Cultural Construction of Sexuality* (New York: Tavistock Publications, 1987), 7.

48. Copeland, "Body, Representation, and Black Religious Discourse," in D'Emilio and Freedman, *Intimate Matters*, 181.

49. Kathy Peiss and Christian Simmons, eds., introduction to *Passion and Power: Sexuality in History* (Philadelphia: Temple University Press, 1989), 6.

50. Linda Brent, *Incidents in the Life of a Slave Girl: An Authentic Historical Narrative Describing the Horrors of Slavery as Experienced by Black Women* (New York: Harvest/Harcourt Brace Jovanovich Publishers, 1973), 53–54.

51. Ibid., 55.

52. Frantz Fanon, for example, speaks of this practice from the perspective of the victims, noting along the way the manner in which these bodies are consumed piece by piece. See Fanon, *Black Skin*.

53. This is because the subjectivity of white bodies was harmed through an unreasonable assumption of superiority and the subjectivity of black bodies was warped through an assumption that they were inferior.

54. Butler, *Bodies that Matter*, 1.

55. Fanon, *Black Skin*, 159.

56. D'Emilio and Freedman, *Intimate Matters*, 86; R. W. Connell, "Bodies, Intellectuals, and the World Society," in *Reframing the Body*, ed. Nick Waston and Sarah Cunningham-Berrley, 14 (New York: Palgrave, 2001).

57. Althaus-Reid, *Indecent Theology*, 88.

58. Butler, *Bodies that Matter*, 178–79.

59. Readers should give attention to George Hutchinson, *In Search of Nella Larsen: A Biography of the Color Line* (Cambridge, MA: Belknap Press of Harvard University Press, 2006), chaps. 12 and 13; Thadious M. Davis, *Nella Larsen, Novelist of the Harlem Renaissance: A Woman's Life Unveiled* (Baton Rouge: Louisiana State University Press, 1994), sec. 3 and appendix A.

60. Nella Larsen, *Quicksand*, with introduction and notes by Thadious M. Davis (New York: Penguin Books, 2002), 114.

61. There is a relationship between a theologically driven reformulation and the socio-logical analysis of the "re-formed" body offered by Philip A. Mellor and Chris Shilling in *Re-forming the Body: Religion, Community and Modernity* (London: Sage Publications, 1997). My initial thoughts on the theological significance of the body as tied to the body's materiality are found in Pinn, *Varieties of African American Religious Experience* (Minneapolis: Fortress Press, 1998), chap. 5; *Terror and Triumph*. Also see: "Sweaty Bodies in a Circle: Thoughts on the Subtle Dimensions of Black Religion as Protest," *Black Theology: An International Journal* 4, no. 1 (2006): 11–26; "Religio-Theological Formations and the (Re)Making of Black Kenyan Bodies: An African American's Perspective, *Africana Studies* 1 (2005): 43–62.

62. See Mellor and Shilling, *Re-forming the Body* for a discussion of the relationship between the sacred, body, nature, and society.

63. Nella Larsen, "Quicksand" in *Quicksand* and *Passing* (New Brunswick, NJ: Rutgers University Press, 1986), 112.

64. See, for example, Shilling, *Body and Social Theory*; Mariam Fraser and Monica Greco, eds., *The Body: A Reader* (New York: Routledge, 2005).

65. Larsen, "Quicksand," in *Quicksand* and *Passing*, 87.

66. Larsen, *Quicksand*, 104.

67. Ibid., 135.

68. James Baldwin, *Go Tell It On the Mountain* (New York: Grosset and Dunlap, 1953), 113.

69. Ibid., 269.

70. For an interesting and insightful discussion of the ramifications of the story of Ham in U.S. race relations, see Stephen R. Haynes, *Noah's Curse: The Biblical Justification of American Slavery* (New York: Oxford University Press, 2002).

71. Baldwin, *Go Tell It On the Mountain*, 267.

72. Michael F. Lynch, "A Glimpse of the Hidden God: Dialectical Visions in Baldwin's *Go Tell It On the Mountain*," in *New Essays on Go Tell It On the Mountain*, ed. Trudier Harris, 37–38 (New York: Cambridge University Press, 1996).

73. Such a connection between sexuality and religion makes perfect sense, if Charles Long is correct in asserting that religion involves the body through a full array of structures, experiences, expressions, and behaviors, in addition to modes of thought, because it was through their bodies and the meaning of their bodies that the oppressed came to be understood and controlled in the context of modernity. The religion of the oppressed, in this case the religion of African Americans, entails an embodiment as they attempt, again turning to Long, to move from their second creation as objects of history back to their first creation as subjects, as fully human. See Long, *Significations*, 7, 197.

74. Wiesner-Hauls, *Christianity and Sexuality*, 38.

75. Anthony Appiah, "Synthesis: For Racial Identities," in *Color Consciousness: The Political Morality of Race,* ed., Amy Gutman and Anthony Appiah (Princeton: Princeton University Press, 1998), 95, 98.

76. Nelson, *Body Theology* , 29.

77. Lynch, "A Glimpse of the Hidden God," in T. Harris, *New Essays*, 39. Connected to this is the reality of sexuality as a construct, a sociopolitical, economic, and culturally constructed something that has a history and which often serves to make some uncomfortable in their skin in order to serve the needs of others. And when connected to additional markers such as race, its importance and power only increases.

78. Vivian M. May, "Ambivalent Narratives, Fragmented Selves: Performative Identities and the Mutability of Roles in James Baldwin's *Go Tell It On the Mountain*," in Harris, *New Essays*.

79. Lynch, "A Glimpse of the Hidden God," in T. Harris, *New Essays*, 52–53.

80. It is clear that the challenge of Larsen and Baldwin to the nature and meaning of sex(uality) and the mechanics and purposes of body construction have implications beyond the church. For example, their framing of the issue also speaks to the construction of "nation" as a framework of meaning. That is a discussion is beyond the scope of this project. However, I address the black body and hemispheric studies more directly in my contribution to a project currently under contract with Palgrave Macmillan: Alexander Byrd, Michael Emerson, Caroline Levander, Anthony Pinn, eds., *Studying and Teaching the Americas* (New York: Palgrave Macmillan, forthcoming).

81. Foucault, *History of Sexuality*, vol. 1, 82–95.

82. (Maryknoll, NY: Orbis Books, 1999) and (Maryknoll, NY: Orbis Books, 2005). Readers may also be interested in the critique I provide in *The Black Church in the Post–Civil Rights Era* (Maryknoll, NY: Orbis Books, 2002), chap. 5. Also see my review of K. B. Douglas, *What's Faith Got to Do with It?* in *Journal of Contemporary Religion* 22, no. 2 (May 2007): 275–77.

83. K. B. Douglas, *Sexuality and the Black Church*, 22–23.

84. Ibid., 7.

85. The problem of a stifled discourse is highlighted when one considers that even the blues, a musical form that seems to celebrate despised sexuality, typically speaks of it in coded terms: Is "jellyroll" always a confectionery treat in the blues? Marketing requirements might have something to do with this issue. However, at certain points in the history of blues recordings, there is still a sense in which nondiscourse sexuality entails a joy that on some level must be linguistically tamed. And when, in rap music, this taming of sexuality is not the case "'cause gangstas celebrate sex," the backlash against certain genres of explicit rap, albeit problematic genres, makes clear a discomfort with sexuality as public.

86. K. B. Douglas, *Sexuality and the Black Church*, 68.

87. Ibid., 114, 127.

88. Cornel West, "Christian Love and Heterosexism," in *The Cornel West Reader* (New York: Basic Civitas Books, 1999), 401–14.

89. Materials related to crisis within black family structures include Robert M. Franklin, *Crisis in the Village: Restoring Hope in African American Communities* (Minneapolis: Fortress Press, 2007); Andrew Billingsley, *Black Families in White America* (Upper Saddle River, NJ: Prentice-Hall, 1968).

90. Frederick C. Harris, *Something Within: Religion in African-American Political Activism* (New York: Oxford University Press, 1999), 169. This quotation and the next are taken from chap. 5 of Pinn, *Black Church in the Post–Civil Rights Era*, 107.

91. Beverly Hall Lawrence, *Reviving the Spirit: A Generation of African Americans Goes Home to Church* (New York: Grove Press, 1996), 142–43.

92. Michael Eric Dyson, "Homotextualities," in Dyson, *Open Mike*, 360.

93. Foucault, *History of Sexuality*, vol. 3, 30–34.

94. On this arrangement of masculinity, see Bordo, *Male Body*, 229–65.

95. Foucault, *History of Sexuality*, vol. 3, 34.

96. K. B. Douglas, *Sexuality and the Black Church*, 105.

97. K. B. Douglas, *What's Faith Got to Do With It?*

98. Foucault, *History of Sexuality*, vol. 3, 36.

99. Bordo, *Unbearable Weight*, 227.

100. Williams and Bendelow, *Lived Body*, 126; Carrette, "Beyond Theology and Sexuality," in Bernauer and Carrette.

101. Williams and Bendelow, *Lived Body*, 126.

102. Bordo, *Unbearable Weight*, 24.

103. Foucault, *History of Sexuality*, vol. 3, 39.

104. Anderson, *Beyond Ontological Blackness*, 21–50. This concept is given some attention in chap. 2, where Anderson's take on race vs. ontological blackness is discussed.

105. Bordo's discussion of the intersections of race, gender, and sexuality is an intriguing take on the topic. See Bordo, *Unbearable Weight*, 234–43.

106. Gudorf, *Body, Sex, and Pleasure*, 15.

107. Ibid., 15. Gudorf uses this term when discussing the manner in which attention to what is sinful about sexuality teaches believers to avoid questionable actions, while failing to teach ways in which to construct productive relationships—those that involve sexual actions and those that do not.

108. Althaus-Reid, *Indecent Theology*, 146.

109. Whereas Jeremy Carrette argues that changes in a doctrine of God precedes changes to discussion of the body, I argue that because of the centrality of Christology for black Christianity (the dominant modality of black religion), this issue must be addressed first. A rethinking of the configuration of desire in ways that challenge heterosexism and homophobia must involve attention to the embodiment of Christ. See Carrette, "Beyond Theology and Sexuality," in Bernauer and Carrette.

110. Readers might be interested in considering this statement in light of Bordo, *Male Body*, 15–104.

111. Ibid., 31.

112. Ibid., 32.

113. Although beyond the scope of this current book, I have given limited attention to a comparative theological discourse in Pinn, *Varieties of African American Religious Experience*, but much work is needed on this topic. Other theological texts pointing in this direction include Dianne Stewart, *Three Eyes for the Journey: African Dimensions of the Jamaican Religious Experience* (New York: Oxford University Press, 2005); Josiah Ulysses Young, *Pan-African Theology: Providence and the Legacies of the Ancestors* (Trenton, NJ: Africa World Press, 1992); Noel Erskine, *Decolonizing Theology: A Caribbean Perspective* (Trenton, NJ: Africa World Press, 1998).

NOTES TO CHAPTER 5

1. This chapter is an expanded version of an article first published as "When Demons Come Calling: Dealing with the Devil and Paradigms of Life in African American Music," in *The Lure of the Dark Side: Satan and Western Demonology in Popular Culture*, ed. Christopher Partridge and Eric Christianson (London: Equinox, 2009). Used by permission of Equinox Publishing Ltd.

2. Eph. 6:10–12 (KJV).

3. Allen Callahan, *The Talking Book: African Americans and the Bible* (New Haven, CT: Yale University Press, 2008); Theophus Smith, *Conjuring Culture: Biblical Formations of Black America* (New York: Oxford University Press, 1994); Vincent Wimbush, *African Americans and the Bible* (New York: Continuum, 2001); Cain Hope Felder, *Troubling the Biblical Waters: Race, Class and Family* (Maryknoll, NY: Orbis Books, 1989); Felder, *Stony the Road We Trod: African American Biblical Interpretation* (Minneapolis: Fortress Press, 1991).

4. Spencer, *Blues and Evil*, 18–27.

5. http://www.cogic.org/dctrn.htm.

6. Paul Tillich, *Theology of Culture* (New York: Oxford University Press, 1959), 42.

7. John Lovell Jr., *Black Song: The Forge and the Flame: The Story of How the Afro-American Spiritual Was Hammered Out* (1972; repr., New York: Paragon House Publishers, 1986).

8. J. H. Cone, *Spirituals and the Blues*, 35.

9. Ibid., 34.

10. "All I Do, the Church Keep A-Grumbling," http://www.negrospirituals.com/news-song/all_i_do_the_church_keep_a_grumbling.htm

11. "Members Don't Get Weary," http://www.negrospirituals.com/news-song/members_don_t_get_weary.htm

12. Bessie Smith, "Devil's Gonna Git You," http://www.geocities.com/BourbonStreet/delta/2541/blbsmith.htm#devil

13. Lightin' Hopkins, "Black Ghost Blues," http://www.geocities.com/BourbonStreet/delta/2541/bllhopki.htm#black

14. Robert Palmer, *Deep Blues: A Musical and Cultural History, from the Mississippi Delta to Chicago's South Side to the World* (New York: Penguin Books, 1982), 18.

15. Ibid., 115.

16. Louisiana Red, "Too Poor to Die." www.geocities.com/bourbonstreet/delta/2541/bllred.htm#Too353

17. This is the working premise of James Cone, *Black Theology of Liberation*.

18. See Spencer, *Blues and Evil* .

19. Palmer, *Deep Blues*, 111–31.

20. Robert Johnson, "Hell Hound On My Trail," http://www.geocities.com/BourbonStreet/delta/2541/blrjohns.htm#Hellhound481

21. Robert Johnson, "Me and the Devil Blues," http://xroads.virginia.edu/~MUSIC/blues/matdb.html

22. Robert Johnson, "Ramblin' On My Mind," http://www.theonlineblues.com/robert-johnson-ramblin-on-my-mind-lyrics.html

23. Robert Johnson, "Me and the Devil Blues," http://www.deltahaze.com/johnson/lyrics.html

24. Richard Wright, *The Outsider* (1953; repr., New York: Harper Perennial, 2003).

25. Whether or not Scarface converted to Islam does not negatively affect this analysis in that the lyrics to the referenced tracks do not clearly indicated an Islamic orientation vs. a Christianity orientation. To the contrary, the imagery and theological language embedded tends to shadow the Christian faith, and the awareness of demons and divine forces appears drawn from the Christian faith.

26. Scarface, "Last of a Dying Breed," *Last of a Dying Breed* (2000).

27. Scarface, "I Seen a Man Die," *The Diary* (2004).

28. Scarface, "Make Your Peace," *Balls and My Word* (2003).

29. 2Pac on Scarface, "Smile," *Untouchable* (1997).

30. Scarface, "Heaven," *The Fix* (2002).

31. Snoop Dogg, with Davin Seay, *The Dogg Father: The Times, Trials, and Hardcore Truths of Snoop Dogg* (New York: William Morrow, 1999), 2–3.

32. Ibid., 41.

33. Readers will find of interest the discussion of countercultural figures found in William L. Van Deburg's *Hoodlums: Black Villains and Social Bandits in American Life* (Chicago: University of Chicago Press, 2004).

34. Snoop Dogg, *Dogg Father*, 149.

35. Ibid., 25–26.

36. Ibid., 188.

37. Snoop Dogg, "Murder Was the Case," *Doggystyle* (1996).

38. Ibid.

39. Foucault, *Discipline and Punish*.

40. Dyson, "Ecstasy, Excess, and Eschatology," in Dyson, *Open Mike*, 307.

41. Dyson's relating of this to the confession is intriguing and certainly plays on Foucault's attention to the confessional. See ibid., 311–12.

NOTES TO CHAPTER 6

1. This chapter is a significantly expanded and revised version of an essay first published as "On a Mission from God: African American Music and the Nature/Meaning of Conversion and Religious Life," in *Between Sacred and Profane: Researching Religion and Popular Culture*, ed. Gordon Lynch, 143–56 (London: I. B. Tauris, 2007). Used by permission.

2. A variety of texts position hip-hop culture and rap music within this "between" period of ideological decline and rebirth. Examples include Marcus Reeves, *Somebody Scream! Rap Music's Rise to Prominence in the Aftershock of Black Power* (New York: Faber and Faber, 2008); Michael E. Dyson, *Between God and Gangsta Rap: Bearing Witness to Black Culture* (New York: Oxford University Press, 1996); Tricia Rose, *Black Noise: Black Music and Black Culture in Contemporary America* (Middletown, CT: Wesleyan University Press, 1994).

3. The purpose of this chapter is more focused than a large-scale analysis of hip-hop culture/rap music as power discourse and technology of self realization. For a recent project offering more general and expansive assessment see Tricia Rose, *The Hip Hop Wars: What We Talk About When We Talk About Hip Hop—And Why It Matters* (New York: Basic Civitas Books, 2008).

4. See Pinn, *Terror and Triumph*, chaps. 7–8.

5. Ibid., chap. 7.

6. "Give Me Your Hand," http://www.negrospirituals.com/news-song/give_me_your_hand.htm

7. 2 Cor 5:17 (KJV).

8. West, "Subversive Joy and Revolutionary Patience in Black Christianity," in West, *Cornel West Reader*, 437.

9. West, "The Crisis in Contemporary American Religion," in ibid., 359. Also see West, *Prophesy Deliverance!*, chaps. 4–5.

10. I have in mind James Cones's response to William Jones's critique of black Christian responses to human suffering. See Cone, *God of the Oppressed*; W. Jones, *Is God a White Racist?*

11. West, "Subversive Joy and Revolutionary Patience in Black Christianity," 438.

12. Ibid., 439.

13. Church of God in Christ: http://cogic.net/cogiccms/default/cogic-history/the-statement-of-faith/. Visited on June 30, 2009.

14. National Baptist Convention USA, Inc., "Baptist Articles of Faith." http://www.nationalbaptist.com/Index.cfm?FuseAction=Page&PageID=1000294. Viewed on June 30, 2009.

15. African Methodist Episcopal Church, "Articles of Faith" (Of Sin After Justification). http://www.ame-church.com/about-us/beliefs.php Viewed on June 30, 2009.

16. West, "Subversive Joy and Revolutionary Patience in Black Christianity," 438.

17. Wilson Jeremiah Moses, *Afrotopia: The Roots of African American Popular History* (New York: Cambridge University Press, 1998).

18. Ibid., 55.

19. Ibid., 94.

20. Ibid., 84–95.

21. Dyson, "Ecstasy, Excess, and Eschatology," in *Open Mike*, 305.

22. Ibid., 305–7.

23. Dyson, "'Searching for Black Jesus': The Nietzschean Quest of a Metaphysical Thug," in *Open Mike*, 271.

24. Dyson says the following concerning a plausible humanistic read of Tupac: "In a sense, Tupac's radical divinization of an imperfect deity in concert with suffering black humanity is much closer to arguments of humanocentric theism put forth by William R. Jones and Anthony Pinn." See Dyson, "'Searching for Black Jesus,'" 285. I explore the humanistic dimensions of Tupac's thought in Pinn, "'Handlin' My Business': Exploring Rap's Humanist Sensibilities," in Pinn, *Noise and Spirit*.

25. Quoted in Michael Eric Dyson, *Holler If You Hear Me: Searching for Tupac Shakur* (New York: Basic Civitas Books, 2001), 138–39.

26. Tupac Shakur, "Trapped," *2Pacalypse Now* (Jive Records, 1998).

27. For information on the term si(g)n, see Anthony B. Pinn, "Sweaty Bodies in a Circle: Thoughts on the Subtle Dimensions of Black Religion as Protest," *Black Theology: An International Journal* 4, no. 1 (2006): 11–26.

28. Dyson, *Holler If You Hear Me*, 210–11.

29. Reeves, *Somebody Scream!* , 170.

30. Dyson, "'Searching for Black Jesus,'" in *Open Mike*, 268.

31. Ibid., 269–70.

32. Ibid., 270.

33. Van Deburg, *Hoodlums: Black Villains and Social Bandits in American Life* (Chicago: University of Chicago Press, 2004), xi, 196.

34. Ibid., 175–76.

35. Reeves, *Somebody Scream!* , 175–76.

36. Dyson, "Ecstasy, Excess, and Eschatology," 306.

37. Drawing imagery from the *Bhagavad Gita* (chapter 11, verse 32) spoken by J. Robert Oppenheimer in a 1965 TV interview, in reference to the 1945 atom bomb detonation.

38. The term "chuch!" has fluid meaning but often references strong agreement and emphatic significance of the statement. However, it can also reference metaphysical authority couched in a given comment or command. For information on this terminology see UrbanDictionary.com.

39. Annie Reed, "Br'er Rabbit and the Briar Patch," in *Talk that Talk: An Anthology of African-American Storytelling*, ed. Linda Goss and Marian E. Barnes, 31 (New York: Touchstone Book, 1989) . Albert Murray offers an assessment of rough life I found useful in developing this perspective. See Murray, *From the Briarpatch File: On Context, Procedure, and American Identity* (New York: Pantheon Books, 2001). This idea of the trickster is further developed in Anthony B. Pinn and Paul Easterling, "Followers of Black Jesus on Alert: Thoughts on the Story of Tupac's Life/Death/Life," *Black Theology: An International Journal* 7, no. 1 (2009): 31–44.

40. See Kevin Powell, "2Pac Shakur," *Vibe Magazine*, April 1995, 50–55.

41. See Howard Thurman, *With Heart and Heart: The Autobiography of Howard Thurman* (New York: Houghton Mifflin Harcourt, 1981), 101–36 (esp. 113–15).

42. In Rob Marriott, "Last Testament," *Vibe Magazine*, November 1996, T7

43. Ibid.

44. Tupac Shakur, "Blasphemy," *The Don Killuminati: The 7-Day Theory* (Interscope Records, 1996).

45. Tupac Shakur, "Black Jesus," *Still I Rise* (Interscope Records, 1999).

46. Tupac Shakur, "Definition of a Thug," *R U Still Down? (Remember Me)*, (Jive Records, 1997).

47. Kevin Powell, "2Pac Shakur," *Vibe Magazine*, April 1995, 52.

48. Tupac Shakur, "So Many Tears," *Me Against the World* (Jive Records, 1995).

49. The lyrics to "Blasphemy" certainly lend legitimacy to this reading of Tupac's doctrine of "God" and eschatology. See n. 14.

50. Tupac Shakur, "I Wonder if Heaven Got a Ghetto," *R U Still Down? (Remember Me)*, (Jive Records, 1997).

51. Tupac Shakur, "Only Fear of Death," *R U Still Down? (Remember Me)*, (Jive Records, 1997).

52. Tupac Shakur, "Hail Mary," *The Don Killuminati, The 7-Day Theory* (Interscope Records, 1996).

53. Murray, *From the Briarpatch File*, 194–95.

54. Pinn, *Terror and Triumph*, 159.

55. Jeffrey O. G. Ogbar, "Slouching toward Bork: The Culture Wars and Self-Criticism in Hip-Hop Music," *Journal of Black Studies* 33, no. 2 (November 1999): 167.

56. The scripture reference is to 1 Cor 1:18, and the quotation is 1 Cor 1:19.

57. On this point, Nick De Genova provides a useful reworking of nihilism within the context of rap music that, using Richard Wright, pushes for a utility and productive dimension of this posture toward the world: "Gangster Rap and Nihilism in Black America: Some Questions of Life and Death," *Social Text* 43 (Autumn, 1995): 89–132, 114.

NOTES TO CHAPTER 7

1. Alice Walker, *The Color Purple: A Novel* (New York: Harcourt Brace Jovanovich, 1982), 178. Also see Walker, *Living By the Word: Selected Writings, 1973–1987* (New York: Har-

court, Brace Jovanovich, 1988). Theological texts making a similar point include Karen Baker-Fletcher, *Sisters of Dust, Sisters of Spirit: Womanist Wordings on God and Creation* (Minneapolis: Fortress Press, 1998) and Jay B. McDaniel, *Of God and Pelicans: A Theology of Reverence for Life* (Louisville, KY: Westminster/John Knox Press, 1989).

2. This chapter is an expanded and revised version of my essay first published as "Shouting at an Angry Sky: Thoughts on Natural Disaster as a Theological Challenge," in *The Sky Is Cryin': Racism, Classism, and Disaster*, ed. Cheryl Kirk-Duggan, 98–104 (Nashville: Abingdon, 2006). Used by permission. In addition, the section dealing with my personal reflections on Hurricane Ike comes from Pinn, "In the Dark Night of Disaster," *Religion Dispatches* (September 18, 2008). Viewed July 1, 2009, on ReligionDispatches.org. http://www.religiondispatches.org/archive/416/in_the_dark_night_of_disaster.

3. See Carolyn Merchant's discussion of the critiques of "recovery" in *Reinventing Eden: The Fate of Nature in Western Culture* (New York: Routledge, 2003), chaps. 8–10.

4. Merchant, "Reinventing Eden: Western Culture as a Recovery Narrative," in *Uncommon Ground: Toward Reinventing Nature*, ed. William Cronon, 154–59 (New York: W. W. Norton, 1995).

5. Merchant, *Reinventing Eden*, 11–63.

6. My concern here is not the historical outlining of African American involvement in the environmental movement. Nor does this chapter purport to offer a framework for African American environmental activism. The focus here involves critique of theodical responses to natural disaster and the promotion of black theological thinking on natural disasters as a matter of embodiment addressed through ethics. For information on African American environmental activism, see Robert Bullard, *Dumping in Dixie: Race, Class, and Environmental Quality* (Boulder, CO: Westview Press, 1990); Bullard, ed., *Confronting Environmental Racism: Voices from the Grassroots* (Boston: South End Press, 1993); Townes, *Breaking the Fine Rain of Death*; Alice Walker, *Living By the Word* (New York: Harvest Books, 1989).

7. Merchant, "Reinventing Eden," 134.

8. Ibid., 140.

9. These lyrics are taken from "Work Is Sweet for God Has Blest." Viewed on July 2, 2009, at: http://nethymnal.org/htm/w/i/s/wis4ghab.htm

10. Cronon, introduction to *Uncommon Ground*, 25.

11. Merchant, "Reinventing Eden," in *Uncommon Ground*, 147.

12. As Merchant notes, the problem in the original garden of Eden stemmed from a white Adam and a black Eve. In that typical interpretation of the early chapters of Genesis portray Eve as the cause of the "Fall," the presentation in some case of Eve as a black woman has significant impact on the perceived nature and meaning of black female bodies. Merchants, however, turner to scholars such as Phyllis Trible also offers counter readings that "rescue" Eve from this negative assessment. See Merchant, *Reinventing Eden*, 154–55.

13. See Cronon, introduction, 51.

14. Merchant, *American Environmental History: An Introduction* (New York: Columbia University Press, 2007), 46.

15. Merchant, *Reinventing Eden*, 162.

16. This term was first used by Benjamin Chavis, in "The Historical Significance and Challenges of the First National People of Color Environmental Leadership Summit,"

Proceedings of the First National People of Color Environmental Leadership Summit (Washington, DC: United Church of Christ Commission for Racial Justice, 1991).

17. For a discussion of the "Eden" framework, see Merchant, *Reinventing Eden.*

18. Ibid., 158.

19. See, for example, Michael Dyson, *Come Hell or High Water: Hurricane Katrina and the Color of Disaster* (New York: Basic Civitas Books, 2007); Spike Lee "When the Levees Broke: A Requiem in Four Acts," HBO Documentary Films. I would argue issues of classism in the United States would mean that white Americans without means would also feel the consequences of natural disasters to be a matter of justice.

20. Big Bill Broonzy, "Southern Flood Blues" (Melotone, 1973). The lyrics were last viewed November 2, 2009, at http://www.foxytunes.com/artist/big_bill_broonzy#/track/southern_flood_blues

21. Cronon, introduction, *Uncommon Ground*, 29.

22. http://www.nytimes.com/2008/09/12/us/12ike.html> Viewed on July 2, 2009.

23. http://www.houstonpress.com/2009-01-08/news/hurricane-ike-s-wake/ Viewed on July 2, 2009.

24. Terence W. Tilley, *The Evils of Theodicy* (Washington, DC: Georgetown University Press, 1991); Tilley, "The Use and Abuse of Theodicy," *Horizons* 11, no. 2 (Fall 1984): 304–19.

25. John Hick, *Evil and the God of Love*, 2nd ed. (New York: Harper and Row/Macmillan, 1987).

26. http://www.cnn.com/SPECIALS/2005/katrina/ Viewed on July 2, 2009.

27. Merchant, *American Environmental History*, 35.

28. http://www.repentamerica.com/pr_hurricanekatrina.html

29. 'Kansas Joe McCoy, "When the Levee Breaks" (1929). Lyrics were viewed on July 5, 2009 at: http://www.geocities.com/bourbonstreet/delta/2541/bljmccoy.htm#When357

30. http://www.beliefnet.com/story/174/story_17418_1.html

31. Ibid.

32. David Jacobson, *Place and Belonging in America* (Baltimore: The Johns Hopkins University Press, 2002), 189.

33. Garth Baker-Fletcher, *Somebodyness: Martin Luther King, Jr., and the Theory of Dignity* (Minneapolis: Fortress Press, 1993), 171–72.

34. Anthony B. Pinn, ed., *By These Hands: A Documentary History of African-American Humanism* (New York: New York University Press, 2001); *African American Humanist Principles.*

35. K. Baker-Fletcher, *Sisters of Dust*, 6.

36. Ibid., 6.

37. See Merchant's *Reinventing Eden.*

38. K. Baker-Fletcher, *Sisters of Dust, Sisters of Spirit*, 26.

39. Ibid., 30.

40. See Pinn, *Terror and Triumph*, chap. 7.

41. I am certainly not the first to propose ecological concerns within the doing of theology. In addition to the work of Karen Baker-Fletcher, readers should also see Sallie McFague, *A New Climate for Theology: God, the World, and Global Warming* (Minneapolis: Fortress Press, 2008); McFague, *The Body of God: An Ecological Theology* (Minneapolis: Fortress Press, 1993); McFague, *Super, Natural Christians* (Minneapolis: Fortress Press,

2000); Jay McDaniel, *Of God and Pelicans: A Theology of Reverence for Life* (Louisville, KY: Westminster John Knox Press, 1989). However, new black theological thought differs in that it does not attempt to "read" and respond to nature in light of the framework of doctrine of God as a sense of cosmic creation to be nurtured. New black theological thought holds open to questioning the sense of divinity as the framework for the beauty and value of nature that many others assume.

Selected Bibliography

Althaus-Reid, Marcella. *Indecent Theology: Theological Perversions in Sex, Gender and Politics.* New York: Routledge, 2000.

Ambler, Charles H. *Kenyan Communities in the Age of Imperialism: The Central Region in the Late Nineteenth Century.* New Haven: Yale University Press, 1988.

Anderson, Victor. *Beyond Ontological Blackness: An Essay on African American Religious and Cultural Criticism.* New York: Continuum, 1995.

——— *Creative Exchange: A Constructive Theology of African American Religious Experience.* Minneapolis: Fortress Press, 2008.

Arthur, Linda B., ed. *Religion, Dress and the Body.* New York: Berg, 1999.

Baker, Houston A., Jr. *Afro-American Poetics: Revisions of Harlem and the Black Aesthetic,* Madison, WI: University of Wisconsin Press, 1988.

Baker-Fletcher, Garth. *Somebodyness: Martin Luther King, Jr., and the Theory of Dignity.* Minneapolis: Fortress Press, 1993.

———, ed. *Voices on the Future: Black Religion After the Million Man March.* Maryknoll, NY: Orbis Books, 1998.

Baker-Fletcher, Karen. *Sisters of Dust, Sisters of Spirit: Womanist Wordings on God and Creation.* Minneapolis: Fortress Press, 1998.

Baldwin, James. *Go Tell It on the Mountain.* New York: Grosset and Dunlap, 1953.

Black, Paula. *The Beauty Industry: Gender, Culture, Pleasure.* New York: Routledge, 2004.

Blassingame, John D., ed. *Slave Testimony: Two Centuries of Letters, Speeches, Interviews, and Autobiographies.* Baton Rouge: Louisiana State University Press, 1977.

Bearden, Romare, and Harry Henderson. *A History of African-American Artists From 1792 to the Present.* New York: Pantheon Books, 1993.

Bernauer, James, and Jeremy Carrette, eds. *Michel Foucault and Theology: The Politics of Religious Experience.* Burlington, VT: Ashgate Publishing Company, 2004.

Bohm, David. *On Dialogue.* New York: Routledge, 1996.

Bordo, Susan. *The Male Body: A New Look at Men in Public and Private.* New York: Farrar, Straus and Giroux, 1999.

———. *Twilight Zones: The Hidden Life of Cultural Images from Plato to O. J. Berkeley.* University of California Press, 1999.

———. *Unbearable Weight: Feminism, Western Culture, and the Body.* Berkeley: University of California Press, 1993.

Brent, Linda. *Incidents in the Life of a Slave Girl: An Authentic Historical Narrative Describing the Horrors of Slavery as Experienced by Black Women.* New York: Harvest/Harcourt Brace Jovanovich Publishers, 1973 [1861].

Butler, Judith. *Bodies That Matter: On the Discursive Limits of "Sex."* New York: Routledge, 1993.

Camus, Albert. *The Myth of Sisyphus and Other Essays*. Translated by Justin O'Brien. New York: Alfred A. Knopf, 1969.

Caplan, Pat, ed. *The Cultural Construction of Sexuality*. New York: Tavistock Publications, 1987.

Carby, Hazel V. *Race Men*. Cambridge, MA: Harvard University Press, 1999.

Carr, David M. *The Erotic Word: Sexuality, Spirituality, and the Bible*. New York: Oxford University Press, 2003.

Carrette, Jeremy R. *Foucault and Religion: Spiritual Corporeality and Political Spirituality*. New York: Routledge, 2000.

———, ed. *Religion and Culture: Michel Foucault*. New York: Routledge, 1999.

Carter, J. Cameron. *Race: A Theological Introduction*. New York: Oxford University Press, 2008.

Castronovo, Russ. *Beautiful Democracy: Aesthetics and Anarchy in a Global Era*. Chicago: University of Chicago Press, 2007.

Chireau, Yvonne, and Nathaniel Deutsch, eds. *Black Zion: African American Religious Encounters with Judaism*. New York: Oxford University Press, 2000.

Clarke, Graham. *The Photograph*. New York: Oxford University Press, 1997.

Coleman, Monica. *Making a Way Out of No Way: A Womanist Theology*. Minneapolis: Fortress Press, 2008.

Cone, James. *A Black Theology of Liberation*, 2nd ed. Maryknoll, NY: Orbis Books, 1986.

———. *God of the Oppressed*. New York: Seabury, 1975.

———. *The Spirituals and the Blues*. Maryknoll, NY: Orbis Books, 1972.

Cone, James, and Gayraud Wilmore, eds. *Black Theology: A Documentary History*. 2 vols. Maryknoll, NY: Orbis Books, 1993.

Cooey, Paula M. *Religious Imagination and the Body: A Feminist Analysis*. New York: Oxford University Press, 1994.

Craig, Maxine Leeds. *Ain't I a Beauty Queen? Black Women, Beauty, and the Politics of Race*. New York: Oxford University Press, 2002.

Cronon, William, ed. *Uncommon Ground: Toward Reinventing Nature*. New York: W. W. Norton, 1995.

Damasio, Antonio. *The Feeling of What Happens: Body and Emotion in the Making of Consciousness*. New York: Harvest Books, 1999.

Danto, Arthur C. *The Abuse of Beauty: Aesthetics and the Concept of Art*. Chicago: Open Court, 2003.

———. *After the End of Art: Contemporary Art and the Pale of History*. Princeton: Princeton University Press, 1997.

———. *The Body/Body Problem: Selected Essays*. Berkeley: University of California Press, 1999.

———. *The Philosophical Disenfranchisement of Art*. New York: Columbia University Press, 1986.

———. *Philosophizing Art: Selected Essays*. Berkeley: University of California Press, 1999.

D'Emilio, John, and Estelle B. Freedman. *Intimate Matters: A History of Sexuality in America*. New York: Harper and Row, 1988.

Desai, Ram. *Christianity in Africa as Seen by the Africans*. Denver: Alan Swallow, 1962.

Dixon, Thomas. *The Clansman: An Historical Romance of the Ku Klux Klan*. Ridgewood, NJ: The Gregg Press, 1967[1905].

Douglas, Kelly Brown. *Sexuality and the Black Church: A Womanist Perspective.* Maryknoll, NY: Orbis Books, 1999.

———. *What's Faith Got to Do With It? Black Bodies/Christian Souls.* Maryknoll, NY: Orbis Books, 2005.

Douglas, Mary. *Natural Symbols: Explorations in Cosmology.* New York: Routledge, 1996.

———. *Purity and Danger: An Analysis of the Concepts of Pollution and Taboo.* New York: Ark, 1966.

Douglas, Tom. *Scapegoats: Transferring Blame.* New York: Routledge, 1995.

Douglass, Frederick. *Frederick Douglass: The Narrative and Selected Writings.* Edited by Michael Meyer. Modern Library College Edition. New York: Random House, 1984.

Dyson, Michael Eric. *Between God and Gangsta Rap: Bearing Witness to Black Culture.* New York: Oxford University Press, 1996.

———. *Holler If You Hear Me: Searching for Tupac Shakur.* New York: Basic Civitas Books, 2001.

———. *Open Mike: Reflections on Philosophy, Race, Sex, Culture and Religion.* New York: Basic Civitas Books, 2003.

Ellison, Ralph. *The Invisible Man.* New York: Random House, 1952.

Ellwood, Robert S. *The Sixties Spiritual Awakening: American Religion Moving from Modern to Postmodern.* New Brunswick, NJ: Rutgers University Press, 1994.

Evans, James H. *We Have Been Believers: An African-American Systematic Theology.* Minneapolis: Fortress Press, 1992.

Fanon, Frantz. *Black Skin, White Masks.* New York: Grove Press, 1967.

Fauset, Arthur Huff et al. *Black Gods of the Metropolis: Negro Religious Cults of the Urban North.* Philadelphia: University of Pennsylvania Press, 2001.

Ferguson, Harvie. *Modernity and Subjectivity: Body, Soul, Spirit.* Charlottesville: University Press of Virginia, 2000.

Fontaine, Pierre-Michel, ed. *Race, Class, and Power in Brazil.* Los Angeles: Center for Afro-American Studies, University of California, 1985.

Foucault, Michel. *The Archeology of Knowledge.* 1969. Reprint, New York: Routledge, 1972.

Foucault, Michel. *Discipline and Punish: The Birth of the Prison.* New York: Vintage Books, 1979.

———. *Ethics: Subjectivity and Truth.* Edited by Paul Rabinow. New York: The New Press, 1997.

———. *The History of Sexuality.* Vol. 1, *An Introduction.* New York: Vintage Books, 1978.

———. *The History of Sexuality.* Vol. 2, *The Use of Pleasure.* New York: Vintage Books, 1990.

———. *The History of Sexuality.* Vol. 3, *The Care of the Self.* New York: Vintage Books, 1988.

Fraser, Mariam, and Monica Greco, eds. *The Body: A Reader.* New York: Routledge, 2005.

Gaehtgens, Thomas W., and Heinz Ickstadt, eds. *American Icons: Transatlantic Perspectives on Eighteenth- and Nineteenth Century American Art.* Santa Barbara, CA: Getty Center for the History of Art and the Humanities, 1992.

Gardella, Peter. *Innocent Ecstasy: How Christianity Gave America an Ethic of Sexual Pleasure.* New York: Oxford University Press, 1985.

Gardiner, James J., and J. Deotis Roberts Sr., eds. *Quest for a Black Theology.* Philadelphia: Pilgrim Press, 1971.

Gayle, Addison. *The Black Aesthetic.* Garden City, NY: Doubleday, 1971.

Geurts, Kathryn Linn. *Culture and the Senses: Bodily Ways of Knowing in an African Community*. Berkeley: University of California Press, 2002.

Giddings, Paula. *When and Where I Enter: The Impact of Black Women on Race and Sex in America*. New York: Bantam Books, 1984.

Gilkes, Cheryl Townsend. *If It Wasn't for the Women: Black Women's Experience and Womanist Culture in Church and Community*. Maryknoll, NY: Orbis Books, 2000.

Girard, Rene. *Violence and the Sacred*. Translated by Patrick Gregory. Baltimore: Johns Hopkins University Press, 1997.

Glaude, Eddie. *Exodus!: Religion, Race, and Nation in Early Nineteenth-century Black America*. Chicago: University of Chicago Press, 2000.

Goffman, Erving. *Stigma: Notes on the Management of Spoiled Identity*. New York: Touchstone, 1986.

Gomez, Michael A., ed. *Diasporic Africa: A Reader*. New York: New York University Press, 2006.

Gordon, Lewis R., ed. *Existence in Black: An Anthology of Black Existential Philosophy*. New York: Routledge, 1997.

Goss, Linda, and Marian E. Barnes, eds. *Talk That Talk: An Anthology of African-American Storytelling*. New York: Touchstone Book, 1989.

Grant, Jacquelyn. *White Women's Christ, Black Women's Jesus*. Atlanta: Scholars Press, 1989.

Griffin, Horace. *Their Own Received Them Not: African American Lesbians and Gays in the Black Church*. Cleveland, OH: Pilgrim Press, 2006.

Gudorf, Christine E. *Body, Sex, and Pleasure: Reconstructing Christian Sexual Ethics*. Cleveland, OH: The Pilgrim Press, 1994.

Guimond, James. *American Photography and the American Dream*. Chapel Hill: University of North Carolina Press, 1991.

Gutman, Amy, and Anthony Appiah, *Color Consciousness: The Political Morality of Race*. Princeton, NJ: Princeton University Press, 1998.

Hackett, David G., ed. *Religion and American Culture: A Reader*. New York: Routledge, 1995.

Hansen, Holger Bernt, and Michael Twaddle. *Religion and Politics in East Africa*. Athens: Ohio University Press, 1995.

Harris, Frederick C. *Something Within: Religion in African-American Political Activism*. New York: Oxford University Press, 1999.

Harris, Trudier, ed. *New Essays on Go Tell It On the Mountain*. New York: Cambridge University Press, 1996.

Haynes, Stephen R. *Noah's Curse: The Biblical Justification of American Slavery*. New York: Oxford University Press, 2002.

Heyes, Cresddia J. *Self-Transformations: Foucault, Ethics, and Normalized Bodies*. New York: Oxford University Press, 2007.

Heywood, Ian, and Barry Sandywell, eds. *Interpreting Visual Culture: Explorations in the Hermeneutics of the Visual*. New York: Routledge, 1999.

Holloway, Joseph E., ed. *Africanisms in American Culture*. Bloomington: Indiana University Press, 1990.

Hopkins, Dwight. *Being Human: Race, Culture, and Religion*. Minneapolis: Fortress Press, 2005.

———. *Shoes That Fit Our Feet: Sources for a Constructive Black Theology*. Maryknoll, NY: Orbis Books, 1993.

Hopkins, Dwight, and Sheila Greeve Davaney, eds. *Changing Conversations: Cultural Analysis and Religious Reflection*. New York: Routledge, 1996.

Howard-Pitney, David. *The Afro-American Jeremiad: Appeals for Justice in America*. Philadelphia: Temple University Press, 1990.

Hughes, Langston, and Arna Bontemps. *The Book of Negro Folklore*. New York: Dodd, Mead, 1959.

Irwin, Alexander C. *E.R.O.S Toward the World: Paul Tillich and the Theology of the Erotic*. Minneapolis: Fortress Press, 1991.

Isherwood, Lisa, and Elizabeth Stuart. *Introducing Body Theology*. Sheffield, England: Sheffield Academic Press, 1998.

Jacobson, David. *Place and Belonging in America*. Baltimore: Johns Hopkins University Press, 2002.

Jalloh, Alusine, and Stephen E. Maizlish, ed. *The African Diaspora*. College Station, TX: Texas A&M University Press, 1996.

Jones, Amelia, and Andrew Stephenson, eds. *Performing the Body, Performing the Text*. New York: Routledge, 1999.

Jones, Colin, and Ray Porter. *Reassessing Foucault: Power, Medicine and the Body*. New York: Routledge, 1994.

Jones, William. *Is God a White Racist?: A Prolegomenon to Black Theology*. 1973. Reprint, Boston: Beacon Press, 1998.

Karp, Ivan, and Steven D. Lavine, eds. *Exhibiting Cultures: The Poetics and Politics of Museum Display*. Washington, DC: Smithsonian Institution Press, 1991.

Kaufman, Gordon. *An Essay on Theological Method*. Missoula, MT: Scholars Press, 1979.

Kayle, Keith. *The Politics of the Independence of Kenya*. New York: St. Martin's Press, 1999.

Kennedy, Dane. *Islands of White: Settler Society and Culture in Kenya and Southern Rhodesia, 1890-1939*. Durham, NC: Duke University Press, 1987.

Klein, Herbert S., and Ben Vinson III. *African Slavery in Latin America and the Caribbean*. 2nd ed. New York: Oxford University Press, 2007.

Koser, Khalid, ed. *New African Diasporas*. New York: Routledge, 2003.

Landes, Ruth. *The City of Women*. Albuquerque: University of New Mexico Press, 1994 [1947].

Larsen, Nella. *Passing*. New Brunswick, NJ: Rutgers University Press, 1986.

———. *Quicksand*. New York: Penguin Books, 2002.

Lawrence, Beverly Hall. *Reviving the Spirit: A Generation of African Americans Goes Home to Church*. New York: Grove Press, 1996.

Lemert, Charles, and Ann Branaman, eds. *The Goffman Reader*. Malden, MA: Blackwell, 1997.

Levine, Lawrence. *Black Culture and Black Consciousness: Afro-American Folk Thought From Slavery to Freedom*. New York: Oxford University Press, 1983.

Lock, Margaret, and Judith Farquhar. *Beyond the Body Proper: Reading the Anthropology of Material Life*. Durham, NC: Duke University Press, 2007.

Locke, Alain, ed. *The New Negro*. New York: Atheneum, 1986.

Long, Charles H. *Significations: Signs, Symbols, and Images in the Interpretation of Religion*. Philadelphia: Fortress Press, 1986.

Lovell, John. *Black Song: The Forge and the Flame; The Story of How the Afro-American Spiritual Was Hammered Out*. 1972. Reprint, New York: Paragon House, 1986.

Lugalla, Joe L. P., and Colleta G. Kibassa, eds. *Poverty, AIDS, and Street Children in East Africa*. Lewiston, PA: Edwin Mellen Press, 2002.

Maaga, Mary McCormick. *Hearing the Voices of Jonestown*. Syracuse, NY: Syracuse University Press, 1998.

Majors, Richard, and Janet Mancini Billson. *Cool Pose: The Dilemmas of Black Manhood in America*. New York: Touchstone Books, 1992.

Mann, Kristin, and Edna G. Bay, eds. *Rethinking the African Diaspora: The Making of a Black Atlantic World in the Bight of Benin and Brazil*. Portland, OR: Frank Cass, 2001.

Martin, James Alfred. *Beauty and Holiness: The Dialogue Between Aesthetics and Religion*. Princeton, NJ: Princeton University Press, 1990.

Martin, Luther H., Huck Gutman, and Patrick H. Hutton, eds. *Technologies of the Self: A Seminar with Michel Foucault*. Amherst: University of Massachusetts Press, 1988.

McElroy, Guy C. *Facing History: The Black Image in American Art, 1710–1940*. San Francisco, CA: Bedford Arts and Corcoran Gallery of Art, 1990.

McHoul, Alec, and Wendy Grace. *A Foucault Primer: Discourse, Power and the Subject*. New York: New York University Press, 1993.

McKittrick, Katherine, and Clyde Woods, eds. *Black Geographies and the Politics of Place*. Cambridge, MA: South End Press, 2007.

Mellor, Philip A., and Chris Shilling, *Re-forming the Body: Religion, Community and Modernity*. London: Sage Publications, 1997.

Merchant, Carolyn. *American Environmental History: An Introduction*. New York: Columbia University Press, 2007.

———, ed. *Major Problems in American Environmental History*. Lexington, MA: D. C. Heath, 1993.

———. *Reinventing Eden: The Fate of Nature in Western Culture*. New York: Routledge, 2003.

Miller, Norman, and Rodger Yeager. *Kenya: The Quest for Prosperity*. 2nd ed. Boulder, CO: Westview Press, 1994.

Miller, Timothy, ed. *America's Alternative Religions*. Albany: State University of New York Press, 1995.

Mohanram, Radhika. *Black Body: Women, Colonialism, and Space*. Minneapolis: University of Minnesota Press, 1999.

Morey, Ann-Janine. *Religion and Sexuality in American Literature*. New York: Cambridge University Press, 1992.

Morgan, David. *The Sacred Gaze: Religious Visual Culture in Theory and Practice*. Berkeley: University of California Press, 2005.

———. *Visual Piety: A History and Theory of Popular Religious Images*. Berkeley: University of California Press, 1998.

Morris, Calvin S. *Reverdy C. Ransom: Black Advocate of the Social Gospel*. Lanham, MD: University Press of America, 1990.

Morton, Fred. *Children of Ham: Freed Slaves and Fugitive Slaves on the Kenya Coast, 1873 to 1907*. Boulder, CO: Westview Press, 1990.

Moses, Wilson Jeremiah. *Afrotopia: The Roots of African American Popular History*. New York: Cambridge University Press, 1998.

Mugambi, J. N. K. *African Christian Theology: An Introduction*. Nairobi, Kenya: Heinemann Kenya, Ltd., 1989.

——, ed. *Democracy and Development in Africa: The Role of Churches*. Nairobi, Kenya: All Africa Conference of Churches, 1997.

——. *From Liberation to Reconstruction: African Christian Theology After the Cold War*. Nairobi, Kenya: East African Educational Publishers, Ltd., 1995.

Muhammad, Elijah. *Message to the Blackman in America*. Chicago: Muhammad's Temple No. 2, 1965.

——. *The True History of Master Fard Muhammad, Allah (God) In Person*. Atlanta: MEMPS Publications, 1996.

Murray, Albert. *From the Briarpatch File: On Context, Procedure, and American Identity*. New York: Pantheon Books, 2001.

Naipaul, Shiva. *Love and Death in a Hot Country*. New York: Penguin Books, 1985.

Nascimento, Abdias Do, and Elisa Larkin Nascimento. *Africans in Brazil: A Pan-African Perspective*. Trenton, NJ: Africa World Press, 1992.

Needleman, Jacob, and George Baker, eds. *Understanding the New Religions*. New York: Seabury Press, 1978.

Nelson, James B. *Body Theology*. Louisville, KY: Westminster/John Knox Press, 1992.

Nettleton, Sarah, and Jonathan Watson, eds. *The Body in Everyday Life*. New York: Routledge, 1998.

Nuttall, Sarah, ed. *Beautiful Ugly: African and Diaspora Aesthetics*. Durham, NC: Duke University Press, 2006.

O'Connor, Francis V. *Jackson Pollock*. New York: Museum of Modern Art, 1967.

Okullu, Henry. *Church and Politics in East Africa*. Nairobi, Kenya: Uzima Press Limited, 1974.

Orvell, Miles. *American Photography*. New York: Oxford University Press, 2003.

Palmer, Robert. *Deep Blues: A Musical and Cultural History, from the Mississippi Delta to Chicago's South Side to the World*. New York: Penguin Books, 1982.

Payne, Daniel A. *Sermons and Addresses, 1853–1891*. New York: Arno Press, 1972.

Patterson, Orlando. *Rituals of Blood: Consequences of Slavery in Two American Centuries*. New York: Basic Books, 1998.

Peiss, Kathy, and Christian Simmons, eds. *Passion and Power: Sexuality in History*. Philadelphia: Temple University Press, 1989.

Perkins, William Eric. *Droppin' Science: Critical Essays on Rap Music and Hip Hop Culture*. Philadelphia: Temple University Press, 1996.

Petersen, Alan, and Robin Bunton, eds. *Foucault: Health and Medicine*. New York: Routledge, 1997.

Pinn, Anthony B. *African American Humanist Principles: Living and Thinking Like the Children of Nimrod*. New York: Palgrave Macmillan, 2004.

——. *The Black Church in the Post–Civil Rights Era*. Maryknoll, NY: Orbis Books, 2002.

——, ed. *By These Hands: A Documentary History of African American Humanism*. New York: New York University Press, 2001.

——, ed. *Making the Gospel Plain: The Writings of Bishop Reverdy C. Ransom*. Harrisburg, PA: Trinity Press International, 1999.

——, ed. *Noise and Spirit: The Religious and Spiritual Sensibilities of Rap Music*. New York: New York University Press, 2003.

——. *Terror and Triumph: The Nature of Black Religion*. Minneapolis: Fortress Press, 2003.

————, ed. *Varieties of African American Religious Experience*. Minneapolis: Fortress Press, 1998.

————. *Why, Lord?: Suffering and Evil in Black Theology*. New York: Continuum, 1995.

Pinn, Anthony B., and Benjamin Valentin, eds. *The Ties that Bind: African American and Hispanic/Latino/a Theologies in Dialogue*. New York: Continuum, 2001.

Putzi, Jennifer. *Identifying Marks: Race, Gender, and the Marked Body in Nineteenth-Century America*. Athens: University of Georgia Press, 2006.

Rabinow, Paul, ed. *The Foucault Reader*. New York: Pantheon Books, 1984.

Raboteau, Albert. *Slave Religion: The "Invisible Institution" in the Antebellum South*. New York: Oxford University Press, 1978.

Rahier, Jean Muteba, ed. *Representations of Blackness and the Performance of Identities*. Westport, CT: Bergin and Garvey, 1999.

Ransom, John S. *Foucault's Discipline: The Politics of Subjectivity*. Durham, NC: Duke University Press, 1997.

Reeves, Marcus. *Somebody Scream! Rap Music's Rise to Prominence in the Aftershock of Black Power*. New York: Faber and Faber, 2008.

Reid-Pharr, Robert F. *Conjugal Union: The Body, the House, and the Black American*. New York: Oxford University Press, 1999.

Roberts, J. Deotis. *Liberation and Reconciliation: A Black Theology*. Maryknoll, NY: Orbis Books, 1994.

Rose, Tricia. *Black Noise: Black Music and Black Culture in Contemporary America*. Middletown, CT: Wesleyan University Press, 1994.

————. *The Hip Hop Wars: What We Talk about When We Talk about Hip Hop—and Why It Matters*. New York: Basic Civitas Books, 2008.

Sadler, Kim Martin, ed. *Atonement: The Million Man March*. Cleveland, OH: Pilgrim Press, 1996.

Sakolsky, Ron, and Fred Wei-Han Ho, eds. *Sounding Off: Music as Subversion/Resistance/Revolution*. Brooklyn, NY: Autonomedia, 1995.

Sansome, Livio, Elisée Soumonni, and Boubacar Barry, eds. *Africa, Brazil, and the Construction of the Trans Atlantic Black Identities*. Trenton, NJ: Africa World Press, 2008.

Sawicki, Jana. *Disciplining Foucault: Feminism, Power, and the Body*. New York: Routledge, 1991.

Segal, Ronald. *Islam's Black Slaves: The Other Black Diaspora*. New York: Hill and Wang, 2002.

Sernett, Milton. *Bound for the Promised Land: African American Religion and the Great Migration*. Durham, NC: Duke University Press, 1997.

Shilling, Chris. *The Body and Social Theory*. 2nd ed. London: Sage Publications, 2003.

Simpson, George Eaton. *Black Religions in the New World*. New York: Columbia University Press, 1978.

Smith, Shawn Michelle. *American Archives: Gender, Race, and Class in Visual Culture*. Princeton: Princeton University Press, 1999.

————. *Photography on the Color Line: W. E. B. Du Bois, Race, and Visual Culture*. Durham, NC: Duke University Press, 2004.

Smith, Jonathan Z. *Map Is Not Territory*. Chicago: University of Chicago Press, 1993.

Smith, Theophus. *Conjuring Culture: Biblical Formations of Black America*. New York: Oxford University Press, 1994.

Singleton, Theresa A., ed. *"I, Too, Am America:" Archeological Studies of African-American Life*. Charlottesville: University Press of Virginia, 1999.

Snoop Dogg. *The Dogg Father: The Times, Trials, and Hardcore Truths of Snoop Dogg*. With Davin Seay. New York: William Morrow, 1999.

Sontag, Susan. *On Photography*. New York: Picador, 1977.

Spear, Thomas, and Isaria N. Kimambo, eds. *East African Expressions of Christianity*. Athens: Ohio University Press, 1999.

Spencer, Michael J. *Blues and Evil*. Knoxville: University of Tennessee Press, 1993.

Stephens, Mitchell. *The Rise of the Image, the Fall of the Word*. New York: Oxford University Press, 1998.

Stoler, Ann Laura. *Race and the Education of Desire: Foucault's History of Sexuality and the Colonial Order of Things*. Durham, NC: Duke University Press, 1995.

Studio Museum in Harlem. *Memory and Metaphor: The Art of Romare Bearden, 1940–1987*. New York: Oxford University Press, 1991.

Sukla, Ananta Ch., ed. *Art and Experience*. Westport, CT: Praeger, 2003.

Sullivan, Nikki. *Tattooed Bodies: Subjectivity, Textuality, Ethics, and Pleasure*. Westport, CT: Praeger, 2001.

Thompson, Robert Farris. *Flash of the Spirit: African and Afro-American Art and Philosophy*. New York: Vintage Books, 1983.

Tignor, Robert L. *The Colonial Transformation of Kenya: The Kamba, Kikuyu, and Maasi from 1900 to 1939*. Princeton: Princeton University Press, 1976.

Tillich, Paul. *Love, Power, and Justice: Ontological Analyses and Ethical Applications*. New York: Oxford University Press, 1954.

Tobin, Jacqueline L., and Raymond G. Dobard. *Hidden in Plain View: A Secret Story of Quilts and the Underground Railroad*. New York: Anchor Books, 2000.

Townes, Emilie M. *Breaking the Fine Rain of Death: African American Health Issues and a Womanist Ethic of Care*. New York: Continuum, 1998.

Trachetenberg, Alan. *Reading American Photographs: Images as History, Mathew Brady to Walker Evans*. New York: Hill and Wang, 1989.

Turner, Bryan S. *The Body and Society: Explorations in Social Theory*. New York: Basil Blackwell, 1984.

Turner, Victor. *The Ritual Process: Structure and Anti-Structure*. Ithaca, NY: Cornell University Press, 1969.

Van Deburg, William. *Hoodlums: Black Villains and Social Bandits in American Life*. Chicago: University of Chicago Press, 2004.

Walker, Alice. *The Color Purple: A Novel*. New York: Harcourt Brace Jovanovich, 1982.

———. *In Search of Our Mothers' Gardens: Womanist Prose*. New York: Harcourt Brace Jovanovich, 1983.

Wallace, Michelle. *Black Macho and the Myth of the Superwoman*. New York: Verso, 1990 [1978].

———. *Invisibility Blues: From Pop to Theory*. New York: Verso, 1990.

Wallace, Michelle, and Gina Dent, eds. *Black Popular Culture*. Seattle: Bay Press, 1992.

Washington, James, ed. *A Testament of Hope: The Essential Writings of Martin Luther King Jr.* New York: Harper and Row, 1986.

Waston, Nick, and Sarah Cunningham-Berrley, eds. *Reframing the Body*. New York: Palgrave Macmillan, 2001.

Welch, Sharon. *A Feminist Ethic of Risk*. Minneapolis: Fortress Press, 1990.

———. *Sweet Dreams in America*. New York: Routledge, 1999.

Welton, Donn, ed. *Body and Flesh: A Philosophical Reader*. Malden, MA: Blackwell, 1998.

Weightman, Judith Mary. *Making Sense of the Jonestown Suicides: A Sociological History of Peoples Temple*. New York: Edwin Mellen Press, 1983.

Weinberg, Jonathan. *Ambition and Love in Modern American Art*. New Haven: Yale University Press, 2001.

Weiss, Gail. *Body Images: Embodiment as Intercorporeality*. New York: Routledge, 1999.

Weiss, Gail, and Honi Fern Haber, eds. *Perspectives on Embodiment: The Intersections of Nature and Culture*. New York: Routledge, 1999.

Wessinger, Catherine. *How the Millennium Comes Violently: From Jonestown to Heaven's Gate*. New York: Seven Bridges Press, 2000.

West, Cornel. *The American Evasion of Philosophy: A Genealogy of Pragmatism*. Madison: University of Wisconsin Press, 1989.

———. *The Cornel West Reader*. New York: Basic Civitas Books, 1999.

———. *Prophesy Deliverance: An Afro-American Revolutionary Christianity*. Philadelphia: Westminster Press, 1982.

Wexler, Laura. *Tender Violence: Domestic Visions in an Age of U.S. Imperialism*. Chapel Hill: University of North Carolina Press, 2000.

White, Shane, and Graham White. *Stylin': African American Expressive Culture from Its Beginnings to the Zoot Suit*. Ithaca, NY: Cornell University Press, 1998.

Wiesner-Hauls, Merry E. *Christianity and Sexuality in the Early Modern World: Regulating Desire, Reforming Practice*. New York: Routledge, 2000.

Williams, Carol J. *Framing the West: Race, Gender, and the Photographic Frontier in the Pacific Northwest*. New York: Oxford University Press, 2003.

Williams, Delores. *Sisters in the Wilderness*. Maryknoll, NY: Orbis Books, 1993.

Williams, Simon J., and Gillian Bendelow. *The Lived Body: Sociological Themes, Embodied Issues*. New York: Routledge, 1998.

Willis, Deborah, ed. *Picturing Us: African American Identity in Photography*. New York: The New Press, 1994.

Wilmore, Gayraud. *Black Religion and Black Radicalism*. Maryknoll, NY: Orbis Books, 1983.

Wilson, Scott. *Great Satan's Rage: American Negativity and Rap/Metal in the Age of Supercapitalism*. Manchester, England: Manchester University Press, 2008.

Wright, Richard. *Black Boy: A Record of Childhood and Youth*. New York: Harper and Brothers, 1945.

———. *Native Son*. New York: Harper and Row/Perennial Library, 1966.

———. *The Outsider*. 1953. Reprint, New York: Harper Perennial, 2003.

Zepp, Ira G., *The New Religious Image of Urban America: The Shopping Mall As Ceremonial Center*. Niwot, CO: University Press of Colorado, 1997.

PARTIAL DISCOGRAPHY

Arrested Development (1994). *Zingalamaduni*. Chrysalis Records.

Arrested Development (1992). *Three Years, 5 Months, and 2 Days in the Life of . . .* New York: Chrysalis Records.

Boogie Down Productions (1989). *Ghetto Music: The Blueprint of Hip Hop*. Zomba Recording Corporation.

Da Lench Mob (1992). *Guerilla's In Tha Mist*. EastWest/Atlantic Records.

Dr. Dre (1992). *The Chronic*. Interscope Records.

Geto Boys (1989). *Grip It! On That Other Level*. Priority Records.

Geto Boys (1992). *Geto Boys Best: Uncut Dope*. Rap-A-Lot Records, Inc.

Public Enemy (1988). *It Takes a Nation of Millions to Hold Us Back*. CBS Records.

Public Enemy (1991). *Apocalypse 91 . . . The Enemy Strikes Black*. Sony Music Entertainment.

Scarface (2004). "I Seen a Man Die." *The Diary*. Scarface, Mike Dean, N.O. Joe.

Scarface (2003). "Make Your Peace." *Balls and My Word*. Mike Dean and Tone Capone.

Scarface (2002). "Heaven." *The Fix*. Scarface, B. Jordan, K. West, T. Jones, K. Price, R. Moore Jr.

Scarface (2000). "Last of a Dying Breed." *Last of a Dying Breed*. Mr. Lee, N.O. Joe, Scarface.

Scarface (1997). *Untouchable*. Noo Trybe Records.

Scarface (1994). *The Diary*. Noo Trybe Records.

Scarface (1991). *Mr. Scarface is Back*. Rap-A-Lot Records, Inc.

Sister Souljah (1992). *360 Degrees of Power*. Sony Music Entertainment.

Snoop Doggy Dogg (1993). *Doggy Style*. Interscope Records.

Tupac Shakur (1999). *Still I Rise*, Interscope Records.

Tupac Shakur (1998). *2Pacalypse Now*. Jive Records.

Tupac Shakur, (1997). *R U Still Down?* Jive Records.

Tupac Shakur (1996). *The Don Killuminati, The 7 Day Theory*. Interscope Records.

Tupac Shakur (1995). *Me Against the World*. Jive Records.

Index

abstract expressionism: emergence of, 26–28; perception of meaning and, 28–31

aesthetics: African American religious experience and, xiii–xiv; black male embodiment and, 66–69; black sexuality and, 81–84; creative disregard of disobedient bodies and, 21–23; of meaning, Danto's discussion of, 32–33; racism and development of, 42–48

African American Christianity: blues music and, 106–12; body/embodiment in, xvii, 137–40; mythologizing of evil in, 102–6; rap music and, 113–15, 130–37; redemption and conversion in, 124–30

African Americans: manhood and masculinity for, 53–54, 65–69; post-World War II art and, 25–28; role of religion for, 38–41; sexuality and embodiment for, 71–97

African artists, Picasso and, 25

African Methodist Episcopal Church, 127

Afrotopia (Moses), 129

agency: body/embodiment and, 17–21; radical consciousness and, 45

Alfieri, Bruno, 26–27

alterity, of African American women, 60–61

American colonialism, sexuality and, 80

Anderson, Victor, 41–48, 50–51, 95, 171n.18, 177n.104

Appeal (Walker), xv, 168n.16

Appiah, Anthony, 88

Aquinas, Thomas, 79

Archeology of Knowledge, The (Foucault), 5

art. *See* musical production; visual arts

Arthur, Linda, 167n.64

Augustine, St., on sexuality and body, 74–76, 80

authenticity, lived religious experience and, 139–40

Baker, Houston, xiii

Baker-Fletcher, Garth, 154

Baker-Fletcher, Karen, 155–56

Baldwin, James, 87–90, 176n.80

banality, beauty and, in pop art, 28–30

Baptist Church, 127

Basquiat, Jean-Michel, 29–31

Bearden, Romare, xiii, 30–31

beauty: blackness and concepts of, 40–41; theological discourse on, 31–33

Bendelow, Gillian, 9–10

Beyond Ontological Blackness (Anderson), 42–48

Bhagavad Gita, Tupak Shakur's theology and, 180n.37

biblical scripture: black theology and role of, 102–6; nature and materiality in, 144

Bigwood, Carol, 162n.32

bi-racial relationships, in Lee's *Get on the Bus,* 56–57

Black Jesus icon, Tupac Shakur's references to, 135–37

black male: African American religious traditions and, 91–96; blues music and, 59–64; body/embodiment and, 53–69; Foucault's discussion of power, 64–65; invisibility of, 60–64; in Lee's *Get on the Bus,* 54–59; theological construction/deconstruction of, 3, 61–64 blackness: black theology and, 38–41; body/embodiment and, 35–52; essentialism and, 42–52; naturalization of, 144–46

"blackness," identity as, 2

black-on-black violence, in Lee's *Get on the Bus*, 56–57

black theology: biblical texts and, 102–6; black bodies and, 53–69; blackness and, 38–41; body/embodiment and, xiv–xvii, 3–4, 8–10, 31–33, 167n.65; demonic force in, 101–2; doctrinal orientations in, 128–30; essentialism and, 50–52; Foucault's influence on, 3–4, 6–10; future trends in, 156–57, 183n.41; historical sources of, 12–13; internal *vs.* external critique in, 49–52, 169n.36; marked body as art and, 24–25; musical production and, 119–21; Obama's election and, 163n.51; ontological blackness and, 43–48; power dynamics of oppression and, 7, 162n.21; rap music and, 123–41; reflection and assessment of, 1–3; sexuality and, 71–76, 90–96; of Tupac Shakur, 130–37. *See also* religious traditions of African Americans

blues music: black manhood and, 59–64; demonic metaphor in, 106–12; rap music and, 116–19; sexuality in, 176n.85

Blumenberg, Hans, 42

"Body, Representation, and Black Religious Discourse" (Copeland), 4

body/embodiment: aesthetic experimentation with, 11–13, 163n.45; African American religious practices and, 84–96, 102–6, 137–40; art and aesthetics and role of, xiii–xiv; blackness and, 35–52; black sexuality and, 78–84; black theology and, 7–10; in blues music, 109–12; disobedience and, 21–23; environmental issues and, 143–57; essentialism and, 42–52; gender and, 53–69; humanism and role, xiii, xv–xvii; marked body as art and, 24–25; music and, 115–19; natural disaster and, 150–52; naturalization of black bodies and, 144–46; ontological

blackness and, 44–48; punishment and, 18–21; redemption and, 123–41; religious struggle located in, 13, 101–21; resistance and role of, 17–21; sexuality and, 71–97; subjectivity concerning, 49–52, 169n.36; terminology and conceptual frameworks for, 4–10; theology of (*see* embodient theology); in Tupac Shakur's theology, 132–36; womanist theology and, 63–64, 171nn.17–18

Bohm, David, 6, 162nn.18, 25

Bordo, Susan, 8–10, 162nn.27, 32; on language and embodiment, 38; on resistance, 23

Bradley, Jordan. *See* Scarface (rapper)

break dancing, 123

Brent, Linda, 82

Broadus, Calvin. *See* Snoop Dogg

Brown, WIllie, 110

Butler, Judith, 162n.32

Callahan, Allen, 102

Candomblé, 97

Cannon, Katie Geneva, 2, 171n.10

Carby, Hazel, 50, 84

Carrette, Jeremy, 177n.109

Carter, J. Cameron, 2, 168n.18

Carter, Philip, 56

Christianity: blackness and, 40–41; black sexuality and, 78–84, 96–97; blues music as critique of, 112; body/embodiment in, xvii, 33, 167n.65; homoeroticism in, 92; hypermasculinity and, 62–64; sexuality in, 72–76

"CHUCH," Tupac Shakur's references to, 134, 181n.38

Church of God in Christ denomination, 103–4, 127

cinematography, post-World War II art and, 25–28

civil rights movement, black theology and, xv

Clark, Elizabeth, 173n.13

Cleaver, Eldredge, 56

Coleman, Monica, 2

Color Purple, The (Walker), 60–61, 143

community: black manhood and, 55–59; sexuality in, 71–72; theological concept of, 49–52

Cone, Cecil, 39–40, 169n.36

Cone, James, 2, 39–40, 109, 169n.36

conjure woman images, reality and memory in, 30–31

Connell, R. W., 83–84

conversion: in African American Christianity, 124–30, 137–40; Tupac Shakur's lived religious experience and theology and, 131–37

Cooey, Paula, 169n.36

Copeland, M. Shawn, xvii, 4, 81–82

creative disregard: body/embodiment and, 21–23; marked body as art and, 24–25; visual arts and, 31–33

Creative Exchange (Anderson), 44, 48

Cronon, William, 144–45, 147

cultural fulfillment: black sexuality and, 95; ontological blackness and, 45, 50–51

cultural production: African American humanism and, xi; black bodies and, 67–69, 144–46; black theology, 49–52, 169n.36; body/embodiment and, 8–10, 162n.32; religious criticism and, 42–48

Danto, Arthur, xiv, 25, 27, 32, 166n.50, 167n.62

Davey, Nicholas, xiv, 30

death and dying, in rap music, 130, 132–36

decorated bodies: as art, 24–25; creative disregard and, 21–23

decorative arts, African American religious experience and, xiii

demonic: African American religious struggle against, 101–21; in blues music, 106–12; rap music and, 113–15

desire: black theology and role of, 94–96; body/embodiment and, 72–76, 90–96; race and, 76–78; religion and, 79–84

Discipline and Punish (Foucault), 5

divine: in African American Christianity, 125–30; in black theology, 101–2; Hurricane Katrina as manifestation of, 150–52; in Tupak Shakur's theology, 136–37

Dodson, Jualynne, 159n.3

Doggystyle (rap album), 117

Douglas, Kelly Brown, 13, 81–82, 90–96, 161n.7

Douglas, Mary, 10

Douglass, Frederick, xv

Dr. Dre, 117

Du Bois, W. E. B.: on black identity formation, 35–38; soul discussed by, 36, 167n.7

DuChamp, Marcel, 166n.50

Dyson, Michael, 76, 92, 119, 130, 132–34, 180n.24

embodiment theology: black bodies and, 67–69; black sexuality and, 96–97; cultural production and, 119–21; current research on, xiv, 159n.10; erotic and, 29, 166n.53; experimentation with, 11–13; formulation of, 3–4, 10–11, 161n.7; future research issues in, 13–14, 163n.50; religious struggle framed by, 101–21

Enfleshing Freedom: Body, Race, and Being (Copeland), xvii

Enlightenment, origins of ontological racism in, 43

environmentalism: humanism and, 155–57; natural disasters and, 150–52; race, gender and class issues and, 143–57, 182n.6

eroticism: African American religious practices and, 84–90, 137–40; embodiment theology and, 29, 166n.53

eschatology, African American Christianity and, 125–30

Essaydi, Lalla, 18–24

essentialism, blackness and, 42–52

ethics, humanism and role of, 155–57

evangelicalism: in African American community, 103–6; natural disasters and theology of, 151–52

evil: in blues music, 106–12; mythologizing of, 103–6; natural disaster as framework for, 148–50

Evil and the God of Love (Hick), 149

existentialism: ontological blackness and, 45; in rap music, 116–19; in Tupac Shakur's theology, 135–37; womanist theology and, 63–64

ontological blackness: Anderson's discussion of, 42–48; black theology and, 50–52, 95, 177n.104
oppression: Foucault on power dynamics of, 7–10; religion and, 175n.73; sexuality and, 83–84
orgasm, theology and role of, 79
Osteen, Joel, 153
Otherness, black sexuality and, 81–84
"Outsider Art," emergence of, 25–26

Palmer, Robert, 108
Pan-Africanism, 55
Patton, Charley, 110
Phillips, Goldie, 92
Picasso, Pablo, 25–27
pleasure: black theology's view of, 93–96; power and, 73–76; religion and control of, 78–84
political structuring, manhood and masculinity for, 65–69
Pollock, Jackson, 26–27
Pop Art, embodiment in, xiv
pop art: emergence of, 27–28; perception of meaning and, 28–31
popular culture, language of, 170n.39
postmodernism, ontological blackness and, 46–48
power: black male embodiment and, 64–69; blackness as affirmation of, 39–41; body/embodiment and role of, 5–10; demonic as force for, 101–2; disobedient bodies as challenge to, 21–23; in Du Bois' work, 35–36; punishment as tool for, 18–21; race and sexuality and, 76–78; sexuality and, 73–76
process thought, liberative theology and, 2
Prophesy Deliverance! (West), 42, 160n.5
"prosperity gospel," 153–54
punishment: aesthetic disobedience and, 23; body/embodiment and, 18–21
Puritanism: meaning of nature and, 144; sexuality and, 80

Quicksand (Larsen), 84–85

quilt art, African American religious experience and, xiii

race and racism: black male embodiment and, 66–69; black theology and, 4, 38–41, 168n.18; body/embodiment and, 36–52; Du Bois on importance of, 35–36; essentialism and, 42–48; Foucault and, 23, 165n.29; in Lee's *Get on the Bus*, 58–59; Obama's election and, 163n.51; sexuality and, 76–78; theological assessment of, 2
Race Men (Carby), 50
racial apologetics, evolution of, 41–48
Rake's Progress, A (Hogarth), 166n.56
Ransom, Reverdy, 43–44
rape, sexuality and, 83–84
rap music: African American religious practices and, 137–40; body/embodiment and, 115–19; demonic metaphor and, 113–15; lived religious experience and, 130–37; redemption motif in, 123–41; sexuality in, 176n.85
reality, in pop art, 30
recovery stories: naturalization of black bodies and, 145–46; redemption theme in, 143
redemption: in African American Christianity, 124–30; body/embodiment and, 123–41; meaning of nature and, 144–45; in recovery stories, 143
Reeves, Marcus, 132–33
Reid-Pharr, Robert, 38, 168n.16
religious criticism: blackness and, 42–48; black sexuality and, 78–84; sexuality and, 72–76, 88, 175n.73
religious pluralism, in African American communities, xi–xiii
religious struggle, popular culture as frame for, 13, 101–21
religious traditions of African Americans: blackness and, 42–48; black theology and, xi–xii; body/embodiment and, 137–40; embodiment and desire and, 90–96; in Lee's *Get on the Bus,* 55–59; normalization of black sexuality and,

Walker, Alice, 60–61, 63, 71, 143, 155
Walker, David, xv, 43, 168n.16
Warhol, Andy, 28–31, 166nn.50, 56
Waters, Muddy, 59–60
Watkins, Gloria, 45
Watson, Jonathan, 17
Weiss, Gail, 10
West, Cornel, 2, 42, 45, 160n.5; on Black Christian eschatology, 125–26; on leadership dilemma, 53; on oppression, 91
What's Faith Got To Do With It? (Douglas), 90–96
Wheatstraw, Peetie, 108
whiteness, race and sexuality and, 77–78
white supremacy, ontological blackness and, 43–48
White Women's Christ, Black Women's Jesus (Grant), 62

Why Lord? Suffering and Evil in Black Theology (Pinn), xi–xii
Williams, Delores, 2, 60, 62–64
Williams, Simon, 9–10
Wilmore, Gayraud, 2
Wimbush, Vincent, 102
womanist theology: assessment of, 2–3; black male deconstructed through, 12–13; black masculine invisibility and, 61–64, 171nn.10, 18; blackness and, 41; body/embodiment and, xiv–xvii; essentialism and, 50–52; Foucault's influence on, 7–10; ontological blackness and, 44–48; sexuality and, 76
women: body/embodiment and, 66–69; nature of black female bodies and, 182n.12
Wright, Richard, 113

About the Author

ANTHONY B. PINN is the Agnes Cullen Arnold Professor of Humanities and Professor of Religious Studies at Rice University. His books include *Varieties of African American Religious Experience, Why Lord? Suffering and Evil in Black Theology,* and *By These Hands: A Documentary History of African American Humanism.*